The Intimate Empire

Literature, Culture and Identity

Series Editor: Bruce King

This series is concerned with the ways in which literature and cultures are influenced by the complexities and complications of identity. Looking at the ways in which identities are explored, mapped, defined and challenged in the arts, where boundaries are often overlapping, contested and re-mapped, it considers how differences, conflicts and change are felt and expressed. It investigates how such categories as race, class, gender, sexuality, ethnicity, nation, exile, diaspora and multiculturalism have come about. It discusses how these categories co-exist and their relationship to the individual, particular situations, the artist and the arts.

In this series:

Nuruddin Farah, *Yesterday, Tomorrow: Voices from the Somali Diaspora*
Mineke Schipper, *Imagining Insiders: Africa and the Question of Belonging*

The Intimate Empire

Reading Women's Autobiography

Gillian Whitlock

CASSELL
London and New York

Cassell

Wellington House, 125 Strand, London WC2R 0BB

370 Lexington Avenue, New York, NY 10017-6550

First published 2000

British Library Cataloguing-in-Publication Data
A catalogue record for this book is available from the British Library.

ISBN 0-304-70599-3 (hardback)
    0-304-70600-0 (paperback)

Library of Congress Cataloging-in-Publication Data
Whitlock, Gillian, 1953–
    The intimate empire: reading women's autobiography / Gillian
Whitlock.
        p.   cm. — (Literature, culture and identity)
    Includes bibliographical references and index.
    ISBN 0-304-70599-3 (hb.) – ISBN 0-304-70600-0 (pbk.)
    1. Commonwealth literature (English)—Women authors—History and
criticism. 2. Autobiography—Women authors. 3. Women and literature
—Commonwealth countries—History—20th century. 4. Women and
literature—Commonwealth countries—History—19th century. 5. English
prose literature—19th century—History and criticism. 6. English prose
literature—20th century—History and criticism. 7. Prince, Mary. History
of Mary Prince, a West Indian slave. 8. Imperialism in literature. 9. Colonies
in literature. 10. Self in literature.   I. Title.   II. Series.
PR9080.5.W47   2000
820.9'9287'09171241—dc21   99-29898
                                                                                    CIP

Typeset by BookEns Ltd, Royston, Herts
Printed and bound in Great Britain by Biddles Ltd, Guildford and King's Lynn

Contents

Acknowledgements

The large comparative research project which led to this book could not have begun, let alone been completed, without the support of an Australian Research Council Grant. I am grateful to Daina Garklavs, Judith Hoey and Tanya Greig for the administration of this Grant. Thanks also to the Inter-Library Loan staff at Griffith University and to library staff at the British Library, the University of Cape Town, the University of British Columbia, the National Library of Canada, the University of Queensland, the Campbell Collections at the University of Natal, the National English Literary Museum at Grahamstown, and the collections in the School of Oriental and African Studies and the Menzies Centre at the University of London.

At Griffith University I am grateful for the enlightened administration and intellectual support of Mark Finnane. My work with Griffith Flexible Learning Services is imprinted on this book, most palpably in the contribution to the cover design by Moira Hogan, and also through my ongoing friendship with GFLS staff. Several chapters of this book were presented to the Postcolonial Research Group at the University of Queensland, and their comments were always helpful. From its earliest drafts Helen Tiffin and Leigh Dale have made careful readings and commentaries. Jackie Huggins and Aileen Moreton-Robinson assisted by reading Chapter 5, and Aileen made her recent doctoral thesis available for my work in that chapter. Only when I came to write did I fully appreciate the research assistance provided by Anna Johnston from the beginning of the project.

I have drawn deeply on the friendship and ideas of David Carter, Pat Buckridge, Kay Ferres, Jill Weber, Ann Motteram, Jacqui Limberger, Russell McDougall, Alan Lawson, Gareth Griffiths, Antoinette Bauer, Susan Sheridan, Margery Fee, Bill and Peggy New, JoAnne Wallace, Sarah Nuttall, Judith Couille, Margaret Daymond, Stephen Gray, Andrew Hassam, Carole Gerson,

Robert Lecker, Michael Peterman, Jan and Steven Homewood, and Christine Boyanoski. Bruce King's reader's report was inspirational. My thinking about women's autobiographical writing begins with the work of Sidonie Smith, Drusilla Modjeska, Leigh Gilmore and Shirley Neuman. In marrying autobiography to postcolonialism, I am always working with Stephen Slemon and Helen Tiffin.

I am delighted that Esmé Robinson will get to read this book, and I regret that there can be no copy to John Matthews at Queen's. My parents, supportive to the end, enabled me to complete this book over a Brisbane summer. My family, Gerry, Annika and Sam, have lived this project with me for a long time, and followed it to Vancouver, London and Cape Town. This book is dedicated to them.

Brisbane
March 1999

Introduction

In the pink: Empire and autobiography

One of the most popular and intricate exhibits at the British Empire Exhibition of 1924 was Queen Mary's Doll's House. Designed by Sir Edward Lutyens, the house was furnished in the finest detail with miniatures made by the artists, craftsmen, purveyors, and authors most prominent at the time. The Doll's House remains today as a centre-piece of the tour of Windsor Castle, where it is viewed by half a million tourists a year. In the library are miniature copies of the works of Shakespeare, many contemporary British writers, and a reference collection that includes several Bibles, the Koran and a miniature atlas of the British Empire. Here is possibly the tiniest map of Empire, for it sits in the middle of the palm of the hand, one inch square and covered with red leather, embossed in gold. As an artefact from the Exhibition of 1924, the map itself is liberally marked in pink: Africa, the Caribbean, Canada, the Mediterranean, Australasia and the 'Far East'.

In this miniature size, the Empire overwhelms the whiteness elsewhere. This is an illusion, of course, but a wonderful metaphor of the fullness of Empire and the emptiness of elsewhere in British colonial discourses. This tiny map is well-hidden and yet a fundamental point of reference in that library. Doris Lessing reminds us in her recent autobiography, *Under My Skin* (1995), that the Empire Exhibition of 1924 has much to answer for and it crops up in unexpected places. It was, for example, this Exhibition which spurred her parents to undertake the purchase of a farm in Rhodesia, and their ill-fated project to become wealthy white settlers there. This is a salutary reminder. The Exhibition was one of a series of occasions designed to promote imperialist sentiment and pageantry, and the atlas remains as a relic of this. That map can, of course, still inspire ill-fated expeditions. Readings of it rarely translate this colonization in terms of its very different enclaves: the township and the reserve, the plantation and the hill station, the pioneering farm and the domestic household. Generations of people outside of Europe found themselves 'in the pink' with pleasure, dismay, ambivalence – rarely indifference. Locating oneself in these coordinates could be a moment of recognition and identification, or a confirmation of resistance or loss. In this book a series of carefully contextualized readings of women's autobiographic writing from 1830 to the present day examines how subjectivity has been produced, imagined, scripted and resisted both then, when much of the world seemed to be pink, and now, in its aftermath. Nostalgia for imperial dominance, the strategic forgetting that this requires, and ways of relating to the ruins of colonialism in 'late imperial culture' will be important issues here.

To conscript writers as diverse as Mary Prince and Susanna Moodie, Audre Lorde and Doris Lessing, Mamphela Ramphele and Ruby Langford Ginibi, and spaces as disparate as Upper Canada and post-apartheid South Africa, into this map of the intimate empire, is an elaborate conceit. In some respects it is as illusory and pretentious as that tiny atlas. There is no simple intertextual passage from map to autobiography. Nor were colonial spaces uniformly, evenly, 'in the pink'. It is part of the illusion, the rhetoric of Empire that all flourished alike. There are marked differences in this map between the conceptual place and colonial relations of, for example, India, Canada and southern Africa, and these continue to affect the formations of cultures in these residual stages of British imperialism. A variety of subject positions arises from this terrain, and there is no single frame for the autobiographic writing I discuss here. In the emergent, dominant and residual phases of Empire the interpellation of the subject is shifting and complex, with different negotiations and authorizations emerging through autobiography. Exactly how the subject negotiates a space to speak, and how she manoeuvres in place and time, is important. The discussion of *The History of Mary Prince* and *Roughing It in the Bush* in the first chapters of this book, for example, suggests this manoeuvring is an ongoing process, as editors, scholars, readers and critics return to autobiographies now and reproduce them for different cohorts of readers. And so Margaret Atwood, Kate Llewellyn, Moira Ferguson and Dervla Murphy, among others, are drawn into the frame of the intimate empire through their various kinds of adjacency to the subjects of autobiography. In drawing these autobiographies together, the question of how, in specific times and places, debates over what the person should be, and how gendered and racial connections are made, come into clearer view. Like Leigh Gilmore, whose work has been germinal in writing this book, I am not interested in female experience as it is sometimes perceived as a 'thematic continuity which makes movement from cradle to autobiography to grave into a more or less shared story of female turning points, crises and conversions.'[1] In short, I do not want to identify with these women, or to argue that they are representative, or to make heroines of them. Rather I mean to locate them in complex and contradictory ways, even within the span of the single life.

The kind of specific, historical and contextual reading that these autobiographies give rise to disperses any sense of a transhistorical female experience, or the notion of the female body as the ground of a unified and consistent meaning. A critical gap looms between anatomy and autobiographical destiny. Bodies are volatile, and their contingency and history are critical when thinking about colonialism's culture in particular. Mary Prince and Susanna Moodie, Karen Blixen and Beryl Markham, Ellen Kuzwayo and Sally Morgan, are interpellated as autobiographic subjects and narrators in very different ways. Nor does psychology, in particular the idea that women are inherently given to constructing a sense of self through others, serve to imagine an enclosure for autobiographies as various as Mrs Seacole's *Wonderful Travels*, Mary Prince's *History* and Karen Blixen's *Out of Africa*. Rather than constructing an identity and history of women, I am interested in difference and intimacy, in the relations between very different female subjects, and the leakage between what might seem to be secure gendered, national and racial identities. For this reason, in what follows I often focus on the interracial relations between the subject and her amanuensis, her editor or her critics, in the production and reproduction of autobiographies. By turning to autobiographies by those who are least authorized – the freed slave Mary Prince, the Creole traveller Mary Seacole, the 'Mother of Soweto' Ellen Kuzwayo, the Aboriginal activist Ruby Langford Ginibi – the ways that autobiographic expression is negotiated and intersubjective come into view. Autobiographic writing by those subjected to the most brutal forms of colonization on the plantations of the Caribbean, in the townships of South Africa and the reserves in Australia allows us to examine the connections between women's texts and the production of truth and authority in autobiography. For autobiographic writing is engaged in an ongoing process of authorization in order to capture not its subject so much as its object: the reader.

The reader is an important element in *The Intimate Empire*. Although the shaping of the autobiography ostensibly follows the mould of the life, the personality and the individual, this is an illusion that is critical to the seduction of the reader. In fact, autobiographers manoeuvre for their public; for the privilege of addressing the reader about her life. What can be said, what must be omitted, and how these parameters shift over time is fundamental to critical reading. By beginning with the autobiography of a former slave, Mary Prince, the ways that discourses of truth, identity and power are fundamental to the autobiographic subject is evident from the very start. As Leigh Gilmore points out, for many women, access to autobiography means access to the identity it constructs in a particular culture and for particular readerships. This is no less true for Ellen Kuzwayo, writing from Soweto in 1985, than it was for Mary

Seacole, who produced her memoir of Crimea in 1857. Although autobiography seems to stabilize truth and the subject who utters it, this is an illusion. For this reason I have followed Gilmore's practice of thinking about 'autobiographics', the changing elements of truth and identity which represent that subject of autobiography, rather than 'autobiography' as it is traditionally understood. This gives precedence to reading for the positioning of the subject, and for recognizing the changing social, cultural and political formations which affect the production and reception of autobiographic writing. Autobiographics asks: Where is the autobiographical? What constitutes its representation and truth, both then and there, and here and now?

Throughout this book I use the agency of the reader to make connections across autobiographical texts. This is the method of a critic in search of the contiguities and the rogue connections that proliferate through autobiography. It makes links using various narratives, discourses, tropes, figures and moments: abolitionism and domesticity, the white hunter and the conservationist, Soweto in 1976 and Sydney in 1988, the ivory fire in Nairobi in 1989, and the memory of the British child in the enclaves of Malaya, Rhodesia and Egypt, among others. Although studies of autobiographical writing may not require this, studies of autobiography and colonialism do. For these encounters and asymmetrical inter-social relationships 'in the pink' highlight the making of identities through relationships, and through social processes. The intimacies of identity formation, the connections between colonial encounters and located subjectivity, are fundamental to both colonialism and resistance. This work adopts a strategy which locates colonial representations and narratives in terms of agents, locations and moments, terms which are conducive to a differentiated vision of colonialisms rather than colonialism, to located projects which can be seen in the context of larger shifts.[2]

This is, in part, to respond to a challenge which is made in Sara Suleri's memoir of life in Pakistan in the 1950s: 'There are no women in the third world.'[3] Suleri calls into question readings of difference through hierarchies, and through generalization. How can we think about women's autobiography in Pakistan, or Africa, or the Caribbean without putting 'women' into 'the third world' (and the first and the second, for that matter)? Is autobiography, the grounds on which many ideas about gender, race and nationality as identities have been constructed and defended, also the site where things fall apart? Suleri returns to this issue in *The Rhetoric of English India*, where she examines literary texts and institutions in terms of the social, cultural and political dynamics of British colonialism and its aftermath. Here too she argues against the 'rhetoric of binaries that informs, either implicitly or explicitly, contemporary critiques of alterity in discourse'.[4] She displaces this way of thinking with a deeper sense of the 'necessary intimacies' between ruler and ruled, and the inseparability of imperial and subaltern subjects. In her criticism and memoir alike, Suleri insists on detail, on quite specific and unpredictable moments and relations. There are, of course, companies of women in Pakistan, and *Meatless Days* is a remembrance of them. They are not, however, predictable or consistent as 'women in the third world'.

Suleri is not alone in finding such categories of postcolonial criticism inadequate.[5] It is no coincidence that women from societies that have been subjected to the most invasive forms of colonization have felt particularly constrained by the trend of reading their work in terms of the collectives 'women' and 'third world'. These identifications miss the intersections, the connections, the ambivalence, which are the grounds from which resistance to colonizing discourses emerges. These questions become particularly acute in reading autobiographical writing out of Empire. Colonialism impacts at the point where the very sense of the possibilities for self-definition are constituted, and autobiographical writing bears the traces of its origins in specific historical relations of power, rule and domination. It is uniquely placed to reflect back on how individuals are categorized and attached to identities, and how identities are invariably produced within the social, political and cultural domain. Autobiographic writing can suggest the multiplicity of histories, the ground 'in between' where differences complicate, both across and within individual subjects. To read for processes of multiple identification, for the making and unravelling of identities in autobiographical writing, for what Suleri calls 'intimacies', is an important gesture to decolonization.

Like Suleri, Trinh Minh-ha looks for a poetics of reading for differences that will recognize more complex identification than categories of 'first' and 'third' world women. Both are critical of the idea of identity as singular and consistent, even within the single life. Multi-layered subjectivity and the shifting self are not the prerogatives of the metropolitan postmodern subject alone. The issue here is complex for, of course, others have argued that poststructuralist and postmodern approaches that decentre the subject and dismantle the referentiality of language threaten to silence minority subjects yet again. Both Suleri and Trinh Minh-ha resist the temptation to generalize, and return to context and to history:

As a focal point of cultural consciousness and social change, writing weaves into language the complex relations of a subject caught between the problems of race and gender and the practice of literature as the very place where social alienation is thwarted differently according to each specific context.[6]

Trinh Minh-ha goes on to suggest that the complexities of 'this subject caught in between' are reduced through ideas of authenticity and origin, which displace the differences that exist both within and between entities: 'Whether I accept it or not, the natures of I, you, s/he, We, they and wo/man constantly overlap. They all display a necessary ambivalence.... Despite our desperate, eternal attempt to contain and mend, categories always leak' (94). The issue here is not what third world subjects may invest in ideas of unified cultures, but how this has served the first world. In particular, how the heterogeneity of Western culture and subjectivity, the implications of other worlds in its own, and the making and unmaking of identities through adjacency rather than separation, are rarely brought into view. If binaries, thinking in terms of origins and authenticity, centre and periphery, and the separation into consistent and homogenous identities are fundamental to colonizing discourses, then the work of decolonization is to return ambivalence and duplicity, and to look to intersubjectivity in cultural formations and texts. All this is implied in 'intimacy' as it is used in *The Intimate Empire*, and it produces its recurrent interest in such different episodes and objects as Kate Llewellyn's visit to the Karen Blixen Museum in Nairobi, Mary Gaunt's hammock in West Africa, the photograph of 'PL, *fellaheen* and photogenic donkey' in Egypt, and Tobias' print which is left on the wall of Doris Lessing's childhood home.

Implicit here is an argument that autobiographic writing is important for thinking about colonialism's culture, and vice versa. The range of texts included in recent studies of women's autobiographical writing in English is seriously (and consistently) limited. The canon is enclosed and almost entirely Euroamerican. The politically charged and historically varying notions of what a 'person' is, the various encodings of gender, race and genre in which autobiographical writing is an agent are rarely considered. We do not need to return to the map of the British Empire to learn these things about autobiography. The operations of colonialism, decolonization and neo-colonialism establish a complex field where the shifting relations of domination and subordination, the making of truth, identity and authority in and through autobiography, come into view. Autobiography is produced in moments and spaces in which subjects are 'driven to grasp their positioning and subjectivity'.[7] The selection of texts for this book highlights encounters, moments, spaces, locations where the effects of colonization and decolonization are the most salient terms for analysis. That these are not the only terms of analysis is evident. A number of the texts included here, for example, *Out of Africa* and *Roughing It in the Bush*, have been often and well read using feminist critical practices. However, reading these texts out of colonialism produces different meanings, subjects and locations. For example, both of these autobiographies are read here in terms of the making of masculinity and femininity through adjacency, rather than the expression of a singular female subject.

The Intimate Empire is about the projection of the self in autobiography through complex negotiations, manoeuvres and display. 'Intimacy' relates to the incorporation of the body in these tactics, and about how deeply, personally embedded colonization and resistance are in thinking and writing about the self – a small pink map at the heart of things. It becomes a way of reading women's autobiographies for connections. Not because of psychological traits particular to their gender, but because what it is, and has been, to write as a freed slave, a settler, an emigrant, a traveller, an expatriate, an Australian, a Jamaican, a Canadian, an African, has always been a matter of negotiation, a balancing act, a process of inventing the self in relation to others. This production is at the heart of autobiography 'in the pink'.

Notes

1   Leigh Gilmore, *Autobiographics: A Feminist Theory of Women's Self-Representation.* Ithaca, NY: Cornell University Press, 1994, p. xii.

2   Nicholas Thomas, *Colonialism's Culture: Anthropology, Travel and Government.* Cambridge: Polity Press, 1994, p. 9.

3   Sara Suleri, *Meatless Days.* Chicago: University of Chicago Press, 1989, p. 20.

4   Sara Suleri, *The Rhetoric of English India.* Chicago: University of Chicago Press, 1992, p. 3.

5   This debate is taken up at some length by Carole Boyce Davies in *Black Women, Writing and Identity: Migrations of the Subject.* London: Routledge, 1994. See also Arun Mukherjee, 'Whose post-colonialism and whose postmodernism?', *World Literature Written in English,* 30(2) (1990): 1–9.

6   Trinh T. Minh-ha, *Woman, Native, Other.* Bloomington: Indiana University Press, 1989. Further references to this edition in text.

7   I am drawing here in part on Ruth Frankenberg and Lata Mani's essay 'Crosscurrents, crosstalk: race, "postcoloniality" and the politics of location', *Cultural Studies,* 7(2) (1993): 292–310, and Caren Kaplan's use of this essay in *Questions of Travel: Postmodern Discourses of Displacement.* Durham, NC: Duke University Press, 1996, p. 184.

1

Autobiography and slavery

Believing the History *of Mary Prince*

The Borderlands are physically present wherever two or more cultures edge each other, where people of different races occupy the same territory, where under, lower, middle and upper classes touch, where the space between two individuals shrinks with intimacy.[1]

Slave narrators came forth to write stories on paper as vivid as the ones engraved on their backs.[2]

Black and white

I want to begin by reading two autobiographies which do not seem to belong together at all and yet, through the course of Empire, are deeply implicated one in the other: Mary Prince's *History* and Susanna Moodie's *Roughing It in the Bush*. The first is the narrative of a former slave born in Bermuda, and first published in 1831. The second, by a Canadian settler, was first published some years later, in 1852. Each of these texts is among the early autobiographical texts in English out of the second empire, although they are brought together here not just because of this chronology. Nor do I begin with Prince and Moodie because they are engaging subjects, although they are, and the manner in which they came together for a brief time makes them even more intriguing as women. They appear together here because the relationship between these subjects, their marked differences and the way this is played out at the writing scene of Mary Prince's *History* raise issues which are fundamental to how we read autobiography. What does it mean to read these texts with colonialism and its aftermath in view?[3]

There is for some autobiographic subjects a kind of extreme, a crisis of authority and expression where as a last resort, in pursuit of the authority which autobiography can confer, body itself becomes text. Gloria Anzaldúa characterizes the self-representations of the most brutally colonized subjects in visceral terms: 'It's not on paper that you create but in your innards, in the gut and out of living tissue – organic writing I call it.'[4] This is the edge which, when all else is said and done, Mary Prince must resort to in order to convince her reader of her veracity and character. What can we make of the particular relations between these two women, Prince and Moodie, whose implications in processes of colonization are so different? More generally, how do we read from them the implications of different gendered, racial, class markings in colonialism's culture? In this and the following chapter the intimacy of these two women is fundamental to reading their autobiographies, 'intimacy' as understood by Anzaldúa in the epigraph to this chapter: the meeting of two very different subjects in borderlands of identity.

As these remarks suggest, I am interested in placing Moodie and Prince through their relationship to each other, not just in terms of their literal contiguity in place and time, but also the way in which their racial, ethnic and gendered identities can be understood to be implicated. Of late a number of critics who draw on both feminist and postcolonial theory to read women's texts have challenged the way we move from text to context, and how we place women whose identity in the scheme of colonialism is very different in terms of discrete 'worlds'. Sara Suleri, for example, says, 'There are no women in the third world.'[5] In particular, Suleri argues against the rhetoric of binarism 'that informs, either explicitly or implicitly, contemporary critiques of alterity in colonial discourse'.[6] She argues that this needs to be displaced in favour of a deeper sense of the 'necessary intimacies' between ruler and ruled, the inseparability of imperial and subaltern subjects. This sense of leakage between what may appear to be very secure and hierarchic identities is useful in approaching Prince's autobiography in particular, and in thinking more generally about autobiographic writing by those who were least authorized, and unlikely to find a way to speak of their own experiences of colonization, unless through processes of intersubjectivity and negotiation. Autobiographies by those subjected to the most brutal forms of colonial rule allow us to examine more carefully the relation of women's texts to the production of truth and authority in autobiography. How could they contest existing conventions? These autobiographical texts are engaged in an ongoing process of authorization to capture not its subject so much as its object: the reader.

The importance of these elements – subject, reader, negotiation and authorization – becomes patently obvious in the first of the two autobiographies I am interested in here, namely, *The History of Mary Prince. A West Indian Slave, Related by Herself.* Mary Prince was the first British woman to escape from slavery and publish a record of her experiences; she is, then, by any reckoning, an unlikely autobiographer. Generically, Prince's *History* could be read within a particular annex of autobiography studies – the slave narrative – although of course it precedes most of the US antebellum narratives by some years. To date, this genre has been formulated by and large through those African-American texts that emerged in the United States in the decades immediately before the Civil War. Although comparison with the best-known American example, Harriet Jacobs' *Incidents in the Life of a Slave Girl*, is useful in thinking about Prince's *History*, the British tradition of slave narrative is in many respects quite different. This becomes an important consideration in reading the *History*, which I will return to later in this chapter. There are other reasons for reading Prince's *History* more broadly, across various genres of autobiographic writing and in relation to other colonial autobiographic subjects. For, although it would be misleading to place this life history of a slave, which necessarily records the most brutal forms of colonial exploitation, as in any way paradigmatic of women's autobiography more generally, Prince's story foregrounds those visceral processes which determined who might speak; how, when, where and why; and how they might engage a 'believing' reader. Prince's *History* becomes something of a limit case, from which we can read on to other, less violent passages into autobiographic writing.

The 'history' of Mary Prince

Mary Prince is, as far as we know, the first black British woman to have escaped from slavery. She was born in Bermuda in about 1788: 'My mother was a household slave; and my father, whose name was Prince, was a sawyer belonging to Mr. Trimmingham, a ship-builder at Crow-Lane.'[7] As Moira Ferguson reminds us in her Introduction, Bermuda was a self-governing British colony at the time of Prince's birth. It was not a plantation colony, and Prince's father worked in one of the two major industries on the island: shipbuilding. The other, salting, would later occupy Mary Prince. At the time of Prince's birth about half the population of 10,000 were enslaved. She was sold for the first time with her mother as an infant, purchased and given to a girl her own age, who regarded her as a 'pet'. Prince lived with her mother and brothers and sisters in a household where the kindness of the mistress allowed the 'piccaninnies' an illusion of freedom. When she was 12 years old she was again traded, hired out to another mistress when her owner could no longer maintain her. Then, around 1805, upon the death of their owner, Prince's mother prepared Mary and her sisters Hannah and Dinah for the slave market, where they were sold 'like sheep or cattle':

> I was soon surrounded by strange men, who examined and handled me in the same manner that a butcher would a calf or lamb he was about to purchase, and who talked about my shape and size in like words – as if I could no more understand their meaning than the dumb beasts. (62)

She fetched about £38, 'a great sum for so young a slave', and became the property of Captain I __ at Spanish Point.

This initiates a long sequence where Prince is traded as private property, with each transaction leading to more abusive relations. This gradual descent into evil and Prince's own deepening understanding of its immoralities shape her *History*. In the household of Captain I __ she learns the difference between the smart of the rope, the cart-whip and the cow-skin when applied to her naked body by Mrs I __: 'a fearful woman, and a savage mistress to her slaves'. 'To strip me naked – to hang me up by the wrists and lay my flesh open with the cow-skin, was an ordinary punishment for even a slight offence' (66). Prince survives five years as a household slave at Spanish Point. She is then sold again, valued at about £100 this time, and sent to work in the salt industry at Turks Island. The working conditions there were appalling; Prince was no longer near her family, nor was she part of a household economy where she could achieve some small measure of independence and autonomy. Prince had hoped for better conditions, 'but I found it was but going from one butcher to another' (72). She works in the salt ponds for some ten years, until her master retires and takes her back to his household in Bermuda where she is hired out to do washing. 'I made myself pretty comfortable. I earned two dollars and a quarter a week, which is twenty pence a day' (78).

There is both subjection and resistance in Prince's narrative. She is powerless to resist the bondage, the trade in slaves that reduces them to the status of cattle, and she submits to demands which cause her shame. And yet the narrative suggests some means of agency. For example, when she returns to Bermuda from Turk's Island she allegedly reminds her master that she cannot be treated 'the same in Bermuda as he has done in Turk's Island' (67). Around 1815, despite being 'pretty comfortable', Prince negotiates to leave 'my indecent master' by asking to be sold into the service of John Wood. This is the fifth and final time she is traded, for about £65, and taken to Antigua as the property of the Woods. Ferguson suggests that the greater liberality of Antigua, where free black men were enfranchised, made it attractive to Prince. There a series of important events takes place: Prince takes in washing and sells yams and coffee to raise money to buy her freedom; she makes contact with Moravian missionaries and becomes part of their congregation; through her association with the Moravians she learns to read; finally she marries Daniel James, who had bought his freedom: 'We were joined in marriage, about

Christmas 1826, in the Moravian Chapel.... We could not be married in the English Church. English marriage is not allowed to slaves; and no free man can marry a slave woman' (74).

Mary Prince's final campaign for freedom was played out before the British public, where it assumed symbolic importance in the abolition campaigns of 1830 to 1831. The Woods took her to London in 1828. After two or three months of abuse, Prince, who 'knew that I was free in England, but did not know where to go, or how to get my living' (78), walked out in search of the Moravian mission house, and renewed contacts she had made in Antigua. Through them Prince took her case to the Anti-Slavery Society in November 1828. Thomas Pringle, the editor of the *History*, was also her employer; she entered service in his house at Claremont Square, where she dictated her *History* to the amanuensis Susanna Strickland 'to let English people know the truth'. Her narrative was subjected to intense and public scrutiny, and republished several times in that first year of publication. Its legitimacy was challenged by the pro-slavery lobby while her character was defended by Pringle and the campaigners for emancipation. This struggle for authority and veracity was played out in the English courts in 1833, the same year the Emancipation Bill came into effect. My interest, in this chapter, is the struggle to authorize Mary Prince as an autobiographic subject in the *History* itself. For this first autobiography by a British black woman is not only eloquent testimony to the inhumanity of slavery, it is also a record of how an unlikely autobiographer can gain access to the British public in 1831, and then again, to a contemporary cross-Atlantic constituency, in 1987.

Marginalia: oppositional reading

The reading I want to pursue here brings into the frame the narratee, Susanna Strickland, Mary Prince's amanuensis, who is the ear and the hand in Prince's text and who went on to become author in her own 'write' as it were of one of the most celebrated settler narratives, *Roughing It in the Bush or Life in Canada*, which is the subject of Chapter 2. There can be no simple equations between these two women's bodies, the prematurely aged black woman in exile in London and the young evangelist and abolitionist, a published poet who married John Dunbar Moodie shortly after transcribing the *History* and, a year later, emigrated to Upper Canada with her husband and baby daughter. However, their collaboration to produce the *History* at Claremont Square in London between late 1830 and early 1831, allows us to consider an autobiographical occasion where quite different ideologies and identifications intersect and dissect one another 'in contradiction, consonance and adjacency'.[8]

Here is a place to examine adjacency, intimacy, and the production of identity through relationship rather than authenticity, through intersubjectivity, and through reversals of attributes that attached to gender, race and class positions there and then. This may seem perverse given the obscurity of Mary Prince – who gains recognition for only a few years and then is lost from view. Why displace her into adjacency rather than pursue what would seem to be the more appropriate approach and recognize the sovereignty she fought so hard to establish?

In part the answer to this is the text itself. The edition now available to us was first reprinted in 1987 in Britain, a mark of the growing and cross-Atlantic interest in the history of black women. Of this edition less than a quarter is the 'History related by herself'. Mary's narrative is embedded in a series of prefaces, introductions and appendices, which proliferate with each edition, and through which Prince's solicitous editors, her contemporary Thomas Pringle and ours, Moira Ferguson, guide the reader's entry and exit with great care. In this respect Prince's *History* is not unusual, for slave narratives in the United States frequently were published with some authenticating documentation – a bill of sale, for example. However, in this *History* the process and strategy of authentication is unusually detailed. We thus have an autobiographical text which is overwhelmed by marginalia, and rather than peeling this away to read the *History* as a core, I want to read it amidst its supplementation. This will not lead to the retrieval of an authentic subject, for it reveals a subject constituted in and through differences as these were understood in two quite precise historical conjunctures: the anti-slavery campaigns of the early 1830s and the Western neo-feminism of the 1980s and 1990s. This writing scene is crowded, and my reading here will focus on the amanuensis Susanna Strickland and the editors Thomas Pringle and Moira Ferguson. It is through the marginalia that we can come to read the *History* not only in terms of its referential context, its place as a document in the history of slavery and what it tells us from a subjective point of view, but also the narrative relationship and the reading context which impinge upon the text. These attributes of the text lead on to ways of thinking about the complexities at the writing scene of the *History* and how these suggest ways of thinking about Prince and Strickland as 'volatile subjects', not as fixed in realms of black and white as it may at first appear.

By bringing the marginalia into the framework of the reading, rather than placing it as a distraction from the main game, I am drawing in part on Ross Chambers' understanding of a politics of oppositionality, and the way that texts can make a form of resistance available to the relatively disempowered. There is, he suggests, between the possibility of disturbance in the system and the system's power to recuperate that disturbance, 'room for manoeuvre', a space of play or leeway in the system where oppositionality arises and change can occur, 'not radical, universal or immediate change; only changes local and scattered that might one day take collective shape and work socially significant transformations'.[9] Prince's autobiography is a particularly complex instance of oppositionality at work in the text, for there is both the explicit agenda of the anti-slavery intelligentsia, her champions who employ her text as an instrument in their campaign for reform; and beyond this the manoeuvrings of the narrator herself within the prescriptions and formulations of the slave narrative which authorize her to speak.

As Chambers suggests, the emergence of opposition through the text is an ongoing process:

> it is the ongoing readability of texts ... that enables them to make all the necessary concessions and compromises with the prevailing power of the moment ... but to do so, so to speak, as a tactic of 'survival', so that their oppositional readability can become available at a later date, and in changed historical circumstances, to a readership that is the true object of their 'address'. (2)

I want to return to this idea of 'ongoing oppositionality' and subsequent readerships later in thinking about Moira Ferguson's recent editions of the *History*. What is particularly useful at this stage is, firstly, Chambers' idea of the oppositional text being characterized by an adroitness in the management of address and, secondly, his argument that we can grasp this adroitness, this oppositionality not by looking to universalities such as authorial agency, but by understanding textual specificity. For Chambers, like Suleri, oppositionality and resistance emerge through reading for the relational character of textual identity: 'one must take account of the role of reading in the production of textual 'meaning', and that consequently

> one must acknowledge and indeed assert the relational character of textual identity ... Textual authority is not determined by the social characteristics of an author so much as it is produced in specific circumstances of reading, and the specificity of a given text will arise from the way the relation of text and reader is mediated, wherever and whenever the text is read ... 'reading oppositional narrative' is ... a reading of the oppositional in narrative, a reading that both produces that oppositionality and is responsive to it, and does so in ways that are themselves situationally mediated. (6)

Mr Pringle: editor

There is another figure to be taken into account in thinking about the writing scene of Mary Prince's *History*: its editor, Thomas Pringle. It is Pringle who reads the text produced by Prince and Strickland. He is Prince's employer and secretary of the Anti-Slavery Society, although he stresses in the Preface that it is in his private capacity that he publishes the tract. The *History* is preceded and succeeded by Pringle's commentaries which position the text precisely and which attempt to secure the reader's belief and allegiance by anticipating disbelief. This is tricky work, for he must both establish Prince's veracity and authority as a subject, yet also offer other affirmations, other authorities to buttress this speaker who is, after all, beyond the pale.

The marginalia of the first editions of the *History*, which went through three editions very quickly, begin with the editor. Pringle's Preface gives us the first glimpse of the writing scene at Claremont Square, stressing Mary Prince's agency in establishing the project:

> The idea of writing Mary Prince's history was first suggested by herself. She wished it to be done, she said, that the good people of England might hear from a slave what a slave had felt and suffered; and a letter of her late master's, which will be found in the Supplement, induced me to accede to her wish without farther [*sic*] delay....
>
> The narrative was taken down from Mary's lips by a lady who happened to be at the time residing in my family as a visitor. It was written out fully, with all the narrator's repetitions and prolixities, and afterwards pruned into its present shape; retaining, as far as was practicable, Mary's exact expressions and particular phraseology. No fact of importance has been omitted, and not a single circumstance or sentiment has been added. It is essentially her own, without any material alteration farther than was requisite to exclude redundancies and gross grammatical errors, so as to render it clearly intelligible. (45)

This, and other marginalia and correspondence, allow us to place this autobiographical occasion in time and space: Claremont Square, London, 1830 to 1831. The case of Mary Prince alerts us that autobiographic texts in the field of colonial and postcolonial cultures will raise issues of power and privilege, marginality and authority, truth and authenticity in ways which may disqualify them as autobiography as it is conventionally understood. Nevertheless, the radically compromised authors, narrators and figurations of the self which Prince and Strickland/Moodie introduce into their texts are characteristic of postcolonial autobiographic writing in particular. In this sense the writing scene at Claremont Square becomes the first in a series of examples where a grasp of the micropolitics and the historical circumstances of writing are vital to understanding what women can and will say, how they can make account of themselves. True, the *History* of Mary Prince is an extreme instance of the crises of authorization which recur in 'the intimate empire', yet as such it foregrounds the stakes in play in the writing, publication and reading of autobiographic texts by colonized subjects. This autobiographical occasion I am describing here is one of those rare examples of what Felicity Nussbaum calls 'literal contiguity' at the centre of Empire,[10] an occasion where metropolitan Englishwomen and a woman from the colonies come into contact in a way that has mutual implications, where the intersection and interdependence of identities and identifications between European and colonial women become apparent – what Suleri might call 'intimacies'. These contiguities were, of course, more commonplace in the colonies themselves, and essential to processes of colonization, as we shall see when we move on to examine autobiographic occasions beyond the metropolis in later chapters. This instance of 'literal contiguity' enacts those processes of identity formation by which ideas of Englishness – ideas about racial, gendered and ethnic characteristics – were produced not at home so much as in a process of interrelationship between home and away, in a process of transculturation.[11]

Pringle remains on the borders of the page, a *sotto voce* presence throughout Mary Prince's first-person narration, which follows his Preface. This editorial presence translates West Indian phrases, assures that 'the whole of this paragraph especially, is given as nearly as possible in Mary's precise words', and points out that 'she refers to a written certificate which will be inserted afterwards'. Ironically he assures us of the truth from Mary's lips – and presents certification of this truth by other, more authoritative individuals. He assures us that Mary's account is characteristic, pointing out, for example, similarities between Prince's account of the slave market in Bermuda and an account of a *vendue* of slaves at the Cape of Good Hope: 'slavery wherever it prevails produces similar effects' (53). As tempting as it is to regard Pringle's assurances as a diversion, we might more usefully keep them in view as a reminder of the crowded autobiographic occasion through which Prince's narration emerged, that writing scene where lips, ears and hand on the page are not embodied in a single authorial presence. Pringle is ever anxious to get this text down 'cold', to prune the narrative, to control the reading. The *History* emerges as an extreme example of Leigh Gilmore's argument that whether and when autobiography emerges as an authoritative discourse of reality and identity has less to do with a text's presumed accuracy about what really happened than with its apprehended fit into culturally prevalent discourses of truth and identity.[12] As we have seen, Prince's *History* fits into an archetypal slave history in many respects, recording experiences which were thought to be typical, proving her suitability to speak for all slaves, both men and women. However, her ability to tell or tell true is always in question, and Prince was ultimately required to show and tell, to authenticate the story on paper with the marks on her body.

Miss Strickland: the 'other' woman

If we read Mary Prince's *History* as a narrative in which 'Mary' is the narrator and the amanuensis the narratee, we can amplify the politics of opposition at work. The presence of the amanuensis alerts us to intersubjectivity in two ways. Firstly, the possibilities and forms of collaboration between these two women can be seen to shape the emergence of the text. Secondly, making this relationship visible allows me to foreground contiguity, the making of identities through relationships rather than essence. It is the differences between Prince and Strickland which enable the production of the text, the presentation of the autobiographic subject 'Mary Prince', even though ultimately the text calls into question the nature of these differences, and the means by which they are anchored in shifting social and cultural domains. Prince gains access to a British reading public at that moment and in that place largely because of the politics of abolitionism. The *History* is precisely located in time, and would not have found a patron and a public in Britain other than at that particular juncture in the anti-slavery campaign being waged by Thomas Pringle and the Anti-Slavery Society of which he was Secretary. Here is a particularly acute formulation of the textual politics which both enable and disable women emerging as autobiographic subjects, and which Strickland herself will later negotiate in very different ways as a settler subject, Mrs Moodie. As Prince's amanuensis, Strickland is the conduit through which the *History* is written down, and the beginning of that process by which the text is shaped for its political and polemical purpose. But, more than this, she is also in every sense Prince's foil: the white English woman who is able to embody the precepts of femininity, domestic respectability and innocent womanhood, an Englishness that casts Prince as 'the other woman'. The writing scene of Prince's *History* is a hall of mirrors, in which the image of each figure is secured by its reverse, the establishment of 'identities through differences' which is germane to colonialist thinking. However, the life story which Strickland records also throws the nature of femininity and its place in the colonial order of things into question and disarray, and the opposition between slave and spinster, between the colony and the metropolis which seem to anchor this writing scene are undermined by what Prince has to tell — and show.

In her collected correspondence we find that in January 1831 the 'lady' visitor to Pringle's household, Susanna Strickland, gives a different glimpse of the writing scene of Prince's *History*. She writes to her friends James and Emma Bird:

> I have been writing Mr. Pringle's black Mary's life from her own dictation and for her benefit adhering to her own simple story and language without deviating to the paths of flourish or romance. It is a pathetic little history and is now printing in the form of a pamphlet to be laid before the Houses of Parliament. Of course my name does not appear. Mr. Pringle has added a very interesting appendix and I hope the work will do much good.[13]

As Strickland suggests to her friends, the function of the amanuensis is to copy the narrator's account. The telling of Prince's story through the benevolence of the collaborator is evident here, but so too is the idea of the scribe 'adhering' to the oral narration. Her task is to take down Prince's simple story without deviating to the 'paths of flourish and romance' which characterize her own writing elsewhere. Strickland was a member of a literary family; her sisters too were active in the urban intelligentsia in pre-Victorian London. As romance and sentimentality was the pre-eminent genre of pre-Victorian English women's writing, the simplicity of Prince's *History* is likewise a marker of her social status. Style is related to identity, both for Strickland and Prince, and certain generic modes set out appropriate ways to address the metropolitan audience.

There are a number of reasons why Strickland's name 'of course does not appear'. By convention an amanuensis remains unnamed, appropriately so in that the appearance of a proper name on the title page suggests authorship, the cohering of identity and style of narration. As we shall see later, Strickland herself was acutely aware of the congruence of name, speech and status for women. Traditionally the 'proper' naming of the text has particular resonance in thinking about autobiographical writing. Phillipe Lejeune stresses the importance of the name of the author on the title page. This is the signature of the autobiographical pact. He suggests this signifies the coherence of textual identity which autobiographical writing seems to guarantee, and the ownership of one's self as property. Lejeune's idea that the autobiographer asserts ownership of the self through naming has particular resonance here, for this is precisely what Mary Prince contests in her autobiographical history. As the supplementary materials prove, the ownership of Mary Prince remains in contention: her owner in Antigua will not relinquish his claim to her, and as a result she is unable to return to the colony to join her husband as a free woman. Her story is all about the ways in which her body was quite literally marketed, traded as currency by slavery. For these reasons, the use of Mary's paternal name of Prince on the title page of the *History* is an affirmation of the legitimacy and truth of what she has to say, and part of a strategy to claim an identity beyond the economy of slavery. It is Mary Prince's name as a free woman in England and her patrilineal name. However, this name is unstable through the text. For her owners in Antigua and Bermuda she has been Mary, Princess of Wales or Molly Wood, and a woman of dubious moral character. For others she is Mary James, wife of Daniel James. This profusion is evident in Appendix One, where we find Mary Prince's petition, which was presented to Parliament on 24 June 1829. It records 'A Petition of Mary Prince or James, commonly called Molly Wood' being presented. Proliferation of naming continues throughout the marginalia. In supplements to the *History* she is Mary Prince, the woman able to speak for all slaves, 'a woman remarkable for decency and propriety of conduct' and delicacy in Pringle's testimony from Claremont Square. On the other hand she is also 'the woman Molly', depraved and base, in the letter from her master in Antigua. The struggle to hold the name of Mary Prince in the title is thus part of her claim to truth and veracity as a speaking subject of an autobiography.

The slippage around the name 'Mary Prince' alerts us to ways that those claiming marginalized identities negotiate round and about the autobiographical 'I' with great difficulty. Ironically, Strickland's letter offers us yet another owner of Mary Prince: 'Mr. Pringle's black Mary.' For Prince, as for Strickland, name is a marker of identity, of one's place in a patrilineal order. However, the shifting names for Prince are also a sign of the fact that the trading of her body through slavery continues to deprive her of any stable history and identity, for each of these titles refers to a different construction of her place, character and status. As we shall see in Chapter 2, transitions from one sphere of womanhood to another are marked by quite specific rites of passage for Strickland, who is deeply conscious of how the shift from Strickland to Moodie, spinsterhood to wifehood, affects her place in society. For Prince there are no clear-cut demarcations related to her gender; rather her rites of passage are related to her status as a slave.

I suggested earlier that there are two oppositional agendas at work here. The first is the most obvious: the editor, Pringle, who wishes to put before the public a slave narrative which will have the marks of authenticity, but not the signs of what would be construed as depravity. The second is the concern of the narrator, Mary Prince, who desires that the good people of England might hear from a slave what a slave had felt and suffered. These two agendas may overlap, but they are not of course coextensive. There is an obvious tension between the need to authenticate and the desire not to alienate or appal the reader. Given these constraints, where does Prince find room for manoeuvre in the text? How does she find ways of inhabiting this space defined by the other? One example is in Prince's own reference to the narrator–amanuensis relationship at the very end of her story: 'I will say the truth to English people who may read the history that my good friend, Miss S __, is now writing down for me' (84). Here, as in Strickland's description of their relationship, the scribe works to and for Prince; the allusion to friendship here stresses the sense of equality and alliance in their relationship.

The amanuensis embodies at the scene of writing the epitome of English womanhood as it was understood in terms of the cult of domesticity. As a young, unmarried woman recently converted to Methodism, Strickland is an innocent scribe. On the other hand, Prince has to tell a story of degradation and punishment, a history about things of which she herself has been 'too ashamed to speak' on occasion. How is decency preserved here? Patterns of exposure and concealment that occur in the text suggest some answers. There are aspects of her life which need to be spoken of, but not by Prince in the narrator–amanuensis framework. For example, it is in Pringle's supplementary materials that the issue of Prince's relationship with a white man in Antigua is discussed and rationalized. It is there that Wood's allegations of depravity and licentiousness are presented edited, given that they are 'too indecent to appear in a publication likely to be perused by females'. The amanuensis does not copy these sections of the text. The section which Prince and Strickland do produce together is a strictly policed first-person narration, with no sexually compromising material. We see here what is 'acceptable'. As I suggested above, this history of a slave is marked by race not gender. Beyond this, it is the life cycle of a slave, quite archetypal and staged: the coming to knowledge of the power which 'white people's law' has over her body to end the innocence of childhood; the sale in the market 'exposed to view' 'surrounded by strange men' and severed from family in adolescence; the cruel hands which 'strip me naked' and 'lay my flesh open', the smart of the rope on her naked body. The descent into bestiality at the hands of the 'Buckra people' is ended only after a process of conversion, marriage and escape from her master and mistress in London, where she enters Pringle's employ as a servant and becomes a champion for the abolitionist movement. One of the marks of vernacular which remain in the *History* is Mary's refrain that the 'thread of my story' is hard to maintain; this must be so, for there are threads which must be excised from the fabric entirely, given that the abuse is 'too, too bad to speak in England' (58). There is much that the 'good people of England' cannot hear, and Prince infers the gap between what she might say and what will be heard in England. The constraints of what might be said and heard were figured right there in the intimacy of the narrator–amanuensis relationship.

In this way the *History* tells us a good deal about the cultural construction of truth and authenticity in autobiography. Prince's amanuensis and editor do not set out to record her experience, and for this woman to tell her life story is not to tell all. The occasion requires truth, not experience. Rarely does an autobiography demonstrate so well how these are not coextensive. The 'truthful' subject position, which Prince is required to embody, is a particular ensemble of race, gender and sexual characteristics that allows her to speak to the good people of England in the abolitionist cause in 1831. A public presentation of self as virtuous, docile and domesticated is mandatory for her to speak with cultural authority then and there. But the conditions which Mary Prince describes in her *History* are hardly conducive to purity and domesticity; the gap between 'experience' and 'telling the truth' in this case is considerable. 'Truth' here allows descriptions of brutal and repeated violence, but there is only the slightest hint of the sexual abuse that more than likely accompanied these beatings, of which she cannot speak 'for shame'. There were of course ways that gender and race intersected to mark the bodies of slave women particularly, but these are not recorded here. The relationship between the amanuensis and narrator, ear and voice must be carefully managed, for the distinctions between permissible entrance into the ear and invasive impropriety are subtle. As Deborah Garfield points out, the challenge for the black female abolitionist was to be an agent without appearing to be one. The aim was to attract public attention through a 'living' word that provoked sensation, yet without provoking lecherous interest or anti-feminist disgust in her sympathetic auditor. The woman had to tell and not tell, to speak of degradation and violence, yet sustain the apparent innocence of the auditor and reader, and her own vocal propriety.[14]

The problem here is not the narrator but the reader. The *History* invited disbelief on two levels: firstly, the narrator must describe behaviours which question the civility of white colonists, the English abroad, quite fundamentally. Secondly, as a black woman, Prince's emergence as an autobiographer, where her life is invested with particular and individual meaning, is unlikely, and letters from her owner which label her base and depraved offer a quite different story, perhaps even a more feasible one. The *History* courts dismissal, and the proliferation of marginalia and silences reflect the struggle to counter and contain these disturbances created by the text. Only an ex-slave might speak with authority of the atrocities of slavery but, of course, black women were not authoritative speakers. Thus 'truth' is dependent on black and white collaborations to authorize a text which, to achieve its objectives, must not only generate readers but also believers for a cause.

The hybrid quality of the text, the proliferation of marginalia, means that the challenge to the narrator's authority is re-enacted in every reading. As Shari Benstock remarks, marginalia of all kinds (prefaces, appendixes, footnotes, afterwords and the like) reflect on the text, engage in dialogue with it, perform an interpretive and critical act on it and break down the semblance of a carefully controlled textual voice: 'they reflect, I think, genuine ambivalence – toward the text, toward the speaker in the text, and toward the audience'.[15] In the slave narrative this struggle for authority encodes a racial divide in the text and each reading of it. The supporting documentation promotes acceptance of the text as historical evidence. Ironically, it also leaves these texts open in literary terms to readings which stress the corrosive interplay of narrator, editor, correspondents and the like. In short, the narrator's character, authority and veracity are called to account as the first-person narration is surrounded by, bound along with, prefatory and supplementary material where collaborators and critics debate the truth.

Authorization: reading the body of the slave

The writing scene at Claremont Square which I have been discussing is succeeded by a quite different episode in a testimonial, which was appended to the third edition of the *History*. This, the final marginal text, had the last word about Mary Prince. It was added following enquiries 'from various quarters respecting the existence of marks of severe punishment on Mary Prince's body' (119). Mary Pringle, the editor's wife, writes to Mrs Townsend, one of the secretaries of the Birmingham Ladies' Society for the Relief of Negro Slaves, from Claremont Square on 28 March 1831:

> My husband having read to me the passage in your last letter to him, expressing a desire to be furnished with some description of the marks of former ill-usage on Mary Prince's person, – I beg in reply to state that the whole back part of her body is distinctly scarred, and, as it were, *chequered*, with the vestiges of severe floggings. Besides this, there are many large scars on other parts of her person, exhibiting an appearance as if the flesh had been deeply cut, or lacerated with *gashes*, by some instrument wielded by most unmerciful hands ...
>
> In order to put you in possession of such full and authentic evidence, respecting the marks on Mary Prince's person, as may serve your benevolent purpose in making the enquiry, I beg to add my own testimony to that of Miss Strickland (the lady who wrote down in this house the narratives of Mary Prince and Ashton Warner), together with the testimonies of my sister Susan and my friend Miss Martha Browne – all of whom were present and assisted me this day in a second inspection of Mary's body. (120)

Here, as is so often the case, the body is seen to represent truth. Although what is taken from Mary's lips remains suspect, her scars on her back, her flesh, cannot lie. Skin determines the deployments of other body parts. The marks of authenticity, which the abolitionist women look for here, are a quite specific requirement. Flogging was a critical issue in provincial women's anti-slavery propaganda campaigns throughout the 1820s:

> In fact flogging was one of the worst punishments evangelical women could imagine — especially, but not only, in the case of females — since it combined absolute control and remorseless abuse of the female body by males ... Flogging, in a word, was anti-Christian. Worst of all, it was a public act, involving an exposed nakedness and an unsolicited male gaze sometimes even attracting spectators and enthusiasts.[16]

Flogging, it seems, still attracted spectators. The scene described by Mrs Pringle can be read as the obverse of the public spectacle for the male gaze; the context here is private and benevolent: only women testify to the sight of the scars. Moira Ferguson points out that Prince would have operated well within her rights (as evangelicals conceived of them) to refuse their request to view her body on grounds of modesty. It is important to note here that the enquiry to which Mrs Pringle responds is a 'benevolent' one, from fellow abolitionists. This final piece of authentication is as managed as the other certifications, and suggests how carefully the various layers of the text were generated to show proof and to anticipate and contain the sceptical reading. In this testimony which completes Prince's *History*, the amanuensis, the auditor, becomes the spectator and speaks under her own name. Here is a final grasp to assert truth on Prince's behalf through a white reading of her body, through recourse to the marks of her history on her back. Thus the relationship between Prince and Strickland, their adjacency, takes a different form. Ultimately the inscriptions of flogging on the body of the Caribbean woman, a body made grotesque and painful by abuse, are what speak authentically to the good people of England. These marks are not spoken of by Mary herself, but by the amanuensis.

There are a number of disturbing features in this viewing, this last cast for truth in the *History*. In each case, the disturbance is produced by leakage from one layer of the narrative into another. Firstly, although benevolence has replaced brutality, the viewing recorded in this Appendix hearkens back to those parts elsewhere in Prince's narration where she was exposed, open to view. This occurs at the market, where she is sold, and the floggings, where she is stripped, hanged and her flesh laid open. These brutalities haunt the viewing at Claremont Square, and bring the good people of England into a different relationship to the West Indies, supposedly a quite different moral and ethical sphere. Secondly, this haunting of earlier scenes is more evident when we go back to those descriptions of flogging and note that in fact Prince was a victim of a savage mistress as well as brutal masters. The pitiless fingers, the licking and flogging of her naked body, the knowledge of corporal punishment are at the hands of a mistress. The brutalization of women in slavery goes both ways. This is stressed in Pringle's remarks in the Supplement: slavery is a curse of the oppressor and the oppressed; its natural tendency is to brutalize both. He includes a description from his friend Dr Walsh to compare with Mary's narrative:

> I saw in the back yard of the house, a black girl of about fourteen years old; before her stood her mistress, a white woman, with a large stick in her hand. She was undressed except her petticoat and chemise, which had fallen down and left her shoulders and bosom bare. Her hair was streaming behind, and every fierce and malevolent passion was depicted on her face. She too, like my hostess at Governo [another striking illustration of the *dehumanizing* effects of Slavery] was the very representation of a fury. (123)

A reversal has taken place here: it is the body of the white woman that is unveiled, grotesque and passionate. The presentation of slavery as a disease of the social body, a debauchery that is written on the bodies of all who are involved, was a common feature of abolitionist rhetoric. This calls into question those constructions of blackness and whiteness which shaped racial identifications and opens white subjects to moral and political scrutiny. The disembodied white reader, like the amanuensis, is drawn into the text, named. The associations of white domesticity and continence and black depravity are called into question; the stereotypical qualities attributed to race and gender, to white women in domesticity and to black slaves who are their property, are confused.

Rhetorically this disturbance is often met by assertions of the separation between England and its colonies, much as the journey north is a progress to freedom in antebellum slave narratives in the United States. However, this separation is not sustained in Mary Prince's *History*. To be sure she remarks that she suffers abuse 'too, too bad to speak in England' at the hands of 'the Buckra people', the white colonists and owners. However, in the final pages she openly questions this separation: 'I have often wondered how English people can go into the West Indies and act in such a beastly manner. But when they go to the West Indies, they forget God and all feeling of shame' (83). This calls into question the character of the English, and dismantles that seemingly fixed opposition between black and white, that anchor of not only racial but also ethnic, class and gendered identities. In the *History* we find monstrous

white women and a slave woman who has all the attributes of English middle-
class domestic gentility: 'she is remarkable for her decency and propriety of
conduct – and her delicacy, even in trifling minutiae, has been a trait of special
remark by the females of my family', says Pringle (105). These are the kinds of
uncertainties and reversals that the unauthorized narrator can induce, even
with little room to manoeuvre.

These complications suggest that although skin fixed identities, the
opposition of black and white needs to be carefully examined in particular
discursive formations. The viewing of Mary Prince's body at Claremont Square
can be compared to those other occasions when black women were presented
as spectacles, and body parts were read. The most infamous example, 'Sarah
Bartmann' or 'Saat-Jee', was displayed naked at the London exhibition in 1810.
Others followed. These spectacles have been discussed at some length
elsewhere.[17] They are invoked here to remark on the contrast, on the fact that
it was not necessarily the case that black women's bodies were used to fix
European identities in terms of the sexual gaze, and these occasions might also
rebound in ways which brought the nature of the racial and gendered
distinctions and their mutability into question. Page du Bois' analysis of how
Athenian torture of slaves emerged from and reinforced the concept of truth as
something hidden in the body is useful here, although the context is quite
different. She points out that in the Athenian state torture performed two
functions. Firstly, as an instrument of demarcation it delineates the boundary
between slave and free, between the untouchable bodies of citizens and the
torturable bodies of slaves: 'The ambiguity of slave status, the difficulty of
sustaining an absolute sense of differences, is addressed through this practice
of the state, which carves the line between slave and free on the bodies of the
unfree.'[18] As we have seen, anxieties and ambiguities about distinctions
proliferate throughout the marginalia of the *History*, both between slave and
free women, and between the 'Buckra' people in the British West Indies and the
English colonizers at home. Secondly, there is a long-established association
between torture and truth, and the supremacy of evidence derived from the
slave's body even above the word of the master. This is, of course, what is at
stake in Prince's *History*, for even as she testified to the abuse she suffered, her
owners and their pro-slavery associates testified to their own propriety and
veracity at her expense. Before returning to Antigua the Woods were able to
prevent a discussion in the House of Commons about their conduct as slave
owners. John Wood brought an act for libel against Thomas Pringle, which he
won by default in 1833 because Pringle could not produce witnesses to prove
his allegations about their abuse of Mary Prince.[19] However, Prince's claim to
truth ultimately rests not on reason or speech but on evidence which
outweighs rhetoric:

Thus, according to Aristotle's logic, representative or not, the slave's truth is the master's truth; it is in the body of the slave that the master's truth lies, and it is in torture that his truth is revealed.... The master can conceal the truth, since he possesses reason and can choose between truth and lie, can choose the penalty associated with false testimony. His own point of vulnerability is the body of his slave.[20]

Volatile bodies

As we have seen, no simple equation can be made between Mary Prince and Susanna Strickland on the basis of their gender alone. Nor can we establish a relationship between them by recourse to terms of doubled, tripled colonizations of women. Race, gender, class and nation have imprinted their bodies in very different ways. Their differences alert us to the appropriateness of Denise Riley's description of women as a 'volatile collectivity'. Female persons, she says, 'can be very differently positioned so that the apparent continuity of the subject "women" isn't to be relied on; "women" is both synchronically and diachronically erratic as a collectivity ... for the individual "being a woman" is also inconstant.'[21] Riley's idea of the volatile collectivity of women alerts us to instability and change not only across the range of women's experiences, but also within the life of the individual. Characterizations of women vary historically and socially between women and within the life history of one woman. Mary Prince and her amanuensis are forceful examples of how women are positioned very differently synchronically, and how carefully they must negotiate access to the public at any one time. They also remind us, as critics of autobiography, that women's access to the status of autobiographer is negotiated through a passage from which subjectivity emerges bearing the imprints of experience and culture, self and society. The body is always embedded in history. However, the imprints, the readings can shift, and *The History of Mary Prince* suggests to us some ways that the identities of women could become implicated in unpredictable ways.

Susanna Strickland, no less than Mary Prince, will go on to be situated as a colonial subject. Silent as she was in Prince's *History*, she nevertheless became acutely aware of her own voice during the stay at Claremont Square. We know this from another piece of correspondence. Within a week of the inspection of Mary Prince's body and the testimony, the relationship between Strickland and Prince took a new turn. Here Mary Prince becomes the spectator, and the amanuensis is the autobiographical subject. A letter written by Strickland on 9 April 1831 reads:

I was on the 4th instant at St Pancras Church made the happiest girl on earth, in being united to the beloved being in whom I have long centred all my affections. Mr. Pringle 'gave me' away, and Black Mary, who had treated herself with a complete new suit upon the occasion, went on the coach box, to see her dear Missie and Biographer wed. I assure you, that instead of feeling the least regret at the step I was taking, if a tear trembled in my eyes, it was one of joy, and I pronounced the fatal obey, with a firm determination to keep it. My blue stockings, since I became a wife, have turned so pale that I think they will soon be quite white ...

I send you twenty copies of Mary's *History*, and two of Ashton Warner. If you can in the way of trade dispose of them, I should feel obliged. I have begun the pudding and dumpling discussions, and now find the noble art of housewifery is more to be desired than all the accomplishments, which are to be retailed by the literary and damsels who frequent these envied circles.[22]

The glimpse of Mary Prince as 'Black Mary', resplendent in a new suit and perched on the coach box of the bridal carriage, is almost the last report we have of her. However, the end of Prince's story is the beginning of Susanna Strickland-Moodie's autobiography, to which I shall return in a later chapter. For now it is of note that in the bridal letter Strickland appears as Prince's 'dear Missie and Biographer'. This confirms our sense of a close relationship and mutual affection between the women, but it is also worth remarking that the title 'Missie' appears in Prince's *History* when Mary refers to Miss Betsey, the little girl from whom Mary Prince was purchased 'as a pet': 'She used to lead me about by the hand, and call me her little nigger. This was the happiest period in my life; for I was too young to understand rightly my condition as a slave' (47). Even in a very different time and place, the title 'Missie' causes seepage and carries connotations of possession, as does the title 'Mr. Pringle's black Mary'. This also appears to be the only occasion where Strickland claims the title of biographer for *The History of Mary Prince*. Of interest to us here is the fact that these names circulate in a letter where she is acutely aware of the shifts and oppositions in identities concerning her own change of status and name, from spinster to wife. Furthermore, these identities are all implicated in notions of appropriate gendered, racial and class behaviors.

To date, no other reference to Prince in Moodie's writing has been uncovered. However, the presence of black Mary clearly inflects Strickland's presentation of her own rite of passage here. Why the 'fatal obey'? Since Mary Wollstonecraft, feminist critiques of marriage associated marriage with a kind of slavery for women, an association which hinged on 'obedience' and the loss of property and independence which by law accompanied marriage for women.

Strickland embraces the association between her change of status and change
of voice; the 'blue-stockings' were intellectual women who took their place
alongside men in urban intellectual circles from the end of the eighteenth
century. The metaphorical change of colour refers to Strickland's profound
sense of the rite of passage that is underway here, for she knew that as a wife
she would leave the urban intellectual circles she had frequented. The disposal
of the slave narratives which she transcribed marks the end of these pursuits,
with new accomplishments to emerge from the 'pudding and dumpling'
discussions, and the role of procreator and nurturer. This is the final glimpse of
Susanna Strickland, 'blue-stocking'. She emerges again out of England, in the
more familiar guise of Mrs Moodie, emigrant, mother, wife, and autobiographic subject. We will return to her in Chapter 2.

In thinking about Prince's *History* I have found much of the recent feminist
work on women's autobiographical writing very useful. In particular, Sidonie
Smith's discussion of subjectivity, identity and the body sets out a framework of
reading for the female body in autobiography through a quite specific series of
questions which pursue the complexities of embodiment and stress the place of
the body in history: Whose history of the body is being written? What specific
body does the autobiographical subject claim in her text? How and where does
the autobiographical speaker reveal or conceal, give or withhold? Does the body
drop away as the location of autobiographical identity, or does the speaker insist
on its founding identification? What are the implications for subjectivity of the
body's positioning? How is the body the performative boundary between inner
and outer, the subject and the world? What regulatory actions of the body
politic impinge on the deployment of the autobiographical body? How are other
bodies arranged in the text? Is the body a source of subversive practice, a
potentially emancipatory vehicle for autobiographical practice, or a source of
repression and suppressed narrative? At the scene of writing does the woman
take up the sanctities of official narratives? How far does she accommodate
inherited forms, the calls to a specific subjectivity, and how far does she stretch
the form to fill her own specific needs and desires? Where does she discover the
narrative elasticity and subversive possibilities of the genre?[23] Each of these
questions is suggestive in thinking about Mary Prince, who works within a very
specific script of female subjectivity, the slave narrative as required by British
abolitionists at the height of their campaign in the early 1830s, and who
manoeuvres and finds ways to suggest that the 'good people of England' may
need to know more than they will hear. She is required to transform herself and
emerge as a good domestic subject despite her history as a slave in the West
Indies, where pre-Victorian English notions of domesticity were alien. She, like
other slave narrators, finally spoke truth by revealing her body and displaying
the marks on her back, the certification that the abuse she had described had

taken place. Prince's *History* presents to us very clearly the complex ways that histories of the subject, discourses of identity, cultural inscriptions of the body, and laws of genre coalesce in the autobiographical 'I' and, as Smith stresses, this notion of the embodied subject takes us away from the universal subject, which is singular, unified and unencumbered by the body. These questions go a long way towards bringing Mary Prince into view, and giving us some ways of reading the complexities of the *History*.

The return of Mary Prince

Although Mary Prince disappears from view after 1832, her career as an autobiographer continues. The *History*, which went to a third edition in the first year of publication, was not republished in Britain until the Pandora edition of 1987, edited by Moira Ferguson with a Preface by Ziggi Alexander. Their commentary places the text for a quite different readership, and offers us yet another layer of interpretation – a quite different series of readings than those of Pringle, Prince's first editor. In 1987, as in 1831, Prince's interest or relevance to the reader as an autobiographical subject is established by the labour of her editor; she remains unknown beyond this text. Ziggi Alexander's Preface begins: 'What is significant about *The History of Mary Prince, a West Indian Slave, Related by Herself* to merit our attention today?' (vii). Ferguson's most recent American edition of the *History* (1997) begins quite differently. There is no preface, and Ferguson's introductory remarks are fashioned in a way which leaves no question about Prince's significance: 'The Voice of Freedom: Mary Prince.' With her first and subsequent editions, Ferguson has in a sense entered the writing scene of the *History*, for her work is to introduce Prince to a quite different cohort of readers, who need to understand not only Prince's story but also the interests of her editor and readers in pre-Victorian England. Here we might return to Ross Chambers' comment that texts may obtain an oppositional readability, which can become available at a later date and in changed historical circumstances. The survival of autobiographical narratives across time, their translation into the idioms and interests of a quite different epoch, depends on the ongoing production and generation of supplementary text around the original. The need for the canny editor to target a readership and package the life remains. For example, the renaissance of Harriet Jacobs' autobiography *Incidents in the Life of a Slave Girl* (1861) owes much to the work of Jean Fagan Yellin, whose literary and historical detective work led to a new definitive edition of Jacobs' text in the United States in 1987, the same year that Ferguson's *History of Mary Prince* was republished in London and Henry Louis Gates' *The Classic Slave Narratives* (which brings together the autobiographical narratives of Olaudah Equiano, Frederick Douglas, Mary Prince and Harriet Jacobs) appeared in New York.

This is of course not coincidental. That three editorial projects should 'midwife' these black autobiographies by Prince and Jacobs into a rebirth simultaneously is evidence of the sea change following a resurgence of interest in both black writers and women writers, and the shift in academic tastes and agendas to 'race, class and gender' in North America and Europe. As Rafia Zafar remarks, it seems to be Harriet Jacobs' fate to be over-exposed or under-exposed, or not exposed at all, and she is as ever dependent on associations between black and white women to establish her authenticity and interest.[24] Zafar writes self-consciously of the role of an editor:

> Where do I stand in relation to this undertaking? That is to say, has my role in putting together this collection, on the autobiography of a long-deceased, female, ex-slave, been overdetermined? What does it mean for black women academics to stand in the midst of ... the traffic jam ... that black feminist studies has become?[25]

Mary Prince has not become as voguish as Jacobs, and discussions of slave narratives are almost exclusively based on American examples. Ferguson is careful to remark upon the differences between American and British traditions, identifying in Prince's *History* elements of eighteenth-century British slave narrative, nineteenth-century US narrative, and the format of cases reported in the *British Anti-Slavery Reporter*, the press organ of the Anti-Slavery Society. The involvement of the Anti-Slavery Society in the publication of slave narratives in general, and in Prince's *History* in particular, leads to an important difference between British and US narratives:

> When black women did write or tell their experiences in the United States, their vivid testimonials frequently focussed on sexual exploitation and disruption of family ties. British female slaves and ex-slaves, by contrast, were either written about in the Anti-Slavery Reporter or had little or no opportunity to chronicle, let alone publish, their experiences. (4)

The form required by the Society and implemented by Pringle leads Ferguson to argue that Prince, unlike American black women, was unable to 'present her authentic experience', and was forced to use strategies for encoding the truth about her sexual experiences in particular. This argument is fundamental to Ferguson's reading of the *History*. To what extent is it based on expectations of truth which are culturally grounded – in American traditions of slave narrative, and in ideas of authenticity which are based upon recent feminist theory?

These are important questions for thinking about Ferguson's work as Prince's most recent editor.

In placing Prince's *History* before a new readership, Ferguson's Introduction supersedes Pringle's Preface as our point of entry to the text. Like Pringle, she has no desire to 'detain' the reader from Prince's narrative; however, she is no less anxious than Pringle that Prince's narrative be received by a 'believing' reader. To invite belief, Ferguson adopts two strategies. Firstly, she documents her extensive and meticulous archival work on Prince and her text. The most recent republication of the *History* includes further historical research in the Caribbean, as well as recognition of the connection between Prince and Susanna Strickland Moodie. Like Yellin's scholarly edition of Jacobs' *Incidents*, Ferguson confronts the question of authenticity at one level with historical detail from sources as diverse as parish records in Bermuda, slave registries, Antiguan law and parliamentary records. In this way Prince's veracity is tested by fact. In his Preface Pringle assures us that once Prince's narrative had been written out by Strickland 'I went over the whole, carefully examining her on every fact and circumstance detailed' (45). One hundred and thirty years later Ferguson's examination of the body of the text is no less meticulous, but the priorities and politics are quite deliberately different. Her research in the Bermuda archives, for example, allows her to identify the slave-owners who abused Mary Prince, as opposed to Pringle's policy of including just an initial and leaving them to answer 'at a more awful tribunal'.

Secondly, Ferguson's Introduction focuses on Prince's first-person narration, and glosses Prince's story in some detail in order to place the contemporary reader closer to Prince's lips, and to rupture that seeming continuum of narrator–amanuensis–editor. Ferguson wishes to bring into view omissions, the strategies for 'encoding truth and inviting interpretation beyond the surface message' through which Prince 'lets the reader know' aspects of her life which were taboo. Ferguson's 'truth' is not the same as that of Prince's first editor, Thomas Pringle. Indeed it is strategically important that the truth of Pringle's Preface be superseded, for Ferguson considers sexual experience and sexual abuse to be vital to our understanding of Prince's *History* (and history). She points out that the Anti-Slavery Society won public support by detailing atrocities and portraying slaves as pure and Christian-like, innocent victims and martyrs. 'They could not be seen to be involved in any situation (even if the women were forcibly coerced) that smacked of sin and moral corruption. Christian purity, for these abolitionists, overrode regard for truth' (3–4). Throughout her summary, Ferguson invites us to 'overread' sections of the *History* for Prince's 'authentic experience', where the 'taboo' policed by Pringle is foiled through encoded messages about abusive sexual experiences. Pringle's docile slave–servant, emblematic of virtue, is replaced by Ferguson's 'unique' and 'authentic' self. The contemporary editor excavates the 'indomitable self-made heroine' and 'voice of freedom' from beneath the layers of abolitionist propaganda and rhetoric.

We can see this approach in more detail when Ferguson considers Mary Prince in her discussion of 'Extending discourse'.[26] Here she draws on colonial discourse theory to examine the 'othering' of Prince by both abolitionists and slave-owners and to understand how Prince 'claims herself as a speaking, acting, thinking subject with an identity separate from Anglo-Africanist constructions of her past and present reality'. Here Ferguson suggests that Prince engages in 'jousts' with her editor, an 'equivocal' narrator with a 'sparring' voice, engaging in double-voiced discourse. This reading suggests that by openly thanking her amanuensis in the last paragraphs of the *History*, Prince effects a power reversal which casts the amanuensis, Susanna Strickland, as 'an archetypal slave-other who takes orders and generates wealth (in this case textual wealth) simultaneously, an embodiment of Mary Prince's literacy'. Thus 'white' scribe becomes 'black' slave; the 'white British texts' that seek to contain and construct Prince cannot rupture the inviolable text she creates for herself.

Power. Truth. Authenticity. How can the association between black and white women be played out? These issues circle about and through the production of Prince's autobiography then, and our readings and uses of it now. To become an editor of Prince's *History* is to enter a force field of anxiety where – to return to Sidonie Smith – cultural ideologies intersect and dissect one another, in contradiction, consonance and adjacency. Ferguson produces another layer surrounding Prince's *History*. As Pringle desired Prince to speak as an authentic subject for abolitionist rhetoric, so Ferguson desires to return to the *History*, to 'Mary's own lips', and exhume the independent, authentic subject pursued by late twentieth-century feminism. This subject has agency; this subject is able to surmount all the prefaces, introductions, apologias, diatribes that encrust the text and establish her own domain, autonomous and independent, an essence free of the text. To be an authentic subject for a white audience now, Mary Prince emerges as a heroine. This is no less conventional than the Mary Prince stage-managed by Pringle, although the conventions are very different. It is less restricting only if we accept that it is implications of sexual abuse, the installation of a sexual history, which lend truth to the *History* and amplification to the self.

In a comment which resonates through discussions of slave narratives, Robert Stepto suggests 'it is the reader – not the author or text and certainly not the storyteller in the text – who is unreliable'.[27] The impulse to be an unreliable reader, to 'escape' the editor and evade his or her appeals to us, in much the same way as Ferguson imagines Prince's escape, is hard to resist. We are amidst a tangle of problems here which are fundamental to thinking about reading and writing autobiography in colonial cultures, and about postcolonial readings more generally. By bringing both of her editors, Pringle and Ferguson, into the writing scene of Prince's text, fanciful as this is, I mean to suggest that the Prince constructed by a contemporary editor in the most recent marginalia is not unalike that created in the next 'layer', Pringle's Preface of 1831. They each seek to convince us that they are close to 'Mary's lips', the source of truth, and yet each must scrutinize, inspect what comes from these lips via other sources of authority to establish the figure of the autobiography. To speak to us, Mary Prince will always be constructed in black and white, in terms of shifting constructions of agency, subjectivity and truth, for the subject that we can hear changes with time, place and intent, untethered by authenticity to an essence. Now, drawing on contemporary notions of identity, sexuality and authenticity, we encounter a different kind of truth.

To return to Rafia Zafar's metaphor, we are in a traffic jam, a critical intersection where we must be highly self-conscious of where we stand, and what our responsibilities are as readers, critics and teachers. We, too, are exposed.[28] As Elizabeth Fox-Genovese suggests, to categorize autobiographies according to the race and gender of those who write them is to acknowledge some relation, however problematical, between the text and its author and, more, between the text and its author's experience.[29] However, is it useful to transpose terms like self and author, or authenticity and experience, into the History? These terms belong to a register that is alien to the negotiations which took place around this hybrid text. They also seem to foreclose on the ongoing and open-ended process of reading and judgement which the History produces. An alternative strategy may be to suggest that what we have bound together before us now, the complex and sometimes tortuous series of oppositional manoeuvres by Prince, by her amanuensis and editor, by abolitionist and pro-slavery interests, and – as I have suggested here – by the most recent editor, may well be a highly appropriate artefact and record of that 'relation, however problematical, between the text and its author and between the text and its author's experience' which Fox-Genovese requires. There is no retrieving the History from its genesis in an autobiographical occasion marked by 'contradiction, consonance and adjacency' into the singularity and comfort of an individual personality and a heroine. The History suggests that gender and race are highly volatile components of a life story, played out in different, unpredictable ways in the life of the individual subject, and in the lives of women.

By reading Prince as an autobiographer out of empire, by thinking about how feminism and postcolonialism together might understand her History, I mean to suggest that colonialism produces particular inflections in answers we might make to Smith's questions for thinking about the body in autobiographical writing. What characterizes colonialism, what makes colonial encounters different? Clearly colonialism doesn't relate to any meaningful category or unitary totality in and of itself. As we have seen, critics who work with colonial and postcolonial materials, like Suleri, increasingly deplore the tendency to totalities such as the 'other', 'imperialism' and 'colonial discourse' which proliferate and make understandings of colonial relations quite clumsy and non-specific. But nor do these critics wish to lose sight of how fundamentally colonialism has produced, and continues to produce, power relations which deeply inflect the subject and subjectivities that emerge out of empire. These have always been, and continue to be, grounds for contestation. By reading Prince's *History* in terms of a colonial encounter, albeit in a quite localized and specific way, the asymmetrical inter-social relationships and the struggle, misrecognition and disingenuous compliance which Nicholas Thomas suggests tend to characterize colonial relations in particular, come into view.[30] As we see, even brutally suppressed colonized subjects might find room for manoeuvre, to make in even the most prescriptive occasions an oppositional text. Most important of all, reading autobiographical writing through processes of colonialism foregrounds the making of identities through relationships and social processes. This is at one and the same time the strength and the weakness of reading texts 'out of empire', for the promise is that we might come to a more complex understanding of how ambivalence, intersubjectivity and inconsistency feature in representations of the self. However, these shifting grounds, these volatile bodies, are obscured in the language of 'others' and 'worlds'.

There is of course much common ground between feminist and postcolonial ways of thinking about autobiography, the idea of shifting subjectivity not being a prerogative of postcolonialism alone. However, postcolonial criticism is distinguished by a particularly strong sense of the intimacies of identity formation, how subjects are formed and reformed in relation to others, with unpredictable intersections, connections and leakage between. These subjects are always to be understood in terms of precise localities, for it is only in specific encounters that the imprint of ideologies of race, gender and sexuality can be read.

To return to Prince, then, I would suggest that we can best understand that body in time and place by reading it alongside and with that very differently gendered subject, Susanna Strickland, a woman who was herself in the process of change. Their identities emerge in relational terms. This is to some extent a 'black' and 'white' issue. Race was an organizing grammar of the imperial order, where policing of the body and the body politic both began and ended with 'blood' and 'skin'. It is after all skin that determines Mary Prince's status and her authority to speak as an autobiographic subject; it is the skin on her back that verifies her speech. We can equally understand Strickland's bourgeois civility as a function of race, and a particular expression of racial gendered identity. However for all that we set out to understand how the modern, bourgeois self was fashioned against the grotesque, undisciplined bodies of 'other women',[31] it is also evident that identities might come adrift; that as a West Indian slave might become a decent, even delicate member of an English household, so too the femininity, self-discipline and restraint of white women and men might come undone out of England. These are the confusions, 'the ground between', where the makings of the black and the white are unravelled. And so, as she looks at her mistress, Mary Prince assures us, 'I saw her change colour' (76).

Notes

1 Gloria Anzaldúa, *Borderlands La Frontera: The New Mestiza*. San Francisco: Aunt Lute Books, 1987, Preface.

2 Stephen Butterfield, *Black Autobiography in America*. Amherst: University of Massachusetts Press, 1974, p. 12.

3 I first discussed relations between Susanna Strickland Moodie and Mary Prince at the 'Colonization and Women's Texts' seminar at the University of Calgary in 1992. A version of this paper, which focuses on settler subjects, was published as 'The silent scribe: Susanna and "Black Mary"', *International Journal of Canadian Studies* (spring 1995): 249–260; an extract appears in Bill Ashcroft *et al.* (eds), *The Post-Colonial Studies Reader*. London: Routledge, 1995, pp. 349–354. Carl Ballstadt discussed Moodie's work as an amanuensis in 'Susanna Moodie: early humanitarian works', *Canadian Notes and Queries*, 8 (November 1971): 9–10.

4 Gloria Anzaldúa, 'Speaking in tongues: a letter to 3rd world women writers', in Cherrie Moraga and Gloria Anzaldúa (eds), *This Bridge Called My Back: Writing by Radical Women of Colour*, 2nd edn. New York: Kitchen Table Women of Color, 1983, p. 172.

5 Sara Suleri, *Meatless Days*. Chicago: University of Chicago Press, 1989, p. 20.

6 Sara Suleri, *The Rhetoric of English India*. Chicago: University of Chicago Press, 1992, p. 3.

7 Moira Ferguson (ed.), *The History of Mary Prince. A West Indian Slave, Related by Herself*. Ann Arbor: University of Michigan Press, 1997, p. 57. Further references to this edition in text.

8 Sidonie Smith and Julia Watson (eds), *De/Colonizing the Subject: The Politics of Gender in Women's Autobiography*. Minneapolis: University of Minnesota Press, 1992, p. xix.

9 Ross Chambers, *Room for Maneuver. Reading Oppositional Narrative*. Chicago: University of Chicago Press, 1991, p. ix. Further references in text.

10   Felicity Nussbaum, *Torrid Zones: Maternity, Sexuality and Empire in Eighteenth-Century English Narratives*. Baltimore: Johns Hopkins University Press, 1995, p. 2.

11   Mary Louise Pratt, *Imperial Eyes: Travel Writing and Transculturation*. London: Routledge, 1992.

12   Leigh Gilmore, *Autobiographics: A Feminist Theory of Women's Self-Representation*. Ithaca, NY: Cornell University Press, 1994, p. ix.

13   Carl Ballstadt et al., *Susanna Moodie: Letters of a Lifetime*. Toronto: University of Toronto Press, 1985, p. 57.

14   Deborah Garfield, 'Earwitness: female abolitionism, sexuality, and *Incidents in the Life of a Slave Girl*', in Deborah M. Garfield and Rafia Zafar (eds), *Harriet Jacobs and 'Incidents in the Life of a Slave Girl'*. New York: Cambridge University Press, 1996, p. 106.

15   Shari Benstock, 'At the margin of discourse: footnotes in the fictional text', *PMLA*, 98 (March 1983): 204–225, p. 204.

16   Moira Ferguson, *Subject to Others: British Women Writers and Colonial Slavery, 1670–1834*. New York: Routledge, 1992, p. 293.

17   Anita Levy, *Other Women: The Writing of Class, Race, and Gender, 1832–1898*. Princeton: Princeton University Press, 1991, p. 71; Sander L. Gilman, *Difference and Pathology: Stereotypes of Sexuality, Race and Madness*. Ithaca, NY: Cornell University Press, 1985; Stephen J. Gould, 'The Hottentot Venus', *Natural History*, 91: 20–27.

18   Page du Bois, *Torture and Truth*. New York: Routledge, 1991, p. 63. I am grateful to Leigh Dale for recommending this reference in relation to Prince.

19   Moira Ferguson's most recent research into these cases and other references to them are included in her 1997 edition of the *History*.

20   du Bois, p. 66.

21   Denise Riley, *'Am I That Name?' Feminism and the Category of 'Women' in History*. Minneapolis: University of Minnesota Press, 1988, p. 2.

22   Ballstadt et al. (1985), p. 61.

23   Sidonie Smith, *Subjectivity, Identity and the Body*. Bloomington: Indiana University Press, 1993, p. 23.

24   Rafia Zafar, 'Introduction. Over-exposed, under-exposed: Harriet Jacobs and *Incidents in the Life of a Slave Girl* ', in Deborah M. Garfield and Rafia Zafar (eds), *Harriet Jacobs and 'Incidents in the Life of a Slave Girl'*. New York: Cambridge University Press, 1996, p. 2.

25   Zafar, p. 1. She also refers here to Ann duCille, 'The occult of true black womanhood: critical demeanour and black feminist studies,' *Signs*, 19(3) (spring 1994): 591, 593.

26   Moira Ferguson, *Subject to Others: British Women Writers and Colonial Slavery, 1670–1834*. New York: Routledge, 1992, pp. 281–298.

27   Robert Stepto, 'Distrust of the reader in Afro-American narratives,' in Sacvan Bercovitch (ed.), *Reconstructing American Literary History*. Cambridge, MA: Harvard University Press, 1986, p. 309.

28   Zafar and duCille are interested in the particular responsibilities and place of black women academics in the field of black feminist studies. As I am thinking through

the connotations of 'black' and 'white' here I am not presuming that the reader is necessarily racially identified as white although, as duCille and Zafar suggest, the stakes for black women readers in debates about how to read black women's texts, their interest in what duCille calls 'critical demeanour', are different.

29 Elizabeth Fox-Genovese, 'To write my self: the autobiographies of Afro-American women', in Shari Benstock (ed.), *Feminist Issues in Literary Scholarship.* Bloomington/ Indianapolis: Indiana University Press, 1987, p. 161.

30 Nicholas Thomas, *Colonialism's Culture: Anthropology, Travel and Government.* Cambridge: Polity Press, 1994, pp. 4–5.

31 See Anita Levy, *Other Women: The Writing of Class, Race and Gender, 1832–1898.* Princeton: Princeton University Press, 1991.

2

Settler subjects

The study of English Canadian literature poses [a] problem: history is too close, or has been made to feel too close.[1]

The recesses of the domestic space become the sites for history's most intricate invasions.[2]

Blood and milk: *Roughing It in the Bush*

The struggle, misrecognition and disingenuous compliance which characterize colonial encounters infect autobiographical writing out of Empire – which, as was suggested in Chapter 1, may also occur through relations in the heart of empire. Radically compromised authors, narrators and complex figurations and displacements of the self are signs of these encounters in autobiographical writing. These signs need to be read in terms of social, historical and cultural scripts for shaping the self in place and in time. Like Mary Prince's *History*, Susanna Moodie's autobiographical sketches *Roughing It in the Bush* emerge through the micropolitics and the historical circumstances of writing 'out of Empire'. Here too the marks of engagement with processes of colonization, settlement and invasion are apparent. As we have seen, the slave narrative is an autobiographical occasion where the script for writing the self as a colonized subject is omnipresent. For settler subjects too there were limits to ways that were available to them – culturally, socially, politically and ethically – to make account of themselves, although the contours of the script, the available discourses, were more flexible and discreet. Both Susanna Moodie and her husband, John Dunbar Moodie, use the sketches of *Roughing It* to present a highly self-conscious and critical account of their experiences as settlers, one which questions explicitly the prevailing representations of

Canadian pioneer life in the literature of emigration. As we saw in Chapter 1, autobiographical texts can be sites where 'things fall apart', and the struggle to assemble a speaking subject remains palpable in the final text. In Susanna and John Moodie's autobiographical sketches, the 'faire' of devising the self in text is apparent.

Susanna and John Dunbar Moodie and their baby daughter left England in July 1832. In the first instance they purchased land near the shores of Lake Ontario, at Cobourg in Upper Canada. A year later they relocated to the backwoods, to Douro. Their backwoods holdings there were about a mile from the property of Susanna's sister and close companion, Catharine Parr, and her husband, Thomas Traill, a Scotsman and fellow officer of John Moodie, who had also emigrated to Upper Canada in the summer of 1832. They were close to their brother Samuel Strickland and his family, who had emigrated some years earlier. In the backwoods at Douro, conditions were harsh and unpredictable. Catharine Parr Traill was also the author of an autobiographic account of pioneering life, *The Backwoods of Canada*, an emigrant handbook published in 1836. I will return to this shortly as an adjacent text for reading *Roughing It*. When rebellion broke out in Upper Canada in December 1837 John left to serve with the militia, leaving Susanna to manage the farm alone. In the autumn of 1839 he was offered an official appointment in Belleville, a town on the shores of Lake Ontario. Susanna and the children set out on 1 January 1840, departing the backwoods with joy and relief which she describes in her last Canadian sketch, 'Adieu to the Woods'.

Roughing It in the Bush is a series of Canadian sketches and poems which form an autobiographical account of the two phases of their life as pioneer farmers: at Cobourg, and then in the backwoods, between 1832 and 1839. The earliest published forms of the Canadian sketches, which were a marked departure from Moodie's other writings in their contemporary Canadian setting and their presentation of the self as autobiographical subject, began to appear in local periodicals, the *Literary Garland* and the *Victoria Magazine*, in 1847. These are the bases for eleven of the twenty-nine chapters that were published as *Roughing It in the Bush* in 1852 by Bentley of London. This first edition included John Moodie's 'Canadian sketches' too. Bentley was familiar with John's work, having published his memoir *Ten Years in South Africa* in 1835. Bentley and the Moodies' London agent, John Bruce, made extensive changes in the process of publication. As John Thurston remarks in his discussion of the production of the text, significant parts of *Roughing It in the Bush* failed to make the Atlantic crossing or arrived shuffled and disoriented.[3] The book, which was a critical success but did not sell well, has subsequently been republished in a variety of editions and is generally accepted as a classic in the canon of Canadian literature.

Recent and extensive bibliographical scholarship on the text of *Roughing It* suggests that Susanna Moodie should be conceived as the initiator and focus of a long process of textual activity called *Roughing It in the Bush*, rather than an autonomous author in the conventional sense. Like *The History of Mary Prince*, this text emerges from complex and ongoing collaborative work: between John and Susanna Moodie; between the Moodies and the publisher and editor of the first edition, Bruce and Bentley; and through a series of editions which have tended to define Susanna Moodie as a Canadian subject. John Thurston has argued that the series of authors, editors, texts, environments of writing, market factors and paths of dissemination around the text are so unstable and open-ended as to vitiate any configuration at the centre which could be attributed to an autonomous author and her final intentions. However, it does not follow from this, as Thurston suggests, that in all its contradictions, irresolution, generic amorphousness and disunity, *Roughing It* tells a story 'of which Moodie had little conscious awareness'.[4] As I have argued in approaching *The History of Mary Prince* through Ross Chambers' notion of oppositional reading, the adroitness and ongoing oppositionality of autobiographical writing is understood in terms of textual specificity rather than the presence or absence of authorial intention, agency or consciousness. The textual complexity of *Roughing It* is evident in Carl Ballstadt's scholarly edition of 1988, which established a readily available variorum edition for the first time. Along with this scholarly edition, the publication of two volumes of correspondence, one drawing on Susanna Moodie's letters and another focusing on correspondence between the couple in particular, interact with the sketches, and complicate and amplify autobiographic readings of them.[5] The scholarly edition and the volumes of correspondence open *Roughing It* to new kinds of oppositional reading, which is to say that of late, Moodie's autobiographic sketches have been opened up to different manoeuvres.

Despite these similarities, *Roughing It* is not like *The History of Mary Prince* at all. Susanna Moodie speaks as a mother and wife. John Moodie writes as a husband and father. For both husband and wife the gendered and sexed self is deeply implicated in the politics of race, class and ethnicity as they converged to formulate the domestic settler subject in the early nineteenth century. In Mary Prince's *History* the politics of race determine that her experience as a gendered, sexed body are written out. For both John and Susanna Moodie marriage and parenthood will be constitutive, the most fundamental element in their articulation of self. In her discussion of the emergence of gendered positions in discourse, Elspeth Probyn argues that the self is never simply put forward in discourse, but rather is reworked in its enunciation, for the ways that sex is constantly re-gendered are never fixed or stable. Because of these fluctuations – 'volatilities' as Denise Riley might say – Probyn designates this self as a *combinatoire*, 'a discursive arrangement that holds together in tension the different lines of race and sexuality that form and re-form our senses of self.... This self therefore represents the process of being gendered and the project of putting that process into discourse'.[6] Although feminist readings of women's autobiographical writing in particular tend to present autobiography as a unifying discourse where certain gendered qualities are constant, by their very nature colonial encounters highlight the inconsistencies and constructions of the self, even within the confines of the individual life. *Roughing It* is a brilliant example of the volatility of the autobiographic subject, for the sketches reveal the work of constructing a sense of self in autobiography when the coordinates of stability and tradition have been called into question.

Colonizer and colonized

Thinking about settlers is deeply unfashionable in postcolonial criticism. Settlers have always been unpalatable subjects. Their writings bring to the fore the 'less defined cadences' of postcolonialism: politically flawed texts which rest uncomfortably on the cusp of coloniality, writings which work with rather than against European models, and feature difficult and sometimes ambiguous engagements with a history of invasion and dispossession.[7] To mark the colour of the white diaspora of settlers requires careful attention to cultural and social practices which often remain unmarked and unnamed. The racialness of white experience tends to be figured as neutrality – 'the apparent emptiness of white as a cultural identity'.[8] This transparency is in itself an effect of its dominance. Little has been done to theorize the settler subject, and there remains active hostility to the inclusion of Australian, Canadian, South African and New Zealand colonial settlements in the framework of the postcolonial.[9] However, if, as one critic has recently suggested, postcolonialism has become conceptually dis/contented, 'a suitcase blown open on the baggage belt ... No one speaks for "the postcolonial". No one place contains its diversity and accord',[10] the time may be ripe for a reading of autobiographies by settler subjects in terms other than the national tradition on one hand, or the minor British literature on the other. Critiques of postcolonial thinking about the third world, which reject monolithic categories of oppression and binary notions of the colonizer and colonized, dominant and subaltern in favour of connections and ambivalence, suggest ways of thinking about settler subjects. As we saw in Chapter 1, what monolithic identifications miss are the leakages and connections, the recognition that identities as gendered, racial subjects are produced in opposition and in confusion. The complexities of the settler subject, who as both colonizer and colonized occupies a uniquely ambivalent position, are a quite distinct domain in the field of postcolonialism – but 'in' it nevertheless. The argument has been rehearsed elsewhere and need not be repeated here.[11]

In this chapter, *Roughing It* will be read as one episode in the process of being gendered through colonial encounters. It is a rare autobiographical account where we see the first-person articulation of both masculine and feminine characteristics as these were understood in adjacency at a clearly discernible historical conjuncture. So 'gender' here is not just femininity; it is a discourse of femininity that is imagined in relation to a particular formulation of masculinity. Feminist readings of *Roughing It* are powerful and persuasive. The emergence of feminist and thematic criticism in Canada in the 1970s produced a new readership for Moodie's autobiography.[12] This is in no small way due to Margaret Atwood, whose sequence of poems *The Journals of Susanna Moodie* includes a spectacular leap of imagination, where Moodie is brought right into the present as a passenger on a bus in downtown Toronto: 'I am the old woman/sitting across from you on the bus.'[13] Moodie also appears in one of Atwood's more recent fictions, *Alias Grace*. Feminist critics who feel autobiographically attached to this early Victorian autobiographer and who write out of a strong sense of intersubjectivity with her have offered other powerful readings of Moodie's work. Most recently this grows from a recognition of how artfully Moodie depicts the maternal body, how thoroughly her sketches are peopled with mothers and children, birth and death.[14] Like Mary Prince, Susanna Moodie has been spectacularly successful in manoeuvring for a late twentieth-century readership.

Reading autobiography for representations of gender and nation can be fundamental to postcolonial readings of the autobiography too, and it will be important in the work of this chapter. However, these readings are less inclined to bring Mrs Moodie 'close', and a subject for identification. Nor should they make her familiar in terms of contemporary understandings of marriage and motherhood. In fact, thinking about Moodie as a settler subject locates her very precisely in a discursive formation which she and her kin sought to embody, articulate and reform: the domestic subject as it emerged through evangelical thinking in pre- to mid-Victorian Britain. This necessarily modifies the sense of *Roughing It* as a narrative of female empowerment, of women surviving together in isolation, for the domestic subject is articulated through the couple and the family, through an interdependent rather than an individualist understanding of identity and subjectivity. Nor does this reading of Moodie's autobiographical writing place it in terms of any distinctively Canadian tradition, where a national self is imagined and invented. Rather it looks to the linking of autobiographic writings by John and Susanna Moodie, and ways they drew upon and contributed to trans-Atlantic discourses of domestication and pioneering in Upper Canada.

The gendered body does not survive this reading practice with any kind of continuity, familiarity or integrity across time and place; rather it is that volatility and the sense of complex intersections of gender, race and ethnicity which emerge. In the Empire, reproductive bodies are invested with particular importance.[15] However, these bodies are deeply embedded in place and in time, in particular formulations of race, class and gender. As Nicholas Thomas suggests, a strategy that situates colonial representations and narratives in terms of agents, locations and periods, terms that are conducive to a differentiated vision of colonialisms rather than colonialism, is required.[16] This strategy localizes colonialism in encounters. By figuring Moodie as a settler subject her autobiographical writing is trained back on to a particular ground, on to a complex location from which *Roughing It in the Bush* emerged. This settler self cannot be seen as an entity which floats free of sexual, racial and ethnic differences. Indeed it is constituted by and through difference, and in history. Colonialism throws that *combinatoire*, that production of the self in the text, into sharp relief. This process of scripting the self in relation to others, through oppositions, intimacies and distinctions with and through others, is germane (although not unique) to colonial encounters. These shape autobiographic writing not through oppositions so much as through adjacencies and intimacies, through associations and dissociations that are complex and ongoing. The relationship between Strickland/Moodie and Mary Prince, discussed at length in Chapter 1, remains significant here. Although Mary Prince is to all intents and purposes left behind as John and Susanna Moodie ride in their bridal carriage, the intellectual, ideological commitment to abolitionism and evangelicalism in the Pringle circle is crucial to ways that the Moodies will represent themselves as domestic subjects in their Canadian sketches.

Grosse Isle, summer 1832

The crossing, the process of departure and distancing from Europe are germinal in nineteenth-century emigrant autobiographies. Here is the birth of the settler subject. For settlers are not travellers, they are not on a circuitous journey where there is prospect of return; they are part of an exodus.[17] In the very first sketch of *Roughing It* there is a quite stunning and textually complex autobiographical presentation of a younger self, as 'Mrs Moodie', an immigrant, leaving England and entering Canadian space on the deck of the *Anne* after an Atlantic crossing of nine weeks in the late summer of 1832. The difficult transformation of the blue-stocking abolitionist Susanna Strickland, which we glimpsed in Chapter 1 through her correspondence from the Pringle household, into Susanna Moodie, Canadian author, wife, mother and creator of 'Mrs Moodie', the fallible, conflicted character at the centre of the sketches, is clear from the very start. This radical textual disturbance in the description of sighting and landing ashore is immediately apparent in 'A Visit to Grosse Isle', the first of the Canadian sketches. The sketch reflects upon an occasion of some personal trauma, and also a moment resonant with ideological implications: 'it is always this beginning moment that the discourse hesitates over'.[18]

Susanna and her sister Catharine Parr Traill chose to shape their recollections of life in the backwoods in terms of quite different generic traditions. *Roughing It in the Bush* is a series of autobiographical sketches. *The Backwoods of Canada* is a series of letters ostensibly written 'home' by 'the Wife of an Emigrant Officer', designed as a handbook for prospective immigrants. And yet each begins the narration of emigration and settlement aboard ship, already apart from England and across the Atlantic in the St Lawrence, on the edge of the new, raw settlements in Upper Canada (later Ontario). Arnold Toynbee has argued that this crossing produces a 'sea change', a new awareness of self and of social issues:

> In transmarine migration, the social apparatus of the migrants has to be packed on board ship before they can leave the shores of the old country and then unpacked again at the end of the voyage before they can make themselves at home on new ground. All kinds of apparatus – persons and property, techniques and institutions and ideas – are equally subject to this law. Anything that cannot stand the sea voyage at all has simply to be left behind; and many things – and these are not only material objects – which the migrants do manage to take with them can only be shipped after they have been taken to pieces – never, perhaps, to be reassembled in their original form.[19]

The crossing initiates a new consciousness of the self through emigration. The different configurations that emerge in the colony begin with these boundaries of departure and arrival, which initiate acute self-awareness and the beginnings of transformation. In his analysis of this 'sea change' David Bentley isolates a number of mythic, archetypal elements which linger around this relocation in settler writing: Homeric, Herculean, biblical (the Ark), and (he suggests) Crusoe.[20] The Swiss Family Robinson may be a more appropriate topos for the domestic, familial process of settlement narrated by Susanna Moodie and Catharine Parr Traill. There is little of Crusoe's masculine individualism, or the encounter with racial others in the form of indigenous peoples as constitutive of a settler subjectivity. In fact there is a quite different model of masculinity at work in *Roughing It*, and it is not produced through domination of racial others. Nor does Crusoe allow for the fantasies about the emigrant wife and mother as a model of spiritual strength and femininity, a Madonna figure, which is a crucial component of settler autobiography in particular.[21] As we will see, Robinson Crusoe is the template for John Moodie's memoir of South Africa, not his very different autobiographical writing from Upper Canada.

There is no doubt that the familiar self is estranged, and the social, cultural and ethical formations of the self are cast into relief at this boundary. This is germinal for thinking about how settler subjectivities emerge in autobiographical writing from the colony. Writing about the transplanted, immigrant 'I' can produce a self-conscious engagement with the available discourses of truth and identity, which foreground processes of negotiation and transformation. At these boundaries, the autobiographer can be led to more self-conscious and experimental autobiographics. The idea that representing oneself to oneself and to others creates discursive spacing, an awareness of discontinuities in identity and a desire to incorporate this in autobiographic representation, did not begin with Stein and Woolf, modernism and the twentieth century.

For example, throughout Susanna Moodie's sketches there is a fluctuating relationship between the autobiographic narrator – a seasoned settler, located in the small provincial town of Belleville who began to write autobiographic- ally in the 1840s after a retreat from poverty in the backwoods; her autobiographic subject – the young Mrs Moodie, arriving in Upper Canada in 1832; and the author – Susanna Moodie. This is evident in the first sketch, where young Mrs Moodie's emotive performance of the sublime response to the St Lawrence landscape is almost always undermined by the intrusive discord around and about them. Glimpses of prosperity and domestication from the deck are similarly deceptive when brought into closer view upon landing. The theme of false expectations and deceptive appearances is sustained throughout the Canadian sketches, most obviously through the device of this gap between the narrator and her younger self. To be sure, there is no consistency in this. The older narrator is capable of vastly different responses to 'the new world'; the irony at the expense of the younger self is not evenly sustained. She is at times scathing of the innocence of that autobiographic character – the young, inexperienced wife of a farmer, she lacks elementary skills in household management and animal husbandry. As the narrator remarks in the sketch 'John Monaghan', 'I was foolish and inexperienced, and unaccustomed to the yoke' (156). At times this is a source of humour at her own expense – for example, the young woman is easily duped by the Yankee neighbours in their first settlement at Cobourg; this is the theme of a whole sketch, 'Our Borrowing'. And yet in other sketches there are continuities between the retrospective narrator and the immigrant. For example, Mrs Moodie is recognizably the younger self of the narrator as the 'blue-stocking' who reads Voltaire aboard ship in the 'Grosse Isle' sketch. The young Mrs Moodie is frequently represented as a writer in search of material, and eagerly gathers such material for characters and scenes at Cobourg. For example, she represents herself as the listener to the story of Jeanie Burns narrated by James, preparing for the imaginative return to these incidents as a writer. It is also evident that writing autobiographically about her younger self in the 1840s becomes a way of representing ongoing ambivalence, nostalgia and estrangement which remain a legacy of emigration. The younger, divided self is in conflict with her surroundings and conflicted in her feelings and intuitions – quite openly so in 'The Charivari', for example, which stresses the fluctuating relationship between the narrator and her subject.[22]

Through the surge of emigration in the 1830s, for a brief period of time, Upper Canada emerged as an extraordinary site of autobiographic writing. A number of middle- and upper-class women, mostly newly married, who emigrated and became settler, mother, pioneer, wrote about that decade in journals, letters, settler guides, memoirs.[23] These are 'prolific' women writing 'prolifically'; this writing scene produced a rare occurrence: women writing autobiographically around and about their years of childbearing. Susanna and Catharine's experience of childbirth in the backwoods, of becoming mother to a large family, wife of a man unsuited to labour, of extraordinary hardship and poverty, and frequent illness and death of loved ones, is shared. The adjacency of birth and death is striking, even if we keep in mind nineteenth-century rates of mortality in urban Britain.

Many of these autobiographers who wrote about pioneering in the backwoods had much in common: well-educated women who went to Upper Canada as close relatives of half-pay military officers, a class of settler particularly attracted to British North America, men who were unable to secure an appropriate living or an inheritance in Britain and were eligible for a land grant in the backwoods. These first-generation settlers were a kind of 'partial society' in the backwoods, a group of emigrants who shared a strong sense of affinity and loyalty to their class, homeland and race. All these writings reflect a sense of well-defined lines of difference which demarcated the groups interacting in the backwoods, although these communities were by no means straightforwardly divided along lines of race or class. In fact it is differences and gradations *within* the white settler community which are keenly marked as points where the text attempts to produce an ideological closure – notably in Moodie's sketch 'The Walk to Dummer', which graphically presents the degradation of their class and kind in the backwoods. This microcosm in Upper Canada in the 1830s emerges as a distinctive writing scene. Sara Mills' suggestion that each colonial relation develops narrative and descriptive techniques particular to its setting and history, which draws on a range of discursive practices, comes into play here.[24] What are the configurations of this autobiographic writing by settler women? How might we read *Backwoods* and *Roughing It* in terms of a particular formulation and episode in a cultural expression of colonial relations? What scripts for male and female subjectivity emerged? Part of the fascination of these writings is the failure of received scripts and the textual rehearsal and reformulation of 'proper' behaviours, appearances and relationships in the context of pioneer settlement.

This profusion of autobiographical writings is a signal of the need to both translate and re-formulate the domestic subject in new circumstances. The conditions for writing in the backwoods were poor: money for paper and postage was scarce as was time, for these women laboured harder with fewer servants than did their English peers. These were not leisured upper-middle-class wives and mothers. Nor were their full kinship networks in place. Although siblings often emigrated in concert – as did the Strickland and Moodie families – older generations were absent, and with them a sense of continuity, precedent and tradition. From when she first steps foot ashore at Grosse Isle, the young Mrs Moodie sees disorder: unruly Irish emigrants who think they be 'gintlemen' on setting foot ashore in North America; Yankees who dupe the British emigrants at every opportunity; servants who don't know their place; and, closest to the bone, middle-class genteel men and women who are reduced to abject poverty and destitution. The pressure to redefine existing notions of gentility is acute, for by conventional standards Moodie and Traill are writing about lives marked by abject failure. Potentially they, too, are symptoms of disorder. By the standards of masculinity and femininity they seek to emulate, their behaviour, households and relationships are found wanting. It was quickly evident that the transposition of the distinctions bred by the English domestic order would be a precarious enterprise for those first-generation settlers. What we see in the autobiographical writing from that 'partial' society, a fragment set apart, is an intense awareness of how gender, race and class coalesce in the production of subjectivity. For Susanna Moodie writing about emigration heightened a sense of the self as tenuous and fragile, in a conflicted relation to experience. It also strengthened the desire to meet this threat by projecting the self as a domestic subject, as wife and mother, through the couple and the family.

Emigration in the time of cholera

The domestic subject, with its entanglements in evangelicalism and abolitionism, was ideological cargo (or 'social apparatus' in Toynbee's terms) aboard the *Anne*, as functional and as fragile as good china, and vital to how John and Susanna Moodie conceived of themselves as a couple. I mean to stress that it is not merely incidental to what follows that Susanna Strickland met her husband in the Pringle household. The background of the anti-slavery struggle and their presence in the evangelical intellectual circle around Pringle is an indication of how both Susanna and John viewed the interdependence of their class, gendered and ethnic identities, how they would set out to reproduce and rework these identifications in Canada. Emigration was an important part of the development and consolidation of the cult of domesticity as Englishness, and as a powerful and emergent script for appropriate femininity and masculinity. In the autobiographical writings of Canadian settlers the familiar elements of nostalgia (the hearkening after England and tradition) and embryonic Canadian nationalism (the 'O Mothers of Canadian Sons' register) too often lead critics back to a centre/periphery framework, where the dynamics and energies across and through the Empire are lost. The autobiographic subjects which are worked through *Roughing It in the Bush* are produced at a specific conjuncture in time. Yet this needs to be understood in relation to those intimacies and contiguities which circulate through the Empire, a larger formation which fuelled the making of identities throughout the nineteenth century and beyond.

In reading emigrant writing we can overestimate the extent to which the Atlantic crossing set emigrants apart from Europe. Ideas of the sea change can underestimate the processes of change and disorder in Britain. For example, that year of the Moodies' emigration, 1832, was at the centre of extraordinary tumult in Britain and Europe more generally. As we have seen, both *Backwoods* and *Roughing It* begin with accounts of the Atlantic crossing as an entry to a new world – as Toynbee suggests, many things they take with them can never be reassembled in their original form. These accounts of the crossing and landing take middle-class subjects to boundaries, frontiers where the making of gendered, racial selves becomes apparent. Yet this process was not unique to the new world, and the responses of these middle-class emigrants work to produce distinctions and subjectivities which were also emerging elsewhere. The representations of the new world hearken back to the old. This is not just in the sense of nostalgia. On the contrary, there is a formative interaction between processes of social and cultural change in colony and metropolis. For example, in Europe too, ideas of the middle-class self were emerging through boundaries, through distinctions based primarily on class and ethnicity. Experience in the colonies was part of this process. We can recognize this by circling back to the first sketch in *Roughing It*, 'A Visit to Grosse Isle', and noting the importance of Mrs Moodie's crossing as an emigration in a time of cholera, and the contiguities between Montreal *and* Manchester.

In fact the opening sketch of *Roughing It* stresses continuity between the old and new worlds: 'The dreadful cholera was depopulating Quebec and Montreal, when our ship cast anchor off Grosse Isle, on the 30th of August, 1832, and we were boarded a few minutes after by the health-officers' (12). The immigrants of that summer arrived in the new world only to be preoccupied with the cholera epidemic which devastated the population of Montreal and Quebec that year. The cholera followed them. As Mrs Moodie remarks, 'We left cholera in England, we met it again in Scotland' (41) – and again in Canada. The cholera epidemics of 1832 ravaged European and American cities. It led to what Nancy Armstrong has called a 'rhetoric of disorder', an acute awareness of decay and degeneration produced by confusion and social disorder.[25] The disease was linked to illicit mixing, to the erosion of social boundaries which were seen to constitute a healthy society. Cholera sharpened and focused the horror at the heaping and intermixing of bodies among the newly urban industrial poor in Britain; this led to a renewed emphasis by middle-class critics on proper domestic management, on the household as the lynchpin of social order and civility. As a number of commentators have remarked, the cholera epidemics of the 1830s produced quite different ways of describing, defining and intervening in the reproductive realm of the individual, the home and the family. They were crucial to the emergence and policing of a series of boundaries between public and private, male and female, productive and reproductive spheres, which were fundamental to the emerging hegemonic formation of English middle-class culture.[26]

For both Traill and Moodie, landing in Canada is deferred because of infection ashore. In *Roughing It* and *Backwoods* the description of what they find when they finally disembark at Grosse Isle and walk the 'infected streets' of Montreal, fearing contamination, bears comparison to the descriptions of poverty and disorder by middle-class observers writing about diseased British cities such as Manchester. Contagion is linked to intemperance, sensuality and degeneration, to spaces where appropriate boundaries are not in place. Their response to this disorder is also characteristic of their class. As Dr James Kay Shuttleworth remarked in his report on the cholera outbreak in the slums of Manchester published in 1832, cholera is 'the strongest admonition of the consequences of insobriety, uncleanliness and that improvidence and idleness which waste the comforts of life, induce weakness and invite disease'.[27] The problem is traced back to the household, the solution is found by consolidating the newly defined domestic configuration centred on the female, in the proper management of the domestic economy, and in masculine temperance. Management of the social body was brought back to the self-discipline of the individual body and proper management of the family by the wife and mother and by the husband and father. In this way, responses to the cholera initiated closer management and regulation of domestic households. As she establishes her household at Cobourg in the first sketches of *Roughing It*, the young Mrs Moodie constantly contrasts her own domestic practices with those of the settlers thereabouts. In the characterizations of Uncle Joe and his family in particular, the comparison consistently suggests the association of domestic disorder and moral dissolution.

In both England and its colonies, the 1830s and 1840s were decades when formulations about what it meant to be white, middle class, male and female, in terms of the contours of the domestic subject, were emergent. These identifications were not imported ready-made, and it is clear that experience in the colonies would be crucial in the ongoing production of ideas about household management, hygiene, and domestic disciplines and regimes more generally. Writings by travellers and settlers offer a crucial insight into the making of the domestic subject, although, as we have seen, the sense of social disorder could be produced by the slums of Manchester as well as the scenes at Grosse Isle, or in the backwoods. Ann Laura Stoler argues that the emergence of the modern bourgeois subject is intimately tied to imperialism. Colonies were boundaries, frontier zones that became key sites in the production of discourses about sexuality. Colonial spaces offered the contrasts, the racially charged ground, from which the bourgeois order of the early nineteenth century emerged:

> Imperial discourses that divided colonizer from colonized, metropolitan observers from colonial agents and bourgeois colonizers from their subaltern compatriots designated certain cultural competencies, sexual proclivities, psychological dispositions and cultivated habits. These in turn defined the hidden fault lines – both fixed and fluid – along which gendered assessments of class and racial membership were drawn. Within the lexicon of bourgeois civility, self-control, self-discipline, and self-determination were defining features of bourgeois selves in the colonies. These features, affirmed in the ideal family milieu ... [t]hese discourses on self-mastery were productive of racial distinctions, of clarified notions of whiteness and what it meant to be truly European.[28]

In these colonial 'laboratories of modernity', household management, which was affirmed in the proliferation of discourses about parenting, servants, hygiene and civility, was critical to the formation of white, middle-class European subjects. Discourses on bourgeois respectability and morality focused on the domestic milieu, the 'privatized habitus' in which European bourgeois values could be cultivated and appropriately socialized children raised. This of course was not a single, unified or consistent project, it was rather made up of a series of what Mary Poovey calls 'uneven developments' at home and abroad.

This idea of 'unevenness' as Poovey develops it is useful in thinking about autobiographic writing. It stresses the apparent coherence and authenticity of ideology on the one hand, and its internal instability and artificiality on the other. The domestic subject – both masculine and feminine – did not emerge ready-made, and attempts to take up or embody the gendered roles appropriate to middle-class British subjects were both critically important, and practically impossible, for those emigrants of 1832. At the crux of the autobiographical writings of Susanna and John Moodie and Catharine Parr Traill is failure, and loss of caste in the backwoods. It is important to keep in mind, as Thurston stresses in his study of the Strickland family, that the Traills, Moodies and Stricklands emigrated because of their impoverishment in England and Scotland. Genteel poverty preceded emigration. However, as pioneers they faced a life of degradation, hardship and humiliation previously unknown.

The connections between the emergence of the Victorian domestic subject and the pre-Victorian anti-slavery campaigns are clear in Catherine Hall's analysis of middle-class behaviour. Evangelicalism was a crucial influence in the struggle over anti-slavery and a more widespread reform of manners and morals that led to a new lifestyle, a new ethic in the celebration of domesticity through a well-ordered, well-managed daily life.[29] A number of threads are sutured together to produce the domestic subject in evangelical discourse. Firstly, there is the separation of the spheres, the association of femininity with dependency through marriage, with the private and domestic life. The anti-slavery campaign was one arena where middle-class women might become politically engaged, however much of their abolitionist work was conducted in and through the domestic sphere (the closeted nature of Susanna Strickland's role in the production of Prince's *History* is an example of this). Masculinity was associated with having dependents and independence, with action in the public sphere. Secondly, this subject is deeply implicated in the rise of the middle classes, so these gendered qualities are quite class specific and emerged with attendant critiques of aristocratic licentiousness and working-class disorder. Thirdly, these realignments were implicated in the elaborate ideological work which constructed or imagined a national community in terms of an 'Englishness' or 'Britishness' which marginalized Welsh, Scottish and Irish ethnicity. Thus a set of class, gendered and ethnic identifications were annealed together around discourses of domesticity to emerge as a powerful definition of 'Englishness'. This was of course contingent and a result of quite specific historical processes, always in contestation, but in evangelical discourse in particular the conflation of a class, ethnic and gendered identity in terms of domesticity was emergent in the late eighteenth century and dominant by 1830.

Conditions in the backwoods made these distinctions of class, gender and ethnicity hard to sustain. For example, the separation of the spheres was threatened by the necessity of engaging in hard physical work. In the second part of the Canadian sketches, when John is away in the militia and the young Mrs Moodie is left alone to manage the household, the survival of the young family depends on her appropriation of 'masculine' traits. On the other hand, John Moodie is similarly found wanting as a domestic subject. He is unable to sustain his family through his own efforts as a backwoodsman. Likewise the class and ethnic distinctions attached to the domestic subject were threatened by the experiences of this settler fragment. The ways these distinctions are stressed and subject to change in the new settlements is evident in Catharine Parr Traill's *Backwoods*, published in 1836.

Conduct books: *The Backwoods of Canada*

Catharine Parr Traill's *The Backwoods of Canada: Being Letters from the Wife of an Emigrant Officer, Illustrative of the Domestic Economy of British America* is adjacent to *Roughing It*, although her autobiographic account of those years in the backwoods appeared much earlier and in a different generic cast. Traill's choice of genre and autobiographic persona for writing about settlement in *Backwoods* makes the cultivation of an exemplary domestic self explicit. She chooses to write as a wife – her proper name does not appear on the title page of the 1836 edition – directly to other wives of her class and race. She is not recounting a particular, individual history, idiosyncratic and personalized. Rather she authorizes herself as the competent, optimistic spouse of an emigrant officer, part of a couple where each partner has clearly defined responsibilities. It is an attempt to anneal her life, aspects of her own experience as a pioneer woman, and the social, cultural, political prescriptions for how she should conduct herself as a domestic subject. *Backwoods* is structured as a series of letters 'home', to the close relations who are left behind and who know nothing of the backwoods. These public 'letters' are very different to the correspondence which later circulated privately among families and friends in the pioneering settlements, as we will see. In public at least, Traill sets out to write for her own class, 'a faithful guide to the person on whose responsibility the whole comfort of the family depends – the mistress, whose department it is "to haud the house in order" '.[30] The well-being of the entire family depends on her skills, on the management of resources and emotions: 'If you would desire to see your husband happy and prosperous, be content to use economy, and above all, be cheerful' (103). In this Traill takes up a major tenet of evangelical prescriptions of femininity in marriage: the well-being and prosperity of the husband is dependent on the ability of the wife to manage the emotional resources of the household.

Backwoods draws on the genres of the conduct book and the memoir, mapping out the appropriate behaviours, morals and competencies for women of the author's rank. Manuals such as this had proliferated throughout the preceding century, presenting a female subjectivity in terms of a grammar that invariably links virtue in a woman to good household management. The domestic woman emerged from conduct books throughout the eighteenth century, which defined the ideal woman in her married state. In fact Nancy Armstrong argues that the conduct books helped to generate the belief that there was such a thing as a middle class with clearly established affiliations *before* it actually existed.[31] It is important to keep this in mind when thinking about *Backwoods*, which is prescriptive rather than descriptive, working to produce an identity and code of conduct for a class fragment under threat. It is constitutive of both the reader and the writer as the 'wife'. The 'letters home' are all about aspiration and the redefinition of masculinity, femininity and gentility in the backwoods, and the emergence of new attributes in middle-class men and women:

> As they maintain a rank in society which entitles them to equality with the aristocracy of the country, you must not be surprised when I tell you that it is no uncommon circumstance to see the sons of naval and military officers and clergymen standing behind a counter, or wielding an axe in the woods with their fathers' choppers, nor do they lose their grade in society by such employment. After all, it is education and manners that must distinguish the gentlemen in this country, seeing that the labouring man, if he is diligent and industrious, may soon become his equal in point of worldly possessions. (62)

Like many of their class, including the Moodies, the Traill family was impoverished in the backwoods. The work of *Backwoods* is to reinvent their rank and gentility in the colonies and to retain the distinctions from others in the community by establishing new terms. In the backwoods, middle-class masculinity and femininity are rearticulated so that it is defined by virtue not income, and by the dignity of labour. Thus *Backwoods* must not only give recipes for the making of maple sugar and the management of the dairy, but also envisage a class structure where this work doesn't contravene the norms of gentility. As Mrs Moodie tells us in *Roughing It*,

> My husband and I had worked hard in the field ... I had a hard struggle
> with my pride before I would consent to render the least assistance on
> the farm, but reflection convinced me that I was wrong – that Providence
> had placed me in a situation where I was called upon to work – that it
> was not only my duty to obey that call, but to exert myself to the utmost
> to assist my husband, and help to maintain my family. (374)

What distinctions of class and gender can be sustained in the backwoods?
Clearly, Canadian conditions produce shifting markers of middle-class
masculinity and femininity, and Traill's 'conduct book' is in response to this.
That conduct books might be quite local or regional in some respects is not in
itself unusual. The book is 'especially intended' for a particular class of men and
women 'in a state of emigration':

> the half-pay officer, by thus leading the advanced guard of civilization,
> and bringing into these rough districts gentle and well-educated females,
> who soften and improve all around them by mental refinements, is
> serving his country as much by founding peaceful villages and pleasant
> homesteads in the trackless wilds, as ever he did by personal courage, or
> military stratagem, in times of war. (3)

Settlement is figured as a process whereby couples take 'civilization' forward,
the epitome of 'civilization' here being understood in terms of English forms of
domesticity which are both fixed and fluid, reproduced and remade, and which
focus on the couple.

The publication in recent years of later correspondence among these
families in the backwoods gives us a quite different set of histories and
establishes more clearly the gaps between experience and rhetoric, between
the exemplary character of the autobiographic Wife of *Backwoods* and
Catharine Parr Traill's subsequent history. The selected edition of Traill's
private correspondence sheds some light on how poorly the family prospered
during many years in the backwoods, and why *Backwoods* advocates such
vigilance about the maintenance of behaviours in difficult circumstances. By
the time *Backwoods* was published, the Traills had already put up their farm for
sale and they were increasingly in debt. It was clear that Thomas Traill was not
suited mentally or physically to the demands of a backwoods life; he was
increasingly susceptible to depression until his death in 1859. *Backwoods* was
an attempt to augment their income. So desperate were the Traills'
circumstances that Susanna Moodie wrote to the lieutenant-governor of
Upper Canada on their behalf in 1838: '[*The Backwoods of Canada*] which has
brought great emolument to the publishers, has done little towards

administering to the wants of the poor author; who is struggling in the Backwoods on a limited income, with four infant children.'[32] Through bad investments and worse luck, the growing Traill family was destitute, dependent on gifts of food, parcels from England and small amounts of money from neighbours. In 1849 Catharine wrote to 'my dearest Suze' (Susanna) describing the contents of a box from England, adding, 'a good pair of boots for myself most acceptable for I was literally shoeless and bootless, and two small pairs for Will and Walter ... I was beginning to think with wonder how I should find clothing for these poor children, now reduced to worse than bareness.'[33] The Traills' fortunes continued to deteriorate; early in 1852 Catharine consults with the Moodies in the following terms:

> Can the bailiffs seize the flour and pork that are in the house ... can they seize the crops in the ground for the ensuing year ... In short dear I am so ignorant of these debtor and creditor matters that I seem puzzled about the most common forms – My husband cannot bear to discuss them with me and indeed I believe he knows as little what steps to take as I do myself – and he is utterly cast down unable to form a plan or think for his own benefit and becomes a prey to everyone ... I feel it is a miserable state to be like a vessel without a pilot drifting before an overwhelming storm on every side rocks and shoals and no friendly port in sight no beacon light to guide us on our perilous way – Do not think dear sister that I lose my faith in God's gracious providence I believe that he can in his good time bring all things to an end of these our troubles, but worldly troubles brought on by human want of prudence and judgement requires human prudence and judgement to aid, and I feel as if these are not in our power to exercise without wiser more calculating heads than our own.[34]

The following year Traill began another emigrant guidebook to raise money: *The Canadian Settler's Guide* was published in 1855. Despite the book's success – it was in its tenth edition by 1859 and the British government made a bulk purchase to encourage emigration – the author received little income from either of her conduct books.

Contrasting Traill's private correspondence and her public persona in this way displaces her autobiographical writing as a privileged insight into Traill's personality or experience. I am reading not for the relation to a life, but for the ways that *Backwoods* engages with the culturally dominant discourses of truth-telling and identity. The later correspondence implicitly reflects back on the exemplary self and prescriptions of appropriate conduct in *Backwoods*. The conduct book figures the settler woman as the wife: active, prudent, resourceful; her husband is independent, physically and mentally strong, still in touch with the military ideals learned in the regiment. In private correspondence, husband and wife are represented in a state of limbo, indecision, paralysis, and 'prey' in the wilderness. The Wife gains mobility by wearing moccasins, and being skilled and mobilized through contact with indigenous peoples. Later, Traill represents their abject poverty and immobility as finding herself 'literally shoeless and bootless'. This is not to say that *Backwoods* lacks factual, historical and autobiographic accuracy in its narration of the Atlantic crossing and migration into the backwoods, in the progress of the newly-wed wife to motherhood and the beginnings of what was to become an extraordinary contribution to the study of Canadian botany.[35] However, Catharine Parr Traill's experiences in the backwoods are not reflected directly in the autobiographic genre she chose for *Backwoods*, which is about conduct rather than experience. The recent publication of her later correspondence suggests that the exemplary wife she created haunts Traill's perception of their failure as settlers; it is the ideal which could not be realized. Susanna Moodie makes this gap between the exemplary settler and the autobiographer fundamental to the structure and theme of *Roughing It in the Bush*.

Autobiography and adjacency: Mr and Mrs Moodie

How could this class of pioneers write of abjection and failure, the irreconcilable gap between expectations and outcomes? How do they engage with failure in their own self-representation? 'Failure' here is to be gauged in terms of those aspirations to independence, self-sufficiency and responsibility that were germane to emigration and crucial to their agency and competence as husband and wife, mother and father. Catharine Parr Traill and Susanna and John Moodie set out quite deliberately to undermine the 'booster' literature about settler colonies. The Moodies write openly of their experience of failure, hoping to counter narratives by the 'artful seducers', the 'speculators in the folly and credulity of your fellow men' (5) who led them to hardship. The tension between their experience of pioneering and writing about it is especially acute because the rhetoric of settler emigration is anchored in teleology, some progress, however modest, towards independence and prosperity, if not for that first generation of emigrants at least for their offspring. What else could justify the hardship, loss and poverty? As Traill's correspondence makes clear, this failure to thrive is made all the more painful because the rhetoric of success for middle-class men and women depended on self-discipline and management, on good government of the self. She spelt out this disciplinary regime clearly in *Backwoods*, which is an exemplar of Nancy Armstrong's argument that prescriptive texts of how middle-class domestic life was supposed to be conducted *antedated* the bourgeois way of life they represented. They were not affirmations of what had already been secured. The internal contradictions and the discrepancies between different textual representations of experience in *Roughing it in the Bush* also reveal the artificiality of the truths they purport to tell.

This might seem to be a rather grandiose scenario for the log cabins which the Moodies, the Traills and their kind established in the backwoods. However, it is in autobiographic writing that these discourses which structured domestic subjects are taken up, rehearsed and reformulated in terms of the individual life; it is a location where gendered, racial identities are embodied, resisted, articulated. *Backwoods* and *Roughing It* are texts which allow us to examine a cusp, a key site where writers struggled to represent themselves and to understand their experiences in ways which we can now recognize as distinctively modern: the emergent discourses of domesticity. It is here we can see what it might mean to think of colonial sites as 'laboratories of modernity', as locations where white, middle-class identities were cultivated in particular terms. Early Victorian autobiographic writing which represents the self in relation to marital, maternal and paternal roles allows us to examine ways in which social and self-disciplinary regimes penetrate the most intimate domains of modern life, for distinctive elements of Victorian bourgeois identity were rooted in the sexual politics of the home. Autobiography reveals how these discourses were taken up, reworked, and became constitutive of ways of thinking about the self in colonial society, a 'new' civilization.

John Moodie is vital to this. Although his contributions to *Roughing It* have no great claims to literary distinction, and were in fact edited out until Ballstadt's 1988 edition, by noting how John Moodie writes as a husband, we can begin to see how Susanna Moodie writes as a wife. Like her sister Catharine, in *Roughing It* the narrator represents the decision to emigrate as a duty of the wife and mother:

Well do I remember how sternly and solemnly this inward monitor warned me of approaching ill, the last night I spent at home; how it strove to draw me back as from a fearful abyss, beseeching me not to leave England and emigrate to Canada, and how gladly would I have obeyed the injunction had it still been in my power. I had bowed to a superior mandate, the command of duty; for my husband's sake, for the sake of the infant, whose little bosom heaved against my swelling heart.... [P]rudence whispered to the father, '...Your family may increase, and your wants may increase in proportion.... When you married for inclination, you knew that emigration must be the result of such an act of imprudence in over-populated England ...'

Alas! That truth should ever whisper such unpleasant realities to the
lover of ease – to the poet, the author, the musician, the man of books, of
refined taste and gentlemanly habits. Yet he took the hint, and began to
bestir himself ...

'The sacrifice,' he said, 'must be made, and the sooner the better. My
dear wife, I feel confident that you will respond to the call of duty, and,
hand-in-hand and heart-in-heart we will go forth to meet difficulties, and,
by the help of God, to subdue them.' (207–209)

The marriage of Susanna Strickland and John Dunbar Moodie was 'imprudent',
a coupling made through desire rather than reason, a choice that led to
emigration. They go forth, in her husband's words, 'heart-in-heart, hand-in-
hand'. From the *Roughing It* sketches we know that Mrs Moodie had a strong
sense of attachment to her husband which included a spiritual, mystical bond
when they were physically apart. Her dependence on him is both material and
emotional:

The hope which had so long sustained me seemed about to desert me
altogether; when I saw him on whom we all depended for subsistence,
and whose kindly voice ever cheered us under the pressure of calamity,
smitten down helpless, all my courage and faith in the goodness of the
Divine Father seemed to forsake me, and I wept long and bitterly. (432)

From the recently published private correspondence between Susanna and
John we know that they remained a passionate couple, writing openly of their
sexual desire, and deeply affectionate one to the other until John's death in
1869. We can move through the personal detail of this marriage to understand
how they viewed their gendered, sexual identities through the couple, through
interdependence, through implication one in the other. For what *Roughing It*
allows us is a rare autobiographical insight into the making of domestic
subjects, man and woman, through contiguity in marriage and parenting.

Much work remains to be done on men and masculinity, manhood and
manliness in Empire. Christopher Lane's recent study focuses on homosexual
desire; so too does Ronald Hyam, who represents the Empire as a site of
consummate non-reproductive sexuality for British men. It is still quite rare to
find men treated historically, as men, socialized into masculinity whose meanings
have changed from one age to another, one society to another.[36] It is almost
unknown to think of men and masculinity in terms of domesticity, although this
may well tell us more about our contemporary interests and fantasies rather than
historical insight. Thinking about settler subjects in particular requires attention
to masculinities and femininities in terms of domestic life.

Anxieties about the generation of the white population and the reproduction of whiteness as a racial identity at settler sites produced concerns about masculinity, virility and potency as well as an idealization of maternity and motherhood. The cult of domesticity was not just about femininity. As they emerged in England, ideas of domestic masculinity and femininity were linked to the rise of evangelicalism: 'Between 1780 and 1820, in the Evangelical struggle over anti-slavery and over the reform of marriage and morals, a new view of the nation, of political power and of family life was forged. This view was to become a dominant one in the 1830s and 40s.'[37] The Evangelicals were champions of married life and domesticity, of domestic man who sought happiness and fulfilment in the home. This conceived of masculinity in terms of temperance and attachment, of masculine sexuality in terms of the couple (rather than coupling) and parenting. This man possesses independence and dependants, and he honours both.

John Moodie's ideas about appropriate masculine conduct can in part be deduced from his circle of attachments prior to his marriage. He frequented Evangelical circles; both Catharine and Susanna Strickland met their husbands in the household of the anti-slavery campaigner Thomas Pringle between 1830 and 1831. Moodie knew Pringle from earlier encounters in South Africa. However, we need not only infer what Moodie's views on manhood and masculinity were from the intellectual company he kept in London: he tells us very directly in *Roughing It*. John Moodie had emigrated before; in 1819 he went to the Cape, to join two of his brothers who had settled in South Africa. He was, he tells us in one of his autobiographical contributions to *Roughing It*, 'The Village Hotel', 'settled as a bachelor in South Africa for about twelve years':

I use the word settled, for want of a better term — for a bachelor can never, properly, be said to be settled. He has no object in life — no aim. He is like a knife without a blade, or a gun without a barrel. . . . In short he is in a false position, as every man must be who presumes to live alone when he can do better ... My very ideas (for I had not entirely lost the reflecting faculty) became confused and limited, for want of intellectual companions to strike out new lights, and form new combinations in the regions of thought; clearly showing that man was not intended to live alone. Getting, at length, tired of this solitary and unproductive life, I started for England, with the resolution of placing my domestic matters on a more comfortable footing. (232–3)

Editing John's contributions from *Roughing It* obscures the couple's idea of the book as a writing partnership, 'hand-in-hand', each with clearly defined roles to play, complementary one to the other, each allowing the other to be eloquent in different ways. As we can see from his reflections on his first settlement, John Moodie was deeply impressed by ideas about the domestic man: 'a bachelor can never, properly, be said to be settled'. For Moodie the idea of settlement involves notions of masculinity which focus on the domestic, on marital and paternal relations, on self-sufficiency, usefulness and independence which were no longer available to him in England or Scotland.

John Moodie's autobiographical account of life at the Cape can be read as the obverse to the account of the husband and father who contributes to *Roughing It*. Moodie's *Ten Years in South Africa, Including a particular description of the wild sports of that country in two volumes* was apparently completed in the spring and summer when Moodie became a father for the first time, and he sailed for Canada as a settler, husband and father shortly afterwards. The earlier account takes up masculinist discourses of a quite different order. Moodie presents a 'true notion of the habits and mode of life of a colonist in the southern extremity of Africa' to produce an accurate idea of the hunting (especially elephant), with anecdotes and particulars of 'Hottentots and Kaffres [sic]'.[38] This colony is represented as a man's world of wild animals, hunting, shooting, male camaraderie. Here is the adventure narrative that is the account of homosocial men in Empire, a figure which is more familiar to us than the domestic, familial man which John Moodie chose to become through marriage and a second emigration. As he tells us in *Roughing It*, he would live to regret representing South Africa in the wild in this way, for Susanna recoiled at the prospect of emigrating there, and he turned to Canada instead. When the couple sail to Canada with their baby daughter, the ideals of settlement and independence through domesticity are paramount. There is some continuity between John Moodie's South African and Canadian writings. In both he represents himself as a writer who avoids the standard narratives of the traveller and the adventurer, which please 'the imagination rather than inform the judgement' (2). He writes not only as an adventurer but also as a colonist, including kinds of agricultural, geographical and economic information which settlers require. In *Ten Years* and the *Roughing It* sketches emigration is represented as the resort of those who can no longer live comfortably 'in the country of their fathers'. In June 1819 and again in July 1832, John Moodie emigrated with a sense of the diminishing opportunities for his class and kind in Britain. The near bankruptcy of Melsetter, the Moodie family's traditional estate in the Orkney Islands, prompted the emigration of three brothers, Benjamin, Donald and John Moodie, to South Africa. John's brothers remained and prospered there, and traces of them appear in contemporary Zimbabwean autobiography, as we shall see in Chapter 6.

Nevertheless, there are differences between the colonial relations in Canada and in South Africa which impact upon Moodie's autobiographical narrative.

This is not just the change in personal status from bachelorhood to married man. Quite different kinds of distinction and stratification organize South African colonial society, and John Moodie spends a great deal of time discussing these, for in his mind there is an absence of moral taint in the Canadian settler colonies which distinguishes them from their South African (and Australian) counterparts. Most obviously this relates to convictism, indentured labour, and slavery in the southern colonies, and the moral contagion and degeneration which Moodie attributes to these relations. The subject of slavery was of considerable interest to the British public when Moodie's South African memoir was published. He links his knowledge of South African affairs to anti-slavery debates in London between 1830 and 1831, confirming on the basis of his experience his views that slavery demeans the master and the slave, and that 'the untutored savage' retains an innate gentility. John Moodie is condescending in his representation of the Xhosa and Khoikhoi; however, as Carole Gerson points out in her analysis of the African writing, Moodie's greatest disapproval is reserved for uncivilized whites.[39] His representation of the Boer is similar to the descriptions of the Irish and the Yankee and the lower classes in general in the later Canadian sketches. Despite his sense of Canadian settlement as somehow morally superior – the view that, as Catharine Parr Traill suggests in *Backwoods*, no matter how bad things were in the backwoods of Canada they must be worse in Botany Bay – in Canada, as in South Africa, white degeneration was a source of constant anxiety. Aristocratic dissolution, the downward mobility of middle-class settlers, the poor and uneducated whites are alike threats to the maintenance of settler authority and the boundaries between colonizer and colonized. Much depended on middle-class propriety. John Moodie left South Africa in 1829: 'I found, notwithstanding all my exertions, that I was not likely to be able to settle comfortably for life, or to have the means of providing for a family, according to my first expectations' (302). In his African and Canadian emigrations he remained vulnerable, unable to provide as domestic man should.

John Moodie's autobiographical narrative in *Roughing It* is intended as a short counterpart to Susanna's expansive, mercurial, chatty sketches; here we find the detailed, more factual exposition of their history which 'is necessary to explain many circumstances in our situation, otherwise unintelligible' (271). The trajectory of emigration in *Roughing It* is 'unintelligible' because it contradicts all those expectations of settlement, and for this the husband and father is called to account. We know from the very outset of *Roughing It* that this retrospective autobiographical account will demonstrate that the Moodies were a class of settlers 'perfectly unfitted by their previous habits and education for contending with the stern realities of emigrant life' (6). Susanna Moodie seems to revel in creating that fallible, emotional character, the 'too sanguine' Mrs Moodie, and her older counterpart, the autobiographic narrator. John Moodie's account of himself, in an intermediate chapter of considerable length that precedes the sketches of Part Two, is no less ironic, but less accepting of that younger self. Innocence is not an appropriate masculine trait. Susanna can represent her emigration as duty, and distance herself from the subsequent fatal error of moving to uncleared land further into the backwoods, which was 'against my wish' (277). It falls to Moodie to account for 'a residence of sixteen years in Canada, during which my young and helpless family have been exposed to many privations, while we toiled incessantly, and continued to hope even against hope' (231). His understanding of his failure, such as it is, struggles to represent the disjunction between the private and public spheres that he inhabits. So the very qualities which make a loving husband and father — temperance, honesty, duty — render him ineffective in the public sphere of the colony, a rough and ready place where business is conducted in the tavern, where land speculation is rife, where a man who is innocent is easy prey:

> I was suddenly thrown on my own resources, to support a helpless and increasing family without any regular income. I had this consolation, however, under my misfortune, that I had acted from the best motives, and without the most remote idea that I was risking the comfort and happiness of those depending upon me.' (271)

Moodie's confessional and painful account of his shortcomings as a settler foregrounds a crisis of masculinity which surfaces elsewhere in *Roughing It* (for example, other male characters such as Tom Wilson, Brian the Still Hunter, or even Uncle Joe). Although there is no husband in his own account alongside the wife in *Backwoods*, we have that image of Thomas Traill, paralysed in the depths of despair and poverty, in Catharine's letter to John and Susanna.

The abjection which Catharine Parr Traill describes in her letter finds its counterpart in Susanna Moodie's penultimate sketch in *Roughing It*, 'The Walk to Dummer', and she makes the relationship between this abjection and appropriate masculine domestic conduct apparent. Although the sequence of sketches in *Roughing It* is open to debate,[40] there is an ongoing descent into hardship and poverty as the Moodie family move deeper into the backwoods. The father and husband leaves the domestic sphere to enter the militia during the unrest of 1837 to 1838, her sister and closest friend departs, and the bitter winter of 1838 unfolds with Mrs Moodie, her servant and the children alone. This pattern of descent is ended only by their deliverance from the backwoods by the benefits of John Moodie's appointment to public office in the provincial settlement of Belleville:

my husband looked upon it as a gift sent from heaven to remove us from
the sorrows and poverty with which we were surrounded in the woods.
Once more he bade us farewell; but it was to go and make ready a home
for us, that we should no more be separated from each other. (501)

The sketch called 'The Walk to Dummer' is the last incident in the backwoods,
and is edited out of the most popular New Canadian Library edition of
Roughing It. As with many sketches, facts and characters of this account can be
verified in relation to experience. What remains to be accounted for is the
emotional intensity of the narration, and its place at the depths, the ground
zero as it were, of life in the backwoods. We might explain this intensity by
keeping in mind that, for those who sought to make, and remake, society in
terms of domesticity, the fact that men abandon their wives and children to
destitution was a particular and urgent concern.[41]

The sketch is an example of autobiography proceeding through adjacency,
for this is about a family without husband and father, about a woman and
children starving on the limits of settlement. Dummer is 'the *last* clearing in the
world', 'Nor to this day do I know of any in that direction which extends
beyond it.' 'Our bush-farm was situated on the border-line of a neighbouring
township, only one degree less wild, less out of the world, or nearer to the
habitations of civilisation than the far-famed "English Line," the boast and
glory of this *terra incognita*' (463). The family which is 'one degree' further out
than the Moodies is a displacement of them: they are of the same class and
station – an ex-military man on half-pay who parts with this income 'in an evil
hour', a gentleman 'unaccustomed to agricultural employment', a young wife
and a small and increasing family, debt from which they 'are unable to extricate
themselves without sacrificing the means which would have secured their
independence' (468), a husband and father who loves his family and yet
reduces them to beggary. Like Mrs Moodie, this wife too is the beloved
mistress of Jenny, the servant who toils 'with the strength and energy of a
man' for each of them. The difference between the two families is wholly in the
'Master's' temperament, for one gives way to drink. This is the critical
difference, and Dunbar Moodie prides himself on preferring his flute and
domestic hearth to the tavern. Temperance is fundamental to his notion of
domestic manhood. The Dummer episode presents the degradation of their
kind; a spectacle that repels her companions and reduces Mrs Moodie to
speechlessness and tears. The sketch is presented as an example of the 'woes
which drunkenness inflicts upon the wives and children of its degraded victims'
(488). It also functions as a presentation of complete abjection, the fragility of
'the English Line' which confronts their kind in the wilderness, and the
dependence of middle-class British immigrant families on the conduct of their

men. The deprivation, helplessness and passivity which Mrs Moodie encounters just one degree further out prefigures Traill's letter:

> I feel it is a miserable state to be like a vessel without a pilot drifting before an overwhelming storm on every side rocks and shoals and no friendly port in sight no beacon light to guide us on our perilous way.

For all that the women might do to embrace the ideal of the settler wife envisaged in *Backwoods*, the well-being of the family is critically dependent on the demeanour of the 'Master'. The horror of Dummer, the threat of the scantily dressed mother and children and the abandoned wife which Mrs Moodie finds is the threat of destitute white settlers, the degeneration of their own race and class at the frontier. The sketch grows from the pervasive anxiety about white degeneration in the colonies, which produced the insistent concern for those Europeans who fell from middle-class grace, and the compendium of manuals and housekeeping guides – such as Traill's *Backwoods* – which spelt out the consequences if certain moral prescriptions and modes of conduct were not met. Dummer is the fate that hovers over them all. In both *Roughing It* and their private correspondence, the Moodies confess to the dire consequences that they 'unwittingly' called down upon themselves.

This 'English Line' is a frontier of settlement that has received little attention in postcolonial or feminist readings. It departs from the individualist heroics that characterize more familiar narratives about the new world, where Crusoe-like man conquers to survive through adventure. This is the cast that John Moodie chose for his adventures at the Cape; as he memorably represents it, this man 'is like a knife without a blade, a gun without a barrel'. It is also quite unlike the frontiers in the travel writings of women such as Mary Kingsley or, closer to Susanna Moodie in place and time, Anna Jameson; for these women, colonial spaces were exhilarating because of the absence of domesticity, routine and English society. Although Mrs Moodie learns to survive amidst a household of women and children in the backwoods, although she learns to labour in the fields, make coffee from dandelion roots and to keep the farm in order in the absence of her husband, to read this in terms of feminist heroics erases Moodie's representation of herself through connection not only to her children, but also to her husband. The domesticated frontier of *Roughing It* is peopled by families, by men and women who understand themselves through familial relationships rather than individual heroics. When the exhausted Mrs Moodie and her friend return home after the excursion to Dummer, Moodie cannot rest without reasserting her connection to her spouse: 'I wrote to Moodie an account of the scene I had witnessed, and he raised a subscription among the officers of the regiment for the poor lady and her children' (488).

When Susanna describes her marriage she embraces both John Moodie and 'the fatal obey', an understanding of marriage which proceeds not through subservience of wife to husband but, following evangelical thinking about domestic life, a coupling which subsumes individual identity in favour of a communion. As she represents this in *Roughing It*, the communion is physical and spiritual; their intercourse is of the body, mind and spirit. In private correspondence both husband and wife represent their separation as unnatural. For Susanna, those last months in the backwoods were not a heroic triumph of women alone but a 'state of widowhood [which] does not suit my ardent affections' (147) and a harbinger of her own death:

> Such another winter as the last will pile the turf over my head ... While I had you to comfort and support me all trials seemed light, but left to myself, in this solitude, with only old Jenny to speak to, and hearing so seldom of you makes my life a burden to me.[42]

Masculinity and femininity are categories whose meanings are historically derived, always in relation to each other and rarely in a simple pattern of binary opposites. In the wake of recent feminist thinking, we tend to look for movements across the binary organization of gender one way: for the translation of passive, domesticated women into freedom from domestic constraint, which we now understand as agency and independence. Feminist readings of *Roughing It* do find these dynamics. However, other radical transformations across gendered boundaries are under way through the sketches, and through the way John and Susanna Moodie set out to the new world 'hand-in-hand, heart-in-heart'. Domesticity as they understood it would involve the domestication of woman *and* man, husband *and* wife. This second emigration for John Moodie would involve a quite different concept of the masculine self:

> come down as soon as I let you know that I have got a house for you. I really long to kiss you all again, and I feel miserably out of my element in a tavern. The Baroness is looking *round* and plump, which is not to be wondered at, as the Baron has little else to do, – and you know a great deal is done in that way in a short time.[43]

Domesticity: the race made flesh

Paternity and maternity are crucial to thinking about the autobiographical writing of settler subjects in particular. In the white dominions domesticity played a fundamental role in the organization of gender, class and race. Pro-natalist policies at settler sites protected the fertility of white women, the welfare of mothers and children, and the potency of white men. As homemakers and mothers, white women helped to maintain and promote the daily and biological reproduction of the settler population. The uterus was singled out not only as the definitive female organ but as the most important organ to the race: 'the uterus is to the Race what the heart is to the Individual: it is the organ of circulation to the species.'[44] In thinking about settler subjects, the race as it were made flesh, the politics of reproduction are critically important; for these reasons the cult of domesticity carried particular implications in settler colonies. The cohesion of Empire and the reproduction of Englishness depended on the vigour, size and racial identification of the white population.

It also depended on the disruption, dispersal and effacement of indigenous populations at settler sites. As colonization sharpened the place of marriage, maternity and paternity as constitutive of pioneer settler subjects, so too the management of colonial populations required that traditions and practices of rearing racially and culturally identified indigenous offspring come under scrutiny and increasingly interventionist 'management'. The generation of white populations in settler colonies and the dispersal of indigenous peoples were co-incident, not coincidental! However, the rhetoric of invasion assumed different forms.

For example, contrary to generalizations about colonial discourse, it is not the indigenous people who appear as the racial 'other' in *Roughing It*. In fact domesticity, the discourse which writes the English middle-class settlers *into* the backwoods, leads to the people of the First Nations being written *out* of the text altogether. As we see in the first Grosse Isle sketch, the strife and disorder which the young Mrs Moodie finds in the New World is not produced by 'savages'. In fact 'the Indian is one of Nature's gentlemen — he never says or does a rude or vulgar thing. The vicious, uneducated barbarians who form the surplus of over-populous European countries, are far behind the wild man in delicacy of feeling or natural courtesy' (21). Mrs Moodie feels a strong sense of mother-to-mother connection with the Indian women whom she writes about in *Roughing It*.[45] In contrast to the lower classes of immigrants, the indigenous peoples are grateful for the Moodies' benevolence as she perceives them; in this way they allow the Moodies to display a gentility appropriate to their class and origins. Thus while the servants regard the 'dark strangers' with horror, Mr Moodie invites them to his own table — a crucial distinction, for class boundaries are preserved at table in the Moodie household. To Mrs Moodie, the indigenous peoples are a finite presence: 'a mysterious destiny involves and hangs over them, pressing them back into the wilderness, and slowly and surely sweeping them from the earth' (318). This disingenuous presentation of invasion as both inevitable and mysterious is not unusual in settler histories. Their disappearance has nothing to do with the Moodies![46]

Several points emerge from this. Firstly, it is important to keep in mind that as abolitionists John and Susanna Moodie were part of that brief order which approached the slave as sister and brother in a discourse of fraternity. The Indian 'friends' of *Roughing It* are residual signs of the abolitionist rhetoric. Secondly, we need to keep in mind how much the Moodies had invested in the idea of a natural gentility. This, you recall, is a negotiation that Catharine Parr Traill performs in *Backwoods*. For impoverished middle-class settlers the idea that gentility resided in manners and intellectual accomplishment rather than wealth or display had much to recommend it, not least in terms of self-interest. For example, the abandoned wife at Dummer retains this distinction even in her extremity. The giving and the acceptance of benevolence define the Moodies and the indigenous peoples in relation to each other.

Discourses of domesticity were put to work to essentialize racial identities and stereotypes. Another example of this is the distinction between the Moodies and the 'vicious, uneducated barbarians who form the surplus of over-populous European countries'. From the very first sketch, 'A Visit to Grosse Isle', we see that the misrule is produced by the fresh cargoes of 'lively savages from the Emerald Isle', and the most depraved are the women: 'We could, perhaps, manage the men; but the women, sir! – the women! Oh, sir!' (23). Here, as in the Dummer sketch, it is the figure of the disordered white woman, the feminine turned savage, which is the focus of anxiety. Whereas the indigenous peoples can be presented as a finite presence, the Yankees, the Irish and the other lower-class immigrants are not grateful, not orderly, and not about to disappear. In fact they thrive even as the middle class degenerate, and at their expense in the Moodies' view. Susanna Moodie was called to account for her representation of the Irish by her contemporaries (xxxi). In her defence she pointed to the character of John Monaghan, who appears in several sketches. Despite this specific, quite positive characterization, clearly the representation of the Irish in the sketches more generally emerges as an example of what Anne McClintock observes as the attribution of domestic degeneracy to a class of 'white negroes'. Although that phrase did not emerge until 1880, it was preceded by a history of distinguishing between Anglo-Saxons and the Irish, and stereotyping the Irish as simianized and degenerate.[47]

In this way *Roughing It* gives us a clearer and more nuanced sense of how race and gender come into play in producing the *combinatoire* of the self in colonial space. Settler autobiography engaged in pursuits of Englishness. The Moodies' sketches participate in the constructions of the 'races' of Britain which were part of the social, cultural and ethical work of discourses of domesticity, and which became more marked in articulations of Englishness toward the end of the nineteenth century. The Moodies' investment in this type of racial characterization is also evident in the representation of the Scots as a racial type in the sketches. Although, as Catherine Hall argues, the terms of Englishness emerged through marginalizing Welsh, Scottish and Irish ethnicity, important distinctions could be made between them. Thus in *Roughing It* the Scots, although marginalized, are also sentimentalized and associated with positive characteristics such as thrift, prudence and loyalty. They are the foil to the unruly Irish, and seen in terms of individual characterizations rather than the mass. Throughout *Roughing It* the Moodies identify themselves in terms of class and ethnicity through their affinity with the Scots — even across class boundaries — and their difference from the Irish. Almost always, racial, gendered and class characteristics are measured and marked in relation to domesticity.

To some extent my interest here has been to dismantle the binary opposition between colony and metropolis as it is played out in this particular text, and more generally in thinking about autobiographical writing by these settlers out of Empire. There were important continuities in the making of the middle-class domestic subject on both sides of the Atlantic, and not just in this time of cholera. Elspeth Probyn's sense of the 'holding together in tension' of different lines of race, gender and sexuality that form and re-form our senses of self alerts us to how autobiographic writing is part of an ongoing process of positioning the self in terms of intimacies, contiguities and distinctions, of recognizing the self in relation to others, and of producing rather than reflecting existing identifications.

By introducing Probyn's *combinatoire* of the self into thinking about autobiographic writing by settler subjects in a very precise context, I have been, as Doris Lessing might say, 'in pursuit of the English', or at least the very complex interactions and implications of Englishness which are characteristic of settler colonies and part of an ongoing legacy of colonization. There were of course fundamental differences between Montreal and Manchester, between the Melsetter which John Moodie lived in as a child in the Orkneys and the 'Melsetter' homestead which he and Susanna tried to establish in the backwoods of Upper Canada. However, we cannot begin to grasp these differences by thinking in terms of binary oppositions between colonized and colonizer, dominant and subaltern, self and other. As we can see from the autobiographic writing which emerged from that class fragment in Upper Canada, colonial encounters blur these boundaries.

Herein lies the difference. For it was much easier to envisage and articulate the spatial, cultural, social and political boundaries of the domestic self back 'home', in the emerging urban spaces of England. In the settler colonies the threat of degeneration, mixing, blurring, comes closer, and remains a constitutive, unique feature of colonial encounters at the frontiers of settlement. Here discourses of self-scrutiny and self-mastery, the racial, class and ethnic distinctions, the clarifications of 'whiteness' which were productive of the middle-class self became what Stoler calls 'precarious vulnerabilities'.[48] Here articulations of difference were not necessarily in black and white, and the process of othering may take some unexpected forms. That fear of what might happen to the English race overseas – the spectre of the disordered white woman which we find in *The History of Mary Prince*, for example – is not confined to the 'torrid zones' alone, although we are more familiar with the formations of racial distinction in the colonies of occupation in the West Indies, Africa and Asia.[49]

I am suggesting then that autobiographical writings from settler sites allow insights into both the tenuousness and the tenacity of these colonial discourses in the making of the self in places where 'the English Line' fractures, where competing notions of civility and sheer anarchy challenge the rhetoric of European authority. In the backwoods of Canada, as in other settler colonies, white prestige was built on middle-class morality and discipline; however, these fragile boundaries were undermined 'close to home' by the transgression of poor whites, and the downward mobility of the middle class itself.[50] For Susanna and John Moodie and Catharine Parr Traill, writing autobiographically as domestic subjects is an attempt to formulate a subjectivity which is not secured by tradition, precedent, environment or birth. Much is at stake around the project to 'haud the house in order'. John Moodie, in search of consolation perhaps given his struggle to speak, suggests that 'a colony bears the same relation to an old-settled country as a grammar does to a language' (262). The idea of Europe as a kind of origin, the colony as a mimic effect remains common.[51] Moodie's metaphor gathers quite different but no less appropriate resonance now, when postmodern linguistics rupture the continuities, repetitions and order which he is seeking to invoke.

It is in some ways an exercise in perversity to read *Roughing It in the Bush*, by any measure one of the most engaging and significant autobiographies out of Empire, focusing on John Moodie at the expense of Susanna. *Roughing It* is by any measure hers, she is its star. I set out to read this autobiography to think about gender in terms of colonialism's culture. In doing this I have wanted to take up the Canadian feminist readings by Atwood, Buss and Friewald most particularly and to carry them into thinking about the gendered politics of settlement, and the very precise context in which the Moodies represented themselves as domestic subjects. Rather than bringing Susanna Moodie close, I have wanted to place her in the past in a very precise way – hence my choice of epigraph from Robert Lecker. With the relatively recent establishment of a readily available full text and the publication of letters, we are now in a position to pursue this kind of reading.

Along the way, I have wanted to use autobiographic writing out of Empire to reformulate my thinking about the emergence of the domestic subject. The ideology of separate spheres, particularly its association of femininity with domesticity, is wholly familiar. However, *Roughing It* opens up this ground in several new ways. It reveals, for example, the complex negotiations and articulations which men and women engaged in around discourses of domesticity. Susanna Moodie was no angel in the house. Upon the occasion of her marriage she self-consciously entered the 'pudding and dumpling club', putting her literary career to one side. But this was of course rhetoric, and throughout her writing the tensions between authorship and appropriately feminine domestic conduct are apparent. As in the bridal letter, Moodie uses the metaphor of the blue-stockings to take up this issue in *Roughing It*. Advised by neighbours to 'lay by the pen, and betake [her] self to some more useful employment', Mrs Moodie protests, 'I tried to conceal my blue stockings beneath the long conventional robes of the tamest common-place, hoping to cover the faintest tinge of the objectionable colour ... I tried to avoid all literary subjects, [and became] more diligent in cultivating every branch of domestic usefulness.'[52] John Moodie too was deeply ambivalent about styles of gendered behaviour available to him. He aspired to independence and masculinity articulated through the domestic rather than the public sphere. He also aspired to be an author. As Susanna remarks, alas that the poet, the author, the musician, the man of books should feel the need to emigrate (208). Although the kind of masculinity Moodie sought to embody may have been particularly fragile in the colonial context, it is also the case that under the gendered logic of domestic ideology a wide array of Victorian intellectual vocations came to resemble models of feminine activity and authority rather than affirmations of masculine identity.[53] For both John and Susanna Moodie, then, the practice of writing, publishing, and generally attempting to engage in a literary life sat uneasily alongside approved styles of gendered middle-class behaviour available to them. The colonial context of their domestic life sharpened this dissonance; it did not produce it.

What thinking about these issues in terms of colonialism's culture does offer here, as before, is a deepened sense of interrelationship, of identities through connections and distinctions. It is this that has led me to place the couple so centrally in this reading of *Roughing It*, perverse as it may be. For we too often think about the separate spheres of Victorian gendered subjectivity as a kind of apartheid, and we read one side in exclusion of the other. Here I have read it as one of the rare autobiographies where husband and wife write together as an intersection, a place where male and female subjectivity is produced through intimacies and engagements which begin with the couple and extend out to the distinctions of race, ethnicity and sexuality which were the accoutrements of the domestic subject. The passage from the private and the individual – John and Susanna Moodie's emigration 'hand-in-hand, heart-in-heart' – to the public and political implications of domestic discourses in empire – evident in Tyler Smith's memorable suggestion in his lectures (1847–1848) that the uterus is at the heart of the race – is complex, and needs to be understood in terms of quite specific engagements. It is nevertheless a passage fundamental to the progression of transmarine migration, invasion and settlement.

Notes

1 Robert Lecker (ed.), *Canadian Canons: Essays in Literary Value*. Toronto: University of Toronto Press, 1991, p. 7.

2 Homi K. Bhabha, *The Location of Culture*. London: Routledge, 1994, p. 9.

3 John Thurston, *The Work of Words: The Writing of Susanna Strickland Moodie*. Montreal: McGill-Queens University Press, 1996, p. 138.

4 John Thurston, *The Work of Words*, p. 166.

5 Carl Ballstadt (eds), *Letters of Love and Duty: The Correspondence of Susanna and John Moodie*. Toronto: University of Toronto Press, 1993, and *Susanna Moodie: Letters of a Lifetime*. Toronto: University of Toronto Press, 1985.

6 Elspeth Probyn, *Sexing the Self: Gendered Positions in Cultural Studies*. London: Routledge, 1993, p. 2.

7 This argument is expanded in Alison Donnell, 'Cultural paralysis in postcolonial criticism', *Ariel*, 26(1) (1995): 101–116.

8 Ruth Frankenberg, *The Social Construction of Whiteness: White Women, Race Matters*. Minneapolis: University of Minnesota Press, 1993, p. 2.

9 See e.g. Aijaz Ahmad, 'Postcolonialism: what's in a name?', in Román E. de la Campa, E. Ann Kaplan and Michael Sprinker (eds), *Late Imperial Culture*. London: Verso, 1995, pp. 11–32; Kenneth Parker, 'Very like a whale: post-colonialism between canonicities and ethnicities', *Social Identities. Journal for the Study of Race, Nation and Culture*, 1(1) (1995): 155–174.

10 Stephen Slemon, 'Introductory notes: postcolonialism and its discontents', *Ariel*, 26(1) (1995): 7–11.

11 See Alan Lawson, 'Un/settling colonies: the ambivalent place of discursive resistance', in C. Worth *et al.* (eds), *Literature and Opposition*. Clayton, Victoria: Centre for Comparative Literature and Cultural Studies, Monash University, 1994, pp. 67–82; Alan Lawson, 'A cultural paradigm for the second world', *Australian-Canadian Studies*, 9(1–2) (1991): 67–78; Stephen Slemon, 'Unsettling the Empire: resistance theory for the second world', *WLWE*, 30(2) (1991): 30–41.

12 Carl Ballstadt includes a useful overview of major lines of enquiry to roughing it in his introduction to the Carleton edition, *Roughing It in the Bush or Life in Canada*.

Ottawa: Carleton University Press, 1988. All further references to this edition in text.

13 The sense of proximity between Moodie and contemporary readers has been fostered by her contemporary editor and champion, Margaret Atwood. Atwood herself feels a strong sense of affinity with Moodie; she writes in the Introduction to the Virago edition of *Roughing It* that 'in some ways we were each other's obverse'. The fragmentation of self, the tensions of language produced by the failure of expectations before the intractability of the present, the estrangement and self-consciousness of gender, class and place, the disappearance of absolute frames of reference, which were the legacy of emigration for Moodie were, for very different reasons, preoccupations of the feminist movement in the 1960s and 1970s.

14 Bina Friewald's argument that Moodie not only brings into existence a universe populated by mothers and their offspring but always also marks herself as a figure of mothering has been germinal for recent critics of *Roughing It*. See ' "The tongue of woman": the language of the self in Moodie's *Roughing It in the Bush*, in McMullen (ed.), pp. 155–172. See also Helen Buss, *Mapping Our Selves: Canadian Women's Autobiography in English*. Montreal: McGill-Queen's University Press, 1993. The work of Friewald and Buss suggests that the maternal body can become a basis for defining personal identity and a place to speak for both the critic and her subject.

15 'Bourgeois women in colony and metropole were cast as the custodians of morality, of their vulnerable men, and of national character. Parenting, and motherhood specifically, was a class obligation and a duty of empire.' See Laura Ann Stoler, *Race and the Education of Desire: Foucault's 'History of Sexuality' and the Colonial Order of Things*. Durham, NC: Duke University Press, 1995, p. 135.

16 Nicholas Thomas, *Colonialism's Culture*, p. 9. Both Anna Davin and Margaret Jolly pursue more 'located' approaches to motherhood and imperialism.

17 Janet Giltrow, ' "Painful experience in a distant land": Mrs. Moodie in Canada and Mrs. Trollope in America', *Mosaic*, 14(2) (1981): 131–144.

18 Peter Hulme, *Colonial Encounters: Europe and the Native Caribbean 1492–1797*. London: Routledge, 1992, p. 193.

19 Arnold Toynbee, 'The stimulus of migration overseas', quoted in D. M. R. Bentley, 'Breaking the "cake of custom": the Atlantic crossing as a rubicon for female emigrants to Canada?', in Lorraine McMullen (ed.), *ReDiscovering Our Foremothers: Nineteenth Century Canadian Women Writers*. Ottawa: University of Ottawa Press, 1990, pp. 91–122, p. 93.

20 Bentley, p. 95.

21 I discuss the Swiss Family Robinson as a settler topos in 'A "white-souled state": across the "South" with Lady Barker', in Kate Darian-Smith *et al.* (eds), *Text, Theory, Space: Land, Literature and History in South Africa and Australia*. London: Routledge, 1996, pp. 65–82.

22 See Thurston's discussion of this sketch in *The Work of Words*, p. 155.

23 Helen Buss's bibliography, *Canadian Women's Autobiography in English* (Ottawa: CRIAW/ICREF, 1991), lists a number of these, including Anne Langton's

A Gentlewoman in Upper Canada: The Journals of Anne Langton, Mary O'Brien's *The Journals of Mary O'Brien 1828–1838*, and Frances Stewart's *Our Forest Home: Being Extracts from the Correspondence of the Late Frances Stewart.*

24 Sara Mills, *Discourses of Difference.* London: Routledge, 1991, p. 87.

25 Nancy Armstrong, *Desire and Domestic Fiction: A Political History of the Novel.* Oxford: Oxford University Press, 1987, p. 171.

26 Anita Levy, *Other Women: The Writing of Class, Race and Gender, 1832–1898.* Princeton: Princeton University Press, 1991, p. 7.

27 Levy, p. 37.

28 Stoler, p. 8.

29 Catharine Hall, *White, Male and Middle-Class: Explorations in Feminism and History.* New York: Routledge, 1992, p. 76.

30 Catharine Parr Traill, *The Backwoods of Canada: Being Letters from the Wife of an Emigrant Officer, Illustrative of the Domestic Economy of British America*, ed. Michael A. Peterman. Ottawa: Carleton University Press, 1997, p. 1. All further references to this edition are included in text.

31 Armstrong, p. 66.

32 Carl Ballstadt *et al.* (eds), *I Bless You in My Heart: Selected Correspondence of Catharine Parr Traill.* Toronto: University of Toronto Press, 1996, p. 15.

33 *Ibid.*, p. 59.

34 *Ibid.*, p. 71.

35 There is a discussion of Traill's considerable achievements as a natural historian in Michael A. Peterman, ' "Splendid anachronism": the record of Catharine Parr Traill's struggles as an amateur botanist in nineteenth-century Canada', in McMullen, pp. 173–186.

36 This is taken up by Marilyn Lake in 'The politics of respectability', in Gillian Whitlock and David Carter (eds), *Images of Australia.* St Lucia: University of Queensland Press, 1992, pp. 156–165. For a discussion of this issue in contemporary Canadian writing see Daniel Coleman, *Masculine Migrations: Reading the Postcolonial Male in 'New Canadian' Narratives.* Toronto: University of Toronto Press, 1998.

37 Hall, p. 82.

38 J. W. D. Moodie, *Ten Years in South Africa. Including a Particular Description of the Wild Sports of That Country* (2 vols). London: Richard Bentley, 1835.

39 Carole Gerson, 'Mrs. Moodie's beloved partner', *Canadian Literature*, 107 (winter 1985): 34–45.

40 See Alec Lucas, 'The function of the sketches in Susanna Moodie's *Roughing It in the Bush*', in McMullen (pp. 146–154) for a convincing argument about the coherence of the sketches.

41 For a discussion of debates about masculinity and temperance in different yet contemporaneous colonial settings, see David Goodman's work on 'Domesticity', in *Gold Seeking: Victoria and California in the 1850s.* Sydney: Allen & Unwin, 1994. Carl Ballstadt's reading of this sketch in relation to correspondence between John and Susanna Moodie suggests she makes a number of changes which shape the

account as a projection of her own experience and attitudes, and a mirroring of her own condition. See '"The Embryo Blossom": Susanna Moodie's letters to her husband in relation to *Roughing It in the Bush*', in Lorraine McMullen (ed.), *Re(Dis) covering Our Foremothers: Nineteenth Century Canadian Women Writers*. Ottawa: University of Ottawa Press, 1990, pp. 137–145.

42   Carl Ballstadt *et al.* (eds), *Letters of Love and Duty: The Correspondence of Susanna and John Moodie*. Toronto: University of Toronto Press, 1993, p. 159.

43   *Ibid.*, pp. 160–161.

44   W. Tyler Smith, 1847–1848 lecture series on obstetrics, quoted in Poovey, *Uneven Developments*. Chicago: University of Chicago Press, 1988, p. 35.

45   See Carole Gerson, 'Nobler savages: representations of native women in the writings of Susanna Moodie and Catharine Parr Traill', *Journal of Canadian Studies*, 32(1) (spring 1997): 5–21.

46   The traveller Anna Jameson presents the connection more astutely in 1838: 'The white population throughout America is supposed to double itself on average in twenty-three years; in about the same proportion for the Indians perish before them.' Quoted in Gerson, 'Nobler savages'.

47   Anne McClintock, *Imperial Leather: Race, Gender and Sexuality in the Colonial Contest*. London: Routledge, 1995, p. 52.

48   Stoler, p. 97.

49   See Felicity Nussbaum, *Torrid Zones: Maternity, Sexuality and Empire in Eighteenth Century English Narratives*. Baltimore: Johns Hopkins University Press, 1995. Nussbaum argues that the contrasts among the torrid, temperate and frigid zones of the globe were formative in imagining that a sexualized woman of Empire was distinct from domestic English womanhood.

50   See Carolyn Martin Shaw, *Colonial Inscriptions*, and Dane Kennedy, *Islands of White* (Durham, NC: Duke University Press, 1987), for discussions of complex lines of difference and the formation of partial societies within the white settler community in Kenya and Zimbabwe.

51   See e.g., David Stasiulis and Radha Jhappan, 'The fractious politics of a settler society: Canada', in Daiva Stasiulis and Nira Yuval-Davis (eds), *Unsettling Settler Societies: Articulations of Gender, Race, Ethnicity and Class*. London: Sage, 1995, pp. 95–131.

52   Misao Dean discusses this at length in *Practising Femininity: Domestic Realism and the Performance of Gender in Early Canadian Fiction*. Toronto: University of Toronto Press, 1998. See also Mary Poovey's discussion of the association between domestic mismanagement and inappropriate sexual behaviour in *Uneven Developments*, p. 115.

53   This is the subject of James Eli Adams' book, *Dandies and Desert Saints: Styles of Victorian Masculinity*. Ithaca, NY: Cornell University Press, 1995.

3

Travelling in memory of slavery

In Antigua, the twenty-fourth of May was a holiday — Queen Victoria's official birthday. We didn't say to ourselves, Hasn't this extremely unappealing person been dead for years and years? Instead, we were glad for a holiday.[1]

... the meanings engendered by hegemonic codes and narratives ... are placed at risk, revalued and distorted, through being enacted and experienced. In colonial encounters, marked not only by struggle but also by misrecognition and by disingenuous compliance, the risks are very real indeed.[2]

Britannia's daughters

In October 1837 the Honourable Emily Eden, described by James Morris as 'a witty and accomplished Englishwoman in her forty-first year' accompanied her brother, Lord Auckland, Governor-General of India, on an official progress up the country from Calcutta.[3] Their journey was a six-month epic that began with steamers and barges from Calcutta up the Ganges to Benares, followed by a succession of carriage, palanquin, sedan-chair, horse and elephant rides through Allahabad and Delhi to the hill station. On 30 October 1837, at dusk, on the banks of the Ganges, alongside some 'picturesque' ruins and with her spaniel Chance on the run, Emily Eden learned of the accession of Queen Victoria to the throne. The news brought a lump to her throat. She wrote back to her sister, 'I think the young Queen a charming invention' (21).

Meanwhile, Anna Jameson was travelling with a small party in the backwoods of Canada. The party is taken by voyageurs up the Mississauga in canoes to the Manitoolin Islands, pitching tents 'gipsy fashion' for a day or two. Somewhere around 4 August 1837 the party began paddling at dawn:

There was a deep slumbrous calm all around, as if nature had not yet awoke from her night's rest: Then the atmosphere began to kindle with gradual light: it grew brighter and brighter: towards the east, the lake and sky were intermingling in radiance; and *then*, just there, where they seemed flowing and glowing together like a bath of fire, we saw what seemed to us the huge black hull of a vessel, with masts and spars rising against the sky — but we knew not what to think or believe!'[4]

Such a black apparition must bring news of death, and so it does:

we rowed up to the side, and hailed him — 'What News?'. And the answer was that William the Fourth was dead, and that Queen Victoria reigned in his place! We sat silent, looking at each other, and even in that very moment the orb of the sun rose out of the lake, and poured its beams full in our dazzled eyes. (261)

Tears come to the narrator's eyes, due not to the blinding sun, nor are they for the dead king who 'in ripe age and in all honour was gathered to the tomb', but for 'that living queen, so young and fair'. 'The idea that even here, in this new world of woods and waters, amid these remote wilds, to her so utterly unknown, her power reaches and her sovereignty is acknowledged, filled me with compassionate awe' (262).

These two moments, one at sunset by the picturesque ruins on the Ganges and the other at sunrise on the Mississauga, the lump in the throat and the tears in the eyes, are wonderful examples of the performance of Englishness in travel writing. The backwoods of Canada and the banks of the Ganges are equally appropriate landscapes for the staging of what is, in Jameson's case in particular, an apocalyptic revelation of imperial power and authority, and a performance of the self as an imperial subject. These are the transcendental points of reference that organize and domesticate the 'foreign'; here Victoria embodies the still point at the centre of the imperium, which is both the origin and the end for the English traveller. In each of these moments Emily Eden and Anna Jameson embody their Englishness apocalyptically. The 'empty' colonial surroundings fall in as backdrop, functioning metaphorically to both amplify and confirm a loss of self, a transportation through awe. The accession of Victoria causes these supplicants to turn as it were towards their Mecca. The banks of the Ganges at dusk and the picturesque ruins are the appropriate setting for recognition of this momentous occasion in British history. The wilds of Lake Huron too are able to become part of a pageant of death and accession. All is subjected to the English queen and animated by her power. The shared conventions apparent in the representation of these two moments

– the picturesque scene, the symbolism of sunrise/sunset, the proximity to water, the transcendence – alert us to the construction, the invention of these symbolic moments, which are both personal and imperial rites of passage. They also alert us to the performative nature of travel writing, the invention of the self in place and time.

Here is the illusion of the Empire as organic, an enactment of that desire to overwhelm difference and discord and orchestrate imperial space so that the new world genuflects to the old. This orchestration, the illusion of simultaneity, the absorption of self into the imperium, was easier to sustain, it is true, in moments of solitary reflection in a natural world, and in a landscape emptied of 'other' people. The capacity to abandon the self in awe, to acknowledge English sovereignty and identify with it viscerally, is to make claim to certain origins, tastes, qualities and competencies in the invention of the self in autobiography. This is a process of identification and sublimation which both Anna Jameson and Emily Eden fail to complete at other moments of their journey.[5] The conditions and limits of this kind of performance need to be clearly defined, for we must not make travellers like Eden and Jameson 'imperial' in order to construct a 'postcolonial subject'. The transits of travel writing produce shifting subjects, with moments of sublimity and coherence being rare. It is no accident that Victoria's accession to the throne should produce this apocalyptic sense of the imperium. Later in her reign both the Jubilee celebrations and the colonial exhibitions gave rise to spectacles where the geographic expanse of the Empire was gathered together and centred around the monarch. On these occasions, the illusion of mapping the Empire in 'imperial pink' (itself a late Victorian development) emerges in elaborately staged theatrics. As Simon Gikandi suggests, the sublime affirmation of sites of Englishness achieved through journeys to the reaches of the Empire confer a certain enunciative authority on the traveller. This authority is important because these narratives are ultimately directed at the domestic English audience, and they address anxieties about the metropolis with an affirmation of English civilization and progress.[6] Travel writing was fundamental to the triumphant narrative of Empire, but it is also a genre where the fragilities and contingencies of Englishness emerge.

In Victorian England, discourses of travel would become a most powerful means for women, largely middle-class and English, to authorize themselves and to write autobiographically. To read travel writing in terms of autobiographics is to sharpen the focus on the production of the self in these texts, to think about how the writer might invent herself in relation to place. In the first book which makes a sustained analysis of British women travellers in the colonial context, Sara Mills sets up an opposition between reading in terms of discourses of travel, with an eye for the complexities of imperial femininity, and reading travel writings in terms of realism, 'as simple autobiographies'. The objection is grounded in the tendency to read these travel writings in terms of the individual, the heroine, the indomitable, eccentric protofeminist struggling against the conventions of her time. As Mills, and others, point out, this type of reading reflects both the cultural baggage of contemporary feminisms and the return to Empire, the 'Raj revival', in Britain during the 1980s and 1990s.[7] Travel writing, always an instrument in colonial expansion, remains seductive in late imperial culture, and too often its role as a medium through which the metropolis obsessively presents and re-presents its peripheries to itself remains unobserved.

There is a canonical version of women's travel writing which places Emily Eden, Anna Jameson and that generation of women who were authorized and empowered by Victoria's reign at the beginning of a trajectory which culminates and begins to decline with Mary Kingsley and the impulses of early modernism. Colonial travellers who were, as we shall see, postmodern before their time, and Victorian well past it, call this trajectory into question. My interest here will not be centred on women like Emily Eden and Anna Jameson, or on how English women embodied a variety of subject positions that we might associate with imperial femininity. Rather I want to escape the orbit of the travelling metropolitan subject and take up an enquiry which began with Mary Prince by looking at what, given the chance, peripheral subjects had to say about the metropolis, and how they navigated across the colonial periphery itself. For women who travelled as colonial subjects, different rhetorical frameworks were in place for projecting the self; different manoeuvres were required. This is to suggest that place matters, both as a destination and as an element in the construction of the narrating subject, the traveller herself. Particularly when we turn to travellers whose origins and destinations are non-metropolitan, we are alerted to how quite regional, specific histories are implicated in the discursive shaping of female subjectivity, and how access to imperial femininity was a matter of careful negotiation rather than an apocalyptic loss of self.

In this chapter I am interested in how travel writing figured in the autobiographies of postcolonial subjects. This is to throw into sharp relief the processes of writing the self through alterities, and through colonial relations. In travel writing the work of enunciation, the articulation of the self in various contexts, becomes very clear. Although these processes are not unique to postcolonial autobiographies, the oppositions and contiguities of colonial encounters thrust what Elspeth Probyn calls the 'faire' of enunciating the self into prominence. The focus of this chapter is decidedly non-metropolitan, putting aside quite explicitly the metropolitan subjects and locales which are almost always the origins, destinations and itinerary of discussions of travel writing.

Jamaica Kincaid reminds us that colonial subjects met the world through England, and if the world wanted to meet them it had to do so through England (33). However, to imagine that all journeys began from England, that empowerment in Englishness was either available to, or desired by, all women travellers, is to displace intricate forms of collaboration and resistance by travelling subjects. I am interested here in how discourses of travel emerged in scripts for writing the self as 'colonial born', or ex-centric. The focus of this chapter will be on the writings of two very different colonial women, which bring into focus the makings of the Creole subject in autobiography by the mid-nineteenth century, and projections of Australianness through settler autobiographics around Federation and its aftermath in the first decades of the twentieth century.

Recently, in her study of Victorian women's travel books about Southeast Asia, Susan Morgan argues at some length that 'place matters' in reading travel writing. She suggests that narrative location, the cultural meanings of both subject voices and geographic places, is a specific, conventional and changing affair: 'in nineteenth century British travel narratives there was no monolithic imperialist or imperialized location and no solidly bounded identity, authorial, narrative, or geographic'.[8] Although Morgan's study remains focused on British subjects, which is to say travellers whose points of departure and return were in Britain, her perspective highlights the dramatic nature of travel writing and of imperial femininity. It suggests that the dynamics of colonialism are best understood not in terms of some unitary representation which extends from the metropolis across passive peripheral spaces, but in a more complex and dispersed process of enactment, enunciation and invention. For both English and colonial travellers, travel writing becomes the means of producing a discursive image of the self which is located not in the traditional discourses of individualism, but in a much more provisional imagining of the self in space and time. This is apparent even in the most sublime moments of coherence. Thus this chapter is concerned with the questions: What if the traveller is herself a colonial subject? What if her conception of self is embedded in the peripheries?

Jamaica: the legacy of the plantation

A different set of dynamics comes into play as we turn to the constant movement of people and ideas around the periphery itself, or from the periphery to the metropolis. These dynamics call into question the tendency to see European culture emanating out to the colonial periphery from a self-generating metropolitan centre, a one-way traffic.[9]

The place I am interested in here is the Caribbean, most specifically Jamaica, and the connections between 'place' and 'colonial relation' which are anchored there. This is not to install additional writers into the canon of celebrated women travellers. The point here is not the individual travellers themselves, but the place of Jamaica in the colonial imaginary of the nineteenth and early twentieth centuries, and how Jamaica figures in autobiographic writing both as a place of origin and as a destination. This is, of course, to return to slavery, for the worst excesses of plantation slavery shaped Jamaican identities, and this remained an integral part of the autobiographic writing in which I am interested. What is at issue here is our grasp on how this colonial relation figured in constructions of the self not just in slave narratives, such as *The History of Mary Prince*, or in the autobiographies of women directly involved in abolitionist campaigns, such as Susanna Moodie. To contain thinking about the subject and subjectivities of slavery to its most immediate and obvious protagonists is to miss the extent to which this colonial relation was, and continues to be, fundamental in the writing of autobiography. The task here is to understand how the subject of slavery is germinal to autobiographic writing out of Empire, even when it is occluded by the transports of imperial femininity on and beside the Ganges and the Mississauga.

Much has been written about slavery in the Empire, but not nearly enough. There are histories of abolition campaigns, and of slavery in the British Empire. There are studies of slavery in the literary imagination, and of the West Indies as a kind of 'other' in the Victorian novel. We now read the islands into *Mansfield Park* and *Jane Eyre* to understand how the wealth of English estates was dependent on slave labour, and how the inventions of Englishness were dependent on the exclusions of Caribbean subjects. There is some work on specific slave narratives, such as *The History of Mary Prince* and the *The Life of Olaudah Equiano*, although critics remain most attracted to learning about colonialism through the prism of the English novel where metaphor can (in Mary Prince's words) 'put a cloak about the truth'. What is missing is the sum which is more than these parts can deliver, a thoroughgoing realization of the extent to which slavery is embedded in colonial relations and is fundamental to the making of colonial and English subjects far beyond the islands themselves. This is not just to argue that the structure and meaning of the core terms of Englishness were invented in colonial space, a case that Simon Gikandi has made very well.[10] Rather it is to place the body of the slave and this particular production and organization of race at the beginning and end of nineteenth-century postcolonial autobiographics. This most brutal, systematic and far-reaching trade in racial difference coloured and shaped autobiographic writing far beyond the campaigns for abolition, and far beyond the autobiographies of black men and women from the Caribbean.

Discourses of slavery are a specific domain, not commensurate with other forms of oppression. In her brilliant analysis of blackness and whiteness in the literary imagination, a reading for the presence of 'conveniently bound and violently silenced black bodies' in the literature of the United States, Toni Morrison points out that 'There also exists, of course, a European Africanism with a counterpart in colonial literature.'[11] The 'of course' here is a cause for reflection, for the kind of discursive analysis Morrison pursues moves from particular instances in texts to the rhetoric of enslavement, to the systematic operations of slavery in black and white. 'Of course' there has been substantial work on European Africanism, but this rarely looks to colonial literature in the way Morrison suggests, and only occasionally attends to the particular operations of discourses of slavery. In Britain, the subject of racial oppression has been examined in relation to colonialism, but much less fully with regard to the problematic of slavery in particular,[12] or the particular discourses of racial oppression and empowerment which have emerged from the construction of blackness, whiteness, creolization and enslavement on the plantations of the Caribbean.

The exception to this proves the rule. In taking racial slavery and the plantation economy as a critical economic, historical and cultural matrix, Paul Gilroy is led to develop a different cultural formation, 'the black Atlantic', a complex unit of analysis that leads to a transnational and intercultural perspective which subsumes national and ethnic boundaries.[13] He suggests that this webbed network produces identities that are syncretic, interdependent, and cultures which are heterogeneous rather than bounded by national formations. Using the memory of slavery as an interpretive device leads Gilroy to unravel bounded notions of 'European' and 'Caribbean' identities, developing a complex view of the mingling of metropolitan and peripheral subjects. Theory follows the passages of the slave ships, shuttling across the Atlantic between Africa, Europe, America and the Caribbean. Here the history of slavery is established as part of the intellectual and ethical heritage of the West as a whole, fundamental to the enlightened rationality and capitalist industrial production of modernity rather than a premodern residue which is the special property of blacks, and which passed into history with abolition. Autobiographic writing has traditionally been one of the most powerful acts of self-creation and self-emancipation for black subjects in this Atlantic web. As we have seen in Mary Prince's *History*, it is personal and representative, both the presentation of a public persona and an assertion of authority and autonomy, fundamental to self-liberation.

My interest here is the legacy of the plantation in black and white autobiographical writing in the period after abolition. What happened when, in British law at least, the binary organization of racial difference in terms of slavery and freedom was dismantled? How did discourses of slavery continue to circulate in autobiographic writing when the narrative of the ex-slave was superseded? As we have seen, the slave narrative used the body of the slave and the authority of her collaborators as anchors to 'truth'. What followed abolition, when slavery became a site of memory and fantasy in autobiography?

By beginning this book with Mary Prince's *History* and insisting on the intimacy of black and white through the figures of Prince and Moodie, I give Prince's story and the institution of racial slavery a primacy in mapping the dynamics of colonization and resistance in nineteenth-century autobiography. However, as is evident in the *History* itself, there is no large and as yet unknown archive of autobiographic writing by British slave subjects themselves.[14] One of the dangers of focusing on the politics of abolitionism, as I have in the histories of Mary Prince and Susanna Moodie, is the construction of a narrative which puts slavery in the past by 1838; after that, so it would seem, slavery becomes an American issue. The slave trade, which began in the 1640s, was outlawed by both Britain and America in 1807. Emancipation campaigns resumed in earnest in the 1820s and full emancipation of slaves was effected in British colonies between 1834 and 1838. However, discourses of slavery continue to circulate through autobiographic writing throughout the nineteenth century and into the twentieth in a variety of ways, with travel writing being among the most common generic pathways for the circulation of both emancipatory and racist polemics.

The colonial relation which is based upon plantation slavery is not confined to a single place. It is the foundation of a network which linked – and, as Gilroy argues, continues to bring together – a disparate collection of colonial and metropolitan sites in West Africa, the Caribbean, and the east coast of the United States and Canada, and Britain. However, the systemic nature of slavery forces connections and interdependencies which are rarely made between, for example, black slavery and the material pleasures of white life; between black misery and the expansion of white pleasure.[15] Slavery, then, established a set of relationships, discourses and institutions which continued to metastasize across the Empire long after the trading ceased, and well beyond the Atlantic itself. In autobiographic writing, the articulations of race, gender and class, which were organized around the slave trade and the plantation economy, continued to shape the autobiographical 'I', offering a repertoire of subjectivities that was deployed to very different ends.

We can explore just how variously slavery continued to emerge in autobiography by turning to two very different colonial subjects. This contiguity is not an encounter, like Mary Prince and Susanna Moodie, or a single writing scene, but a relation produced through place: Jamaica, and through the colonial relations produced by the slave trade and the plantation.

The first of these subjects is Mary Seacole, a Jamaican Creole whose *Wonderful Adventures of Mrs. Seacole* was published in England in 1857, in that interlude between abolition in Britain and the Civil War in the United States. Seacole narrates her travels from Kingston, Jamaica to Panama, to London and ultimately to the Crimea, where she becomes (and the italics are hers!) a *heroine*, one of the first Creole travellers. The second traveller is an Australian, Mary Gaunt. An author of a number of fictions as well as travel narratives, Gaunt, in a mystifying if not improper desire, imagines herself as a slave in a former life. In a series of travel narratives — *Alone in West Africa* (1912), *Where the Twain Meet* (1922) and *Reflection — in Jamaica* (1932) — she reconnoitres the Gold Coast and Jamaica to authorize herself as the 'white missus' and the 'Buckra lady'. Both Seacole and Gaunt belong in part to the traditions of imperial femininity, yet they also use discourses of travel to authorize themselves as colonial subjects, to rehearse what it might mean to be 'Jamaican', 'Australian', at the same time as they identify as 'Britons'. In both contexts, what we might now represent as a 'national' or 'regional' identity is spelt out through a version of imperial supremacy.

What is at issue here is how the colonial relations established around plantation slavery remained fundamental to constructions of the self in autobiographic writing. To contain thinking about the subjects and subjectivity of slavery to its most immediate and obvious protagonists is to miss how fundamental this colonial relation was, and continues to be, in autobiographic writing after abolition.

The Wonderful Adventures of Mrs. Seacole

In 1857, some twenty-five years after Mary Prince disappears from view, the autobiography of another Caribbean woman was published in England. Whereas the occasion for Mary Prince's appeal to the British public was the abolitionist campaigns of the early 1830s, Mary Seacole's *Wonderful Adventures of Mrs. Seacole in Many Lands* is part of the small industry of autobiographical and biographical writing that emerged from the Crimean War. Predictably, much of this celebrated the exploits of military men. Less predictably, the Crimean War was a stage where women entered the theatre of war and the lives of women assumed heroic status; the life of one woman in particular — Florence Nightingale — became the focus of attention. For Mary Seacole the conditions and limits of autobiography would be quite different from those obtaining for Mary Prince. A freeborn Jamaican, she was never in bondage, and asserts her freedom to 'adventure' unshackled by any obligations, familial or economic. Yet for Seacole, as for Prince, questions about authorization, the making of the subject through autobiographic writing, arise. How is this autobiographer authorized by her text? What was her means of access to a British readership? What are the terms and conditions of her emergence as an autobiographer? Like her precursor, Seacole manoeuvres within discursive constraints, which stage her appearance before metropolitan readers.

Mary Seacole (1805–1881) tells us many things about the external appearance of her autobiographic subject; she is, for example, very explicit about her colour, her dress and her spirit of adventure, yet she is coy about her age throughout her autobiography. She is, she tells us, 'young with the century'. She is thus part of that generation of women travellers like Anna Jameson and Emily Eden who would be empowered by the ascension of a young and female monarch in 1838. And yet for Seacole, being a Victorian subject would be a 'chequered' experience.

Seacole's *Wonderful Adventures* reverses the usual pattern of 'home' and 'away' in Victorian travel writing. Mrs Seacole does not look longingly at the English shore as the ship sails for the Antipodes or the Americas. England, London specifically, is her destination, not her 'home'. Metropolitan encounters in the book are important tableaux of the kind of exchange which Seacole brings to pass between metropolitan and Caribbean locations. For example, the narrator recollects an earlier trip to London when, as a young woman from Jamaica, she learns the implications of her appearance in the metropolitan view:

> I shall never forget my first impressions of London; Of course, I am not going to bore the reader with them.... Strangely enough, some of the most vivid of my recollections are the efforts of the London street-boys to poke fun at me and my companion's complexion. I am only a little brown – a few shades duskier than the brunettes you all admire so much; but my companion was very dark, and a fair (if I can apply the term to her) subject for their rude wit ... our progress through the London streets was sometimes a rather chequered one. (4)

Seacole reverses the ethnographic gaze here, for the young woman comments on the irrational, the 'strange' and certainly uncivilized behaviour of the inhabitants in a place far from home. There is some displacement through class – it is street boys who mock the girls – and through humour – the pun on 'fair' – but the point remains. The narrator stresses that, in this metropolis, she is always read for her skin. She speaks of this later, as a transparent, unspoken yet vital component of imperial femininity – whiteness. She can practise the domesticity and the maternal qualities of Englishness; in her autobiographic narrator there is complete suppression of the erotic body which stereotypes the coloured woman in colonial discourse. Nevertheless, imperial femininity remains above all a racialized category. Her career will continue to be 'chequered' by the meaning of her skin. Mrs Seacole habitually remarks on her appearance with an eye to how she might look 'different', 'colourful', a cause for surprise: 'a stout female tourist, neatly dressed in a red or yellow dress, a plain shawl of some other colour, and a simple straw wide-awake, with bright red streamers' (86).

Born in Kingston, Jamaica, Mrs Seacole is a Creole, her father a soldier of an 'old Scotch family', her mother a Creole with skills as a doctress 'in high repute with officers of both services' − as she would be herself. The narration begins with Mrs Seacole already widowed. Her childhood and married life glossed very briefly in the first chapter, it is the departing from Jamaica that begins to drive the narration. Mrs Seacole is a peripheral subject *par excellence*. Whereas abolitionist rhetoric offered a part to Mary Prince, the place of a freeborn Creole Jamaican was by no means scripted so clearly in terms of class, race and gender. Both abolitionist and planter agitation in Britain championed the interests of black and white, slave and planter, throughout the late eighteenth and nineteenth centuries, and these interests would emerge again in the debates about 'the nigger question' following the Morant Bay rebellion in Jamaica in 1864. However, what it meant to be Jamaican in anything other than these binary terms was unclear. Mrs Seacole lays claim to ethnic characteristics of both the Scots (diligence, reliability) and Creole (the capacity to empathize and nurture). She is also marked by slavery:

I have a few shades of deeper brown upon my skin which shows me related − and I am proud of the relationship − to those poor mortals *whom you once held enslaved*, and whose bodies America still owns. And having this bond, and knowing what slavery is; having seen with my eyes and heard with my ears proof positive enough of its horrors − let others affect to doubt them if they will − is it surprising that I should be somewhat impatient of the airs of superiority which many Americans have attempted to assume over me? (14; my emphasis)

This is a volatile mix, particularly so in that she follows the Creole trade of the 'doctress'. At a time when roles of 'doctor' and 'nurse' were in the making as professions in England − and the Crimea was central to this − Seacole presents a creolization of both. She has the skills and knowledge of a doctor (for example, she trains with British doctors in the West Indies and conducts a post-mortem to acquire knowledge) and the particularly feminine characteristics of the nurse.

Seacole is, then, by any measure 'exotic' from a metropolitan viewpoint. She is a marvellous example of transculturation at work. This is the process of selection and invention which occurs in contact zones, where subordinated or marginal groups select and invent from materials transmitted to them by a dominant or metropolitan culture. These selections are sutured to local traditions and circumstances to produce quite different cultural and social forms.[16] Furthermore, she has a clear sense of belonging to an English community that was both of and apart from the British Isles. For Seacole, again like her mother, serves the imperial diaspora, the military officers, administrators and their wives, the men of the British army and navy. This floating population circulates about the colonial peripheries, and produces such unexpected convergence as, for example, the important place of Governor Edward John Eyre in both Australian and Jamaican histories.[17] So when Seacole sets out to become 'a Crimean *heroine*' it is in a desire to serve a constituency familiar to her, 'the regiments I had known so well in Jamaica'. And yet when Seacole arrives in England after the battles of Balaclava and Inkerman in 1864, she is an alien, indubitably coloured: 'the authorities would not listen to the offer of a motherly yellow woman to go to the Crimea and nurse her "sons" there ... In my country, where people know our use, it would have been different' (78). How can a Creole doctress be translated into metropolitan language?

My interest here is in how this autobiography deals with this conjuncture, how a Jamaican – one might say *peculiarly* Jamaican – woman can authorize herself for a British readership. Like Prince's *History*, Seacole's narrative is authenticated by the inclusion of various kinds of letters, statements and affidavits. Here they are incorporated into the text itself by Seacole, rather than clustering as appendices and prologues. *Wonderful Adventures* is dedicated (by permission) to Major-General Lord Rokeby by 'a humble and most grateful servant'. Another sign of an unauthorized narrator is the place of the editor, in this case *The Times* correspondent in the Crimea, W. H. Russell. This editor is less anxious and intrusive than Mary Prince's Mr Pringle, but his place as a legitimating device is apparent: 'I have witnessed her devotion and her courage; I have already borne testimony to her services to all who needed them.' Russell restricts himself to one footnote in the text itself, correcting Seacole's reference to *Macbeth* (she confuses the ghosts and the witches).

Seacole's text reveals, then, some of the shifts and continuities which enabled the emergence of a Jamaican subject in the period after abolition. *Wonderful Adventures* is located at the intersection of several autobiographic genres: the slave narrative, the war memoir and the travelogue. And yet it is not quite any of them. The slave narrative was redundant by then in the British sphere (even as it continued apace in the United States) and in any case Seacole tells us in the very first paragraph that she was born free as a Creole. And yet as a Caribbean woman Seacole, no less than Mary Prince, needs to align herself very carefully with metropolitan interests and British politics, domestic and other. She needs to secure patronage. This must be made very explicit in the text. She appeals to a reader who is British – not one of her own people – and frequently defends her presumption in doing so. What authorizes this kind of autobiography is knowledge based on experience. Ostensibly, in *Wonderful Adventures* this experience is based on Seacole's exploits in the Crimea. However, other kinds of firsthand experience, other things which Seacole speaks of 'having seen with my eyes and heard with my ears', come into play. To relate *Wonderful Adventures* to the slave narrative is thus to suggest that some of the dynamics of that autobiographic genre continue. In particular, the capacity of the 'seeing eye' and 'hearing ear' of black (and slightly brown) Caribbean subjects to witness slavery, and in turn to destablize the binary organization which discourses of slavery draw upon. What Seacole has to say about the Crimea will be shaped by what she has to say about Jamaica.

Wonderful Adventures is part of a proliferation of writing around and about the Crimean War. Seacole is very explicit that this appears to be the 'one and only claim I have to interest the public ear' (26). Narratives about the West Indies following abolition no longer have the kind of currency that gave Prince access to the British public at the height of the abolition debates in 1830. The Crimea does. Like Prince, this narrator knows that the limelight is surrounded by obscurity. Her claim to significance hangs upon her service to a British cause. Seacole's relationship to the female figure that was created quite spectacularly out of Crimea is important. As critics have observed, the celebration of Florence Nightingale reveals delicate transformations in thinking about the role of women in the mid-nineteenth century, and she came to embody her contemporaries' complex ideas about what a woman could, and should, be.[18] Her nursing expedition to the East in 1854, when she led a team of thirty-eight nurses to the hospital at Scutari, captured public attention in this the first war to be covered by the modern technologies of photography and telegraphy. The authorization of women through this war brought together two narratives about patriotic service which were culturally available in the mid-nineteenth century: a domestic narrative of maternal nurturing and self-sacrifice, and a military narrative of individual assertion and will. Mary Poovey argues that the convergence of these narratives and the archetypal feminine and masculine qualities associated with each in the figure of Florence Nightingale reveals that the domestic ideal always carried an aggressive component (170). As we have seen, the convergence of the domestic and the military, the association of domestic management with processes of invasion and settlement, is evident in autobiographical writing from the British colonies some time before the Crimean War.

Seacole, no less than Prince, has things to say which sit uneasily with what the English knew of themselves, most particularly the imperial femininity which was emergent in the mid-nineteenth century. Seacole is authorized by the Crimea, but very differently. She has things to say about Florence Nightingale which cast the negotiations of gender roles in mid-Victorian England in relation to issues of race and class, for she went to the Crimea as a Caribbean subject. For Seacole there had been no passage from Jamaica into the kind of imperial femininity that was mythologized in Florence Nightingale, *the* Crimean heroine, although she embodies the qualities which it celebrated. When Seacole returns to the streets of London and lays siege to the 'great house' in London where nurses were recruited to join Nightingale in the Crimea, her offer of assistance 'could not be entertained'. In an interview with one of Miss Nightingale's companions, 'I read in her face the fact, that had there been a vacancy, I should not have been chosen to fill it.' Seacole goes on to speculate: 'Was it possible that American prejudices against colour had some root here? Did these ladies shrink from accepting my aid because my blood flowed beneath a somewhat duskier skin than theirs?' (79). This is the second metropolitan episode in the autobiography and here, as before, on the streets of London Seacole is relegated to her skin.

Seacole's questions remain rhetorical. In asking them at all she is drawing upon all the privilege that her patrons confer, for she is calling into question the whole project of emancipation, the opposition of America and Britain, and suggesting continuities if not origins of American slavery in British prejudice. She is also casting a quite different light on Nightingale's project and the ways that the English domestic subject was both gendered and ethnicized. The way in which Seacole does this is also significant:

> I laid the same pertinacious siege to [the Secretary-at-War's] great house in __ Square, as I had previously done to his place of business.
>
> Many long hour did I wait in his great hall, while scores passed in and out; many of them looking curiously at me. The flunkeys, noble creatures! marvelled exceedingly at the yellow woman whom no excuses could get rid of, nor impertinence dismay, and showed me very clearly that they resented my persisting in remaining there in mute appeal from their sovereign will. (79)

Here, as before, Seacole is 'looked at', a subject of the imperious gaze, set apart by her skin. However, here, as before, the 'yellow woman' turns the tables. For by bringing the nomenclature and architecture of the plantation — the 'great house', the 'great hall' — into play, Seacole also invokes the racial organization at work in metropolitan space, and collapses its difference from the planter discourse she knew so well in the Caribbean. The separation between Jamaica and England, the distinction between the planter culture and the English, is drawn into question here. It is precisely the kind of exchange which occurs in Mary Prince's narrative.

It is not just coincidence that a Jamaican Creole would bring this convergence of gender and ethnicity in the invention of Englishness into the open. English representations of Jamaica and its peoples between the 1830s and 1860s were critical for, in characterizing, defining and identifying those others, they characterized, defined and identified themselves:

> Englishness was what the planters were not; the freed slaves might be, the freed slaves were not. In the turbulent decades between emancipation and the rising at Morant Bay in 1865, the changes in English perceptions of Jamaican blacks and the debates about those perceptions not only revealed changing attitudes to blacks but also to 'whiteness' itself and what it meant to be English.[19]

The period after emancipation was unstable. In 1833 the dominant definition of Englishness included the gratifying element of liberator of enslaved Africans. By 1865 English middle-class views on Jamaican blacks had become much more explicitly racist, displaced by a more aggressive biological racism rooted in the assumption that blacks were not brothers and sisters but a different species, born to be mastered. The public campaigns organized in the wake of the rebellion at Morant Bay flushed these shifts into the open,[20] whereas at the peak of the abolitionist campaign in 1830, respectable middle-class opinion was against the planters. By 1846 Thomas Carlyle, who publicly challenged the anti-slavery position in his 'Occasional discourse on the Negro Question' in 1849, had taken up their case.[21]

Seacole's memoir was published towards the end of a decade when a more racist, pro-slavery position was increasingly legitimate. In Jamaica itself sugar production declined dramatically after emancipation, and almost half the plantations were abandoned by 1854. Events elsewhere in the Empire were crucial, most notably the 1857 uprising in India, which brought the term 'niggers' into common use in Britain.[22] Thus in the (almost) thirty years between the appearance of *The History of Mary Prince* in 1830 and *Wonderful Adventures of Mrs. Seacole in Many Lands* in 1857, public discourses round the issue of slavery and racial difference fundamentally changed. We know this by reading Mill and Carlyle, where the politics of emancipation and abolition, brought to a crisis again by the Governor Eyre controversy, became a site of struggle over the dignity, sexual identity and status of whole categories of people: blacks as opposed to whites, Jamaican whites as opposed to the English, the middle class as opposed to the working class, men as opposed to women.[23]

One way of reading Seacole's autobiography is to place it as a kind of captivity narrative, where the colonial subject is thoroughly ensnared in the mapping of the class, ethnic and gendered boundaries of Englishness. Here the colonial autobiographer is a subject of lack, of the failure to 'lose oneself' in the sublimity of Empire. She is condemned to speak from an unfulfilled desire for Englishness: 'you have to speak to exist, but you can utter only what the dominant allows you to utter; even when you speak against the culture of colonialism, you speak its language because it constitutes what you are.'[24] But are colonial subjects destined to speak only in terms established by the imperium? What happens when the 'other woman' speaks as the subject of an autobiography? As we know from Prince and Seacole, autobiographic narration can bring about reversals and exchange, a blurring of social and cultural borders which are allegedly constitutive of the subject.

Creole travelling

Seacole's autobiography is tactical, using British patronage and finding room for manoeuvre, places where the system turns in upon itself, where the rhetoric of slavery can turn into discourses of emancipation. As we have seen for Mary Prince, access to autobiography, albeit in a highly mediated, edited and patronized form, allowed her to reach beyond that place of the mute 'other' woman, foil to the English domestic subject, and to call into question the distinctions which constituted white femininity. That is to say, although Prince is authorized to speak within clearly defined discursive constraints, she nevertheless uses 'the mysterious phenomenon of *authority*' to change the situation, to generate an oppositional authority which has the 'tricky ability' to erode 'insidiously and almost invisibly' the very power from which it derives.[25] To read for the oppositional in these autobiographical narratives is to look for the special oppositional status which might be achieved in the historically specific narrative situation of the text, to understand how structures of power might be exploited for quite different ends.

To do this, we might return to *Wonderful Adventures* with the genre of the travelogue in mind, and approach Seacole as a travelling subject, and an ex-centric one at that. To presume that 'other women' like Seacole are defined by lack, driven by a desire to lose the self in an imperial cause, obscures what Seacole, no less than Prince, understood very well: that the exclusion of colonial subjects was fundamental to the making of imperial femininity. Seacole narrates her experiences at the 'great house' where Nightingale's campaign is organized in a way which foregrounds the processes of silencing and negation at work very clearly. Here one of the most potent mythologies which gave meaning to the national and imperial project are cast into a different light, and the ways in which English identity was constructed through the active silencing and management of disruptive relations of ethnicity, gender and class is foregrounded. In England and among the metropolitan English, Seacole can be defined only by her skin, and in terms of negation. Yet other, quite different interactive and improvisational ways of subject formation are at work in the text, generated by Seacole's making of herself as a Creole.

The dynamics of Creole self-fashioning emerged elsewhere from the Americas in the 1820s, 1830s and 1840s, a process of invention among Creole intellectuals associated with the emergence of the newly independent decolonized states in Spanish America. Pratt relates this process to the first wave of decolonization, and a sign of peripheral improvisation quite beyond the experience of European societies: 'it was not in Europe, after all, that "European" institutions like colonialism, slavery, the plantation system, the mita, colonial tribute, feudal missionism, and so on had been lived out as history, language, culture amid everyday life' (175).

Although it would be grossly misleading to transpose thinking about decolonization in Spanish America to the British West Indies, it is nevertheless increasingly evident that to split Caribbean writing in terms of English, French, Dutch and Spanish colonialism is to take a metropolitan perspective which obscures synchronicities across the region. This is nowhere more evident than in thinking about the nature and function of literary creoleness and creolization, which is particular to neither British, French nor Spanish colonialisms.[26] Seacole's narrative coincides with the emergence of Creole travel writing in the newly decolonized Spanish America. Although they were coincident, there is no question of direct influence between the writings of the Creole intelligentsia of Spanish America and Seacole's autobiography. Yet Pratt's insistence on the association between creolization and decolonization, the improvisation of self in terms of experiences which were non-European (such as slavery and the plantation system) is very useful in thinking about Seacole's *Wonderful Adventures*. If we look to the writings of other postcolonial Creole subjects, for example, Sarmiento's *Travels* (1849), and how they position themselves in relation to Europe, we can perceive distinctively peripheral practices of self-invention in autobiography. 'One can more accurately think of Creole representations as transculturating European materials, selecting and deploying them in ways that do not simply reproduce the hegemonic visions of Europe or simply legitimate the designs of European capital.'[27] If we return to Seacole's *Wonderful Adventures* and read it as a travelogue, where the earlier sections of the narrative set in the Isthmus of Panama are not just a prelude to the arrival in England and the 'real' adventures in Crimea but are in themselves constitutive, the project of Creole self-fashioning is much clearer.

In 1850 two things happen which are fundamental to the making of Mrs Seacole in the text. This was the year when cholera 'swept over the island of Jamaica with dreadful force' and Seacole sharpens her skills as a doctress, a woman able to act decisively and usefully when social disorder and chaos erupt. Here she begins to represent herself as a 'heroine'. Secondly, in 1850 Seacole heads to Chagres on the Isthmus of Panama. Loaded with clothing, guava jelly, preserved meats and vegetables, she leaves Jamaica prepared to cater for the travellers trekking through the Isthmus on their way to the gold fields of California. When cholera arrives there 'Mrs Seacole' is again heroic in the battle against disease, with the knowledge of a doctor and the gentleness of a nurse. At Cruces the second element of the hybrid character which is 'Mrs Seacole' comes into play when she establishes the 'British Hotel'. Here, as the name suggests, a regime of domestic order, cleanliness and propriety is put into place amidst chaos, where law, order and appropriate gendered and sexual behaviour are non-existent. The 'British Hotel' is a precursor of 'Spring Hill', the establishment which Seacole manages near Balaclava. The point is that from the outset of her *Wonderful Adventures*, Seacole invents herself as a woman produced by contact zones, by raw social spaces where chaos and disorder prevail, where boundaries and appropriate behaviour are not in place.

The experiences on the Isthmus in the early 1850s, prior to her expedition to England and the Crimea, suggest that a crucial component of Seacole's improvisation is not just the fusion of the Creole doctress and the hotel-keeper, but also the working through of racial identity at places where different bodies of land and ocean meet, and different kinds of social organization and racial identification compete. In the 1850s in particular, the Isthmus was at a crossroads: between the Atlantic and the Pacific, 'America' and 'California', crossed by passengers to and from Chile, Peru and Lima, with many travellers specifically from the southern states of America. Although 'it is one of the maxims of the New Granada constitution – as it is I believe of the English – that on a slave touching its soil his chains fall from him' (52), nevertheless British and American, abolitionist and pro-slavery discourses confronted each other then and there. Seacole herself is conscripted into a variety of racially based identities: a nigger, a 'yaller woman', viewed by a traveller 'as he would eye a horse or nigger he had some thoughts of making a bid for'. Even here her status as a traveller is racially marked as, refused passage on an American steamer, she must await passage on a British ship to return to Jamaica. Yet Cruces is also the place where slaves are elevated by freedom and equality, 'the same negro who perhaps in Tennessee would have cowered like a beaten child or dog beneath an American's uplifted hand, would face him boldly here, and by equal courage and superior physical strength cow his old oppressor' (43). It is here that colour is shown to be such an arbitrary marker of difference.

Seacole openly speaks on the subject of her colour, its association with slavery, and the crucial difference between herself and 'you', the British reader: 'I have a few shades of deeper brown upon my skin which shows me related — and I am proud of the relationship — to those poor mortals *whom you once held enslaved'* (14). Slavery establishes a fundamental difference between Creole and British subjects, and although the binaries of slavery and freedom have collapsed in law, the moral economies they denote are by no means superseded from Seacole's perspective; in fact they are invoked anew. The British reader carries the taint, and is constituted as a national and imperial subject by it.

At the Isthmus in 1853, in a unique convergence of place and time, two quite different discourses of slavery meet, an enactment of the space between Britain and the United States in those years between abolition in the British colonies and the southern American states. To a degree, Seacole's narrative works to confirm the opposition of 'American' and 'British', 'plantation' and 'emancipist' ideologies. She does constitute herself in part by drawing upon those supremely Victorian virtues of self-help and feminine domesticity. She also identifies with the English in their desire for Britannic supremacy. However, to suggest that she aspires to Englishness is to displace the marks of ex-centricity, the ways that Seacole draws upon the periphery in her self-invention, and looks at the making of Englishness from the perspective of a woman of colour. This is, after all, how she is perceived during her brief sojourns in the London streets. As a Creole subject Mrs Seacole is uniquely placed to speak from, and about, the space between black and white which is opened up in post-emancipation Caribbean autobiography.

Slavery removes any possibility of Mrs Seacole being an innocent traveller. Her adventures are not 'wonderful' in the sense of that transcendence, the loss of self in the experience of awe, that we find in so many Victorian women's travel narratives. The search for the sublime, the 'out of body' experience and delight was not the prerogative of a woman traveller who was so often seen in terms of her skin, profoundly embodied by the making of English subjects through alterities. As I have suggested, the narrative always presents Mrs Seacole with an intense awareness of that Creole body, its appearance in the metropolitan view, and the shifting constructions of that body in place and time. Yet she also deploys the ethnographic gaze back on to metropolitan subjects and spaces, so that the arbitrariness of the distinctions is brought into view. The narrator displays a self-consciousness of her subjectivity, a sense of herself as both inside and outside her surroundings and her body. This is not just to say that Mrs Seacole travels with the burden of colour. More specifically than this, she travels with the burden of slavery at her back, with the movements of black people in the slave trade as commodities always at her heels. This occurs not just in the Isthmus, where she is refused free passage on the passenger steamer, and regarded as a commodity herself. The shadow of the plantation and the middle passage shapes her experiences in the metropolis, where the 'great house' and the 'great hall' reappear. They also haunt the very notion of travel itself.

The question arises as to how Seacole can draw on the discourses of travel to represent herself. The idea that all travel can be seen in the light of the classic formations of imperial travel in the West is called into question by *Wonderful Adventures*. In his discussion of the 'inherited schema or doxa' of travel, Gikandi draws attention to the established ethos of travel, to its association with immutable values such as progress, the quest for knowledge, freedom to move, self-awareness as an Odyssean enterprise, and the need to understand the self by appropriating the strangeness and difference of the other:

> In the case of English travelers ... there is no doubt that Englishness is always the stable point of reference, even when those authors have grave doubts about the value and identity of the English domestic space. In this sense, Englishness is the equivalent of the *oikos* in earlier narratives of travel: it acts as a 'transcendental point of reference that organizes and domesticates a given area by defining all other points in relation to it. Such an act of referral makes all travel a circular voyage insofar as that privileged point or *oikos* is posited as the absolute origin and absolute end of any movement at all.'[28]

Whether this centre, figured so vividly by Eden and Jameson in those moments of transcendence, can hold for ex-centric travellers is open to question.

Mrs Seacole takes every opportunity to express her debt and gratitude to her patrons and holds her editor in due deference. There is, however, ongoing dialogue through the text about the usefulness, or at least the use, of élite knowledge. As we have seen, the editor sets us straight in a footnote on Mrs Seacole's knowledge of *Macbeth*. Elsewhere there is an ongoing parry about bringing literary and mythic references to cast Mrs Seacole's adventures in a classic and archetypal frame. She tells us at the very start: 'Some people, indeed, have called me quite a female Ulysses. I believe they intended it as a compliment; but from my experience of the Greeks, I do not consider it a very flattering one' (2). The irony and humour here are deployed by Mary Seacole to some extent at Mrs Seacole's expense, but the issue returns later: 'Upon my word, I think if the poor things had possessed as many legs as my editor tells me somebody called the Hydra (with whom my readers are perhaps more familiar than I am) had heads, I should have found candidates for them' (119). Mrs Seacole draws attention here to a shared knowledge of mythology by the reader and her editor, and *their* predisposition to read travel writing with a classic framework in mind. This is, to some extent, deferential. It also grows from her determination to draw upon her experience, and the cultural heritage of 'her people' in Jamaica.[29] The memory of slavery, very recent for Seacole, casts the ship, freedom, 'home', and the notion of the circular passage, the return, in a quite different light. The brutal excesses of the slave plantation and then the memory of it called into question foundational moves of Western philosophy and social thought. This certainly includes the place of Greek mythology as the template for experiences of travel.

I want to hold on to not just race in reading Seacole's autobiography but the very specific organization of racial difference in terms of plantation slavery. This becomes difficult, as the Creole and creolization are increasingly read as the archetypal postcolonial subject and process, part of a 'global mongrelization of métissage' and as the idea of 'travelling theory' and poststructuralist nomadologies construct a global cosmopolitan subject. Against this we can pose bell hooks' reminder that travel 'is not a word that can be easily evoked to talk about the Middle Passage, the Trail of Tears, the landing of Chinese immigrants, the forced relocation of Japanese-Americans, or the plight of the homeless.'[30] Seacole's *Wonderful Adventures*, an anomaly in the plethora of Victorian travel writings in its ex-centricity, is a reminder of the cultural specificity of travel, a spectrum with one edge defined by privilege, time and choice, and the other marked by the violence of forced passages through slavery and indenture. As one of the first Creole travellers to travel to the metropolis and represent it 'from the outside', Seacole uses her marginality as a colonial subject to assert, as Pratt so memorably suggests in a quite different context, 'your fictions are my realities; your past is my present; your exotic is my everyday' (191). Mrs Seacole travels to the metropolis as both an infiltrator and a pilgrim, a transcultural subject who is more British than the British in her aspirations to domesticity and independence. She confesses to her 'general enthusiasm' for British campaigns, and yet is under no illusions that the boundaries of Englishness extend to herself. This Creole subject is made on both sides of the Atlantic and authentic in neither, a product of the intercultural dynamics that were established, and linger, as a legacy of slavery in the West Indies.

As Caribbean autobiographers, Prince and Seacole play upon a complex circuitry of colonial relations. In the process of becoming autobiographic subjects they shift the binary organization of racial, gendered and ethnic identities into something altogether more duplicitous: implicating Susanna Moodie and Florence Nightingale into their autobiographies, pulling the English drawing-room into the dynamics of the plantation economy. Within the historical, political, geographic, cultural and imaginative boundaries of

Empire, the making of subjectivity in this way, through contiguities, adjacencies, oppositions and associations − that is, 'intimacies' of all kinds − was a constant process which defies the centrifugal force of a single historical centre. In their autobiographic writing, constrained as they are by metropolitan expectations and patronage, we see what Toni Morrison means when she suggests that the slave experience marked out black women as the first truly modern people, handling in the nineteenth century dilemmas and difficulties which emerge in European autobiographics a century later:

> modern life begins with slavery ... From a women's point of view, in terms of confronting the problems of where the world is now, black women had to deal with post-modern problems in the nineteenth century and earlier. These things had to be addressed by black people a long time ago: certain kinds of dissolution, the loss of and need to reconstruct certain kinds of stability. Certain kinds of madness ... These strategies for survival made the truly modern person.[31]

The autobiographic texts of both Mary Prince and Mary Seacole confirm Morrison's argument. For all the differences in their genesis, genre and contexts, both *The History of Mary Prince* and *Wonderful Adventures of Mrs. Seacole in Many Lands* foreground the analytical and experiential categories of 'the self' and the limits of its representation. They alert us to the ways in which the cultural, historical and textual expectations of self-representation affect their particular performances as autobiographic subjects.[32] As a piece of travel writing which experiments with the process of creolization in autobiography, Seacole's *Wonderful Adventures* looks forward to contemporary debates about mapping the self in terms of 'between-ness', of thinking through a hybridity which links distinct, historically connected postcolonial spaces.[33]

Mary Gaunt: writing a master narrative

Slavery remained active in other kinds of autobiographic writing. It was, for example, invoked in constructions of whiteness. Here we find the forms of what Morrison calls the 'master narrative', where Africans are spoken 'of' and 'for', where the place of the master in the transactions of slavery is brought into view. The question of how the imaginative encounter with Africanism enabled white writers to think about themselves has particular resonances in the establishment of white settler culture in the United States. Morrison suggests that the master narrative remains intact in other colonial literatures too, for Africanism serves to 'limn out' and 'enforce' the inventions and implications of whiteness. Furthermore, it establishes the grounds for exploring the fantasies, desires and suppressions which are part of the making of white identities in settler cultures, 'a fabricated brew of darkness, otherness and alarm' (38).

To bring Mary Gaunt into these circuits is to explore some of the unpredictable intersections of postcolonial autobiography. Gaunt plays upon a complex series of interconnections between Jamaica and Australia, working through the legacies of the slave trade almost a century after abolition with a different series of collaborations and distinctions in view. That a traveller should seek to secure her identity in terms of an Australianness explicated through slavery is unexpected. It suggests that the gendered, racial and sexual markers of plantation slavery emerged in very different ways after the demise of those who had witnessed the Jamaican plantations with the 'seeing eye'. And yet, with Morrison's argument about the ongoing production of master narratives in settler cultures in mind, perhaps the emergence of an Australian deployment of Africanism in autobiographical writing should not surprise, for in Australia, too, European colonists were in the process of becoming national subjects.

Mary Gaunt (1872–1942) was a prolific writer across a number of genres. She is best known for her novel, *Kirkham's Find* (1897), in which she uses the romance plot to explore the constructions of gender in the colonial Australian landscapes of her childhood. Her travels produced a number of travelogues and the material for the 'ripping yarns of adventure' by which she sought to make her living as an expatriate writer. She grew up in Australia where her father was Governor of the Victoria Goldfields, and she was one of the first women to enrol at the University of Melbourne. She sailed to England as a young widow in 1901, hoping to find more congenial circumstances to pursue an independent career as a writer. It is worth noting that she is one of the first Australian women to publish a travel book, with *Alone in West Africa* (1912) being preceded only by Margaret Thomas' volumes on Spain, the Middle East and Denmark. I will focus on her trilogy of writings which emerged from her travels in Africa and Jamaica: *Alone in West Africa, Where the Twain Meet* (1922) and *Reflection – in Jamaica* (1932). Gaunt also published extensive travelogues about her experiences in China.[34]

Gaunt produces an autobiographical self by inserting herself into landscapes of slavery, as the 'white missus' in West Africa (in *Alone in West Africa*, 1912) and the 'Buckra lady' in Jamaica (in *Never the Twain* and *Reflection – in Jamaica*). We know from Mary Prince's *History* that the 'Buckra lady' is an unstable ensemble of gender and race, subject to metamorphosis and mutation, where the boundaries of Englishness and colonial identities intersect. For Gaunt it is a subjectivity which is on a threshold of gendered and racial characteristics, where she pursues what it means to be 'colonial born', a 'woman of the South'. We need to ask what this delivers to Gaunt as an autobiographer, why she desires to deploy discourses of slavery and this particularly violent arrangement of black and white bodies. Why does this particular colonial encounter figure in Gaunt's enunciation of independent womanhood and Australianness?

This immediately involves a shift from memory to fantasy. Whereas both Mary Prince and Mary Seacole were authorized as autobiographers through their ability to testify and witness, to invoke slavery as a site of memory, for Gaunt it becomes a site of performance, of romance. By travelling to West Africa and to Jamaica, Gaunt places herself at thresholds of terror and desire, savagery and primitivism. It is from here that she can invent her own identity as a Briton and a colonial subject.

The racial and gendered aspects of settler colonialism as it was shaped in Australia are important in understanding Gaunt's autobiographic 'I'. Each volume of the travel trilogy begins with recollections of her Australian childhood, memories that are fundamental to the ways in which she seeks to identify herself through travels to Africa and the Caribbean. In the first, *Alone in West Africa*, Gaunt traces her interest in the African coast and the slave trade back to an Australian childhood, to a storybook read as a child, or part-read at least. The tale of a small boy called Carl who was shipwrecked on the coast of West Africa remains unfinished when a bushfire breaks out in a paddock and takes the young girl from the romance of savagery to the realities of bush life. This recollection sets in place both gendered and racial markers. Firstly, it privileges romance, for reading romance remains one of the few escapes from the restricted roles open to women of her generation in Australia. For the child narrator and her sister: 'There was really nothing for a woman to do but to marry, and accordingly we both married and I forgot my entrance into that world which is so old and yet always so new, my vague longings after savage lands.'[35] Ironically, for Gaunt, romance is not the story of love and marriage but its obverse. Romance is the 'wild' and the 'savage', romance is in opposition to domesticity. It is also in opposition to all that she recalls of her childhood and young womanhood in Australia. Secondly, from the outset, the recollection associates Africa with those familiar tropes of Africanism: 'the Dark Continent', primitivism; places and peoples outside time and history.

This recurs in the recollection that begins the second book, *Never the Twain*, where the narrator recalls a trip 'home' to England when she was a child. There, in the household of Liverpool shipowners whose forebears had been African traders, she comes upon the relics of the slave trade: an old slave account book from their estates in Jamaica, models of their factories on the Guinea Coast, pictures of the slave ships in the Oil Rivers. Here that interest in savagery and romance is traced back not just to Africa but to the slave trade in particular, and the connections between Africa and Jamaica. Was I a slave in a former life, she asks, 'for some haunting memory of a past life has shaped my career'.[36] The association of slavery with 'haunting memory' indicates the cluster of attributes which Gaunt pursues through slavery, and through travel to West Africa and Jamaica. What becomes available to her through relics and landscapes of slavery is a kind of theatre for romance, a backdrop for a performance of the self which draws on the most brutal and violent forms of colonization. There is no consistency in this self-projection. It veers from imagining the self as a slave in a former life to, at one point, identifying with Simon Legree, the infamous slaver of *Uncle Tom's Cabin*. By shuttling between childhood recollections and the travel memoir of a middle-aged, widowed writer, Gaunt seeks to use the relics of slavery in Jamaica and West Africa to write herself into narratives of conquest.

In the third and final book of the travel trilogy the narrator rehearses quite explicitly her search for a discursive framework to express these oppositions through the development of a gendered and Australian discourse of travel writing. In the Author's Note to *Reflection – in Jamaica* (1932) she again recalls her childhood in Ballarat, Australia, with the same gendered and racial oppositions in mind:

> I was once given to reading every book of travel I could lay my hands on. When I was a little girl a volume telling of the discovery of the Victoria Nyanza was in the bookcase beside which I was condemned to practise music three hours daily ... The lure of the unknown was irresistible. I propped the book on the music rack and endeavoured to absorb it while playing my scales ... There was no chance of reading Captain Speke at any other time or perhaps I should not have misbehaved ... There was always in me a desire for independence considered by mothers in my youth very unwomanly and likely to spoil my chance of marrying. I wanted to travel, a most improper desire for a young lady I was often told. Since that was not possible I wanted to see how other people managed in the wilds. Civilized travelling didn't interest me in those days.[37]

For Gaunt the African travel book is a kind of illicit knowledge hidden in the rituals of the music practice, and a metaphor of the opposition between travel and marriage – the former unwomanly and associated with the 'wild' and the independent, with unpredictability and savagery. The discipline and docility of practising scales, the acquiring of appropriate feminine and domestic skills in rural Australia finds its antithesis in the fantasy and romance of the 'uncivilized' in Africa, 'the Dark Continent'. Captain Speke is the interloper on the music rack: 'I cannot hear his name mentioned even now without a thrill, as if he belonged to me, though I never got nearer to him than those stolen readings.' Gaunt aspires to the masculine attributes which Speke represents: adventure, freedom, agency, independence. Yet she does not aspire to speak as Speke does, for 'truth compels me to state his book was dull, leaving out a great many things I wanted to know'. What is left out by Speke and pursued by Gaunt in her African and Jamaican travels are, ironically, desires which are not so improper for women after all: the 'everyday life of the peoples', the romance of the 'wild', the epic and romantic narratives of colonization and conquest.

These childhood fantasies and their Australian locations are fundamental to understanding why and how Gaunt proceeds to write herself into the landscapes of slavery. They suggest the making of an Australian woman in reaction against the gender role expectations which shape her life in Australia in compliance with the racial organization of the settler society. Of course Gaunt did not have to leave Australia to observe the legacies of indentured labour as an instrument of colonization, or to find an imaginative and historical terrain shaped by the presence of a racial other. The transportation of convicts to Australia during the first quarter of a century of white settlement was part of a larger international and intercontinental flow of forced migration, which included the recruitment of slaves for America.[38] However, by the end of the nineteenth century the role of the pioneer settler – both man and woman, both white – rather than the indentured labourers of the penal colony were placed at the forefront of histories of settlement. Likewise the place of Aboriginal Australians was suppressed. 'Terra nullius', the idea of the Australian continent as an empty land, belonging to no one, and unoccupied before the arrival of British settlers in 1788, was fundamental to the logic and legitimacy of white settlement. It was also germane to the ongoing invasion and dispossession, dispersal and disposal of indigenous Australians which proceeded apace, largely unobserved and unrecognized. This blend of convictism, invasion and dispossession, of indentured labour and race, is a uniquely Australian inheritance. It lacked the complete articulation of race and indentured labour which was a feature of plantation slavery; nevertheless, transportation and dispossession were fundamental to the making of white Australia – as we can see in Gaunt's autobiographic writing. However, these elements of colonial history were thoroughly repressed in the decades before and immediately after Federation in 1901, Mary Gaunt's Australian years.

Through her travels to West Africa and Jamaica, Gaunt identifies a series of purportedly Australian attributes. Most notably these relate to race – the idea that Australians have 'strong feelings about race' – and to gender: 'Because I am an Australian and have had a harder bringing-up I resent the supposition that a woman cannot go where a man can go' (*AWA*, 46). In particular she stresses the independence of Australian women. The legacy of settler colonialism is their superior capacity to labour and establish settlements in the wilderness alongside their men, and the necessity for white women in Australia to thrive without the resources of slave labour which settlers in British West Africa and the West Indies had to hand: 'The people who grumble should live in Australia and do their own work, cooking, washing, scrubbing. Do it for a week with the temperatures averaging 100 in the shade, and they wouldn't grumble in West Africa' (333). The elements of the pioneer legend of Australian settlement, dominant in the Federation period at the turn of the century, are apparent here. This celebration of the pioneers who settled and worked the land was a cornerstone of popular histories of the nation, a national rural myth that was deeply conservative in its concerns for national and racial health, and the preservation of white settler hegemony.[39]

Placing Gaunt in terms of the gendered and racial dynamics of Australian settlement is important, because the articulations of gender, sexuality and white supremacy, which follow in her travel writing, are deeply implicated in Australian settler racism around Federation. Histories of British feminism and abolition by Vron Ware and Moira Ferguson, among others, have led to a focus on the association between feminism and abolition, and the ongoing interest of British feminists in race relations. Elsewhere, different relations between feminism and anti-racism pertained. In fact, Gaunt's desire for independence and autonomy, her commitment above all to the equality of women, leads to a construction of the self in terms of colonialist discourses of racial supremacy, terms which are deeply embedded in the gender dynamics of Australian settler colonialism.

The particular construction of white femininity which Gaunt attempts to deploy through the black Atlantic thus has its origins in the place which Gaunt always calls 'far away Australia'. In Gaunt's Australian years the colonies were engaged in extensive debates about Federation and the character of Australian society. Although these fitted into frameworks derived from political movements common to all Western democracies, they developed in particular ways in the Australian context. Ideas of race based on social Darwinism were used to sanctify a ruthless dispossession of the Aborigines, to restrict the rights of Asian and Pacific immigrants, and to secure the interests of the white population. The white settlers' search for a separate identity as Australians was implicated in their sense of themselves as Anglo-Saxon and fundamentally superior to other racial types, most particularly those who lacked the badge of superiority: fair skin.[40] The pressure on white women to be healthy and fertile, wives and mothers, and so secure white Australia, was of course a component of the racial politics of the settler society. The pressure on women to marry and the establishment of pro-motherhood social policies was championed across the political spectrum, for feminists also valorized motherhood as a means of socially empowering women.

Gaunt leaves Australia to escape these pressures, to make a living by the pen in England. However, this ensemble of ideas about race and gender, a clear sense of white supremacy secured through colonialism, remains with her. They suggest why she was so attracted to the tropes of Africanism, and to one of the few contact zones which was even more violent and repressive than the one with which she was familiar. Discourses of slavery offered Gaunt sharply defined oppositions of black and white, savagery and civilization. These oppositions – which were present in Australian colonization but suppressed and hidden from view in settler histories – were clearly articulated in the discourses of plantation slavery. Gaunt goes to West Africa in 1911 with a commission to write a book about the old forts along the Gold Coast, decaying establishments which are the relics of slavery and the operations of French, British, Danish and German colonization. In *Alone in West Africa* Gaunt proceeds to write herself into a master narrative organized around a thoroughly racialized landscape, a geography of forts and islands of white amidst darkness and decay. She produces an Africanism which serves the articulation of herself as an Australian traveller and, in taking up the 'White Man's burden', she finds that imperialism gives her more authority and independence than she could have aspired to at home.[41]

The Buckra lady

Gaunt's determination to be 'Alone' in West Africa obliterates not only the black men and women who carried her and her belongings from one place to another. It also erases the discursive tracks left by earlier women travellers who were themselves empowered through writing about allegedly the most nefarious corner of 'the Dark Continent'.[42] Unlike Mary Kingsley, who travelled in West Africa some twenty years earlier with a strong sense of the historicity of African peoples, Gaunt 'went to see a savage land, I went to seek material for the only sort of story I can write, and to tell the prowess of the men who had gone before and left their traces in great stone forts all along the three hundred miles of coast' (11). Whereas Kingsley travelled wherever possible by foot or in canoe, using the localized networks of the traders, Gaunt travels by hammock, staying whenever possible in the official outposts of white settlement under the patronage of the colonial administration. In fact, when she leaves the coast after six months' travel along the rivers and beaches where slaves were sold and corralled in barracoons, Gaunt is proud to remark that she has travelled some seven hundred miles in a hammock, reaching places where no white woman had gone before. Allegedly her very appearance introduces history into places outside of time: 'for these people whose lives move in the same groove from the cradle to the grave all things will bear date from the day when the white missus and the white master had chop on the Chief's verandah' (107).

This hammock is axiomatic to the narrator's self-projection, and a symbol of the social relations established around the white woman and the way she seeks to empower herself. In fact, this traveller is constituted as the 'white missus' most unequivocally not in the arrival but in the transit itself, during those 700 miles in the hammock. The hammock is the focus of the narrative. It is the centre-piece of an entourage of porters and carriers, baggage, boxes and beds which are arranged around 'the missus' herself, and which need to be orchestrated by negotiations and power plays between 'the missus' and the 'negroes'. It is in these transits that the traveller fulfils those fantasies of independence through the mastery and domination of an 'inferior race': 'I was the white woman all over dealing with the inferior race and I had not a doubt as to what should be done' (130). As the journey progresses across the beaches of the slave coast she comes to identify with Simon Legree, to regard the carriers as her property, 'the captures (*sic*) of my bow and spear', to 'fairly purr with pride' when she is carried over treacherous rocks 'without setting foot out of my hammock', to long for a slave-driver's whip. It is from the hammock too that the 'romance' of Africa can take hold:

All the glories of the ages, all the delights of the world were in that night. The song of the carriers took on a softness and a richness born of the open spaces of the earth and the glorious night, and for accompaniment was the pad-pad of their feet in the dust of the roadway. (203)

Here, supine yet in control, protected by her Burberry raincoat within the gauzy material of the hammock, the narrator can entertain the fantasies, horrors, ghosts of darkest Africa. From this perspective she can generalize and philosophize about 'the negro mind', the march of civilization, and the need for white governance in Africa in perpetuity. The hammock and all it connotes is a mode of travel that allows the re-emergence of the dynamics of slavery in the complete domination and infantilization of African peoples. It allows Gaunt a narrative location where she can reproduce and inhabit the most violent and intrusive form of white presence in Africa, a position mapped out clearly in the discourses of slavery.

There are places where this traveller perceives another view, although this emerges from a quite different vantage point. On one of the few occasions when Gaunt visits a Mission House, she is introduced to a polygamous household which she sees 'with understanding eyes': 'It was quite delightful staying here ... and seeing quite a new side of African life, seeing it as it were from the inside' (288). Here, albeit briefly, the narrative no longer dramatizes the narrating self in terms of racial superiority and an aggressive female independence. A moment of ambivalence emerges, when the imperial and patriarchal conventions briefly lose their hermeneutic force. This 'inside' is a very different narrative space, in which the narrator is no longer defined in terms of difference and racial supremacy.

Gaunt is by any measure a belated traveller. What Ali Behdad calls the 'predicaments of belatedness', the struggle to produce an orientalist epistemology amidst late colonial relations of power, are everywhere apparent. There is no prospect of discovery or the shock of the new here. Gaunt is recording relics, and her appearance as the 'first white woman' is a fantasy which has no meaning beyond her own need to be at the centre of a self-empowering colonizing narrative. This is nowhere more evident than when she is mistaken for a tourist, an identification which she must 'disclaim promptly', for the tourist is a consumer and a follower rather than a traveller. Discourses of tourism do not derive authority from the interpretive power of a centralized subject of enunciation, the 'meaning-making "I" of the travelogue',[43] but the ideological limitations of the terms in which Gaunt is seeking to inscribe herself as that centre of authority are clear. The fantasy is that she herself initiates the entry into time for some African peoples, that she is being carried across 'the same shore, the very same' as the great days of the slave trade, is belied by the marks of change and time all around. Evidence of this includes self-government in Liberia, the brass dishes as common in London markets as in the West African village and the glimpses of an 'inside' story which alter the dynamics of the narration centred on the 'white missus'. At the end of the final book she glimpses the tourist at her heels and her own belatedness:

> So Jamaica, the land of wonderful hills, of rushing streams, of palm-clad shores and painted seas, is beginning to cater for the tourist, dotting her shores with luxurious hotels. The tourist clamours for luxury. The result of luxury is commonplaceness. Romance departs. Perhaps it is just as well. For romance is seldom romantic to the people who live in it.[44]

At the conclusion of an evening's entertainment in Jamaica the gathering listens to a concert from New York on the radio. For a narrator given to visions of the old world, apparitions of Columbus and Yssassis, gentlemen in wigs and buckled shoes in Jamaican great houses, it is a sharp reminder of the modern synchronicities of Jamaican life.

Familiar as we now are with the argument that colonial discourse operates according to ambivalent protocols of fantasy and desire, we might miss the quite specific uses to which slavery is put in Gaunt's self-fashioning as a settler subject. By turning to the landscapes of slavery and the torrid zones, this 'Buckra lady' is able to entertain the classic fears of the colonizer, 'what the white people feared sub-consciously all the time' (*WTM*, 156): miscegenation, the violation of white women, the precariousness of the authority on which white supremacy depended. The Guinea Coast and Jamaica become sites where these fantasies and self-projections can be entertained, seemingly remote from the domesticity in the 'land of liberty', Australia. From this vantage point, Australasia appears as the land of peace and plenty from which a superior colonizing race of Britons will emerge. And yet of course the Australian national subject has been produced no less by colonial invasion and dispossession, and expressed in terms of white supremacy and black degeneration. Gaunt's invention of a sense of Australianness in landscapes where relics of slavery are to hand allows an expression of the anxieties and ambivalence, the fears and desires, which would not be expressed openly and self-reflectively in Australian autobiography until very recently. In West Africa and Jamaica, Gaunt can both act out and articulate a national subjectivity and a complete mastery as a white settler woman. She can also draw on the trope of the white woman as vulnerable, an object of forbidden desire, which is one of the classic embodiments of femininity in allegories of Empire. In this trope, black and white are absolutely differentiated in the figures of the white woman and the black rapist, a trope which functions to justify the extreme exercise of control and retributive justice. This is a process of 'gathering identity unto herself from the wholly available and serviceable lives of Africanist others'.[45]

Romance and slavery

Romance facilitates this process for, as Toni Morrison suggests, romance emerges in colonial literatures as a way of transacting the fears, hopes and forces of colonizing cultures:

> It has been suggested that romance is an evasion of history (and thus perhaps attractive to a people trying to evade the recent past). But I am more persuaded by arguments that find in it the head-on encounter with the very real, pressing historical forces and the contradictions inherent in them as they came to be experienced by writers. Romance, an exploration of anxiety imported from the shadows of European culture, made possible the sometimes safe and other times risky embrace of quite specific, understandably human, fears. (36)

In his Introduction to *The Scarlet Letter* (1850), the American writer Nathaniel Hawthorne describes the space of romance as 'somewhere between the real world and fairy-land, where the Actual and the Imaginary may meet, and each imbue itself with the nature of the other'.[46] This intermediate space finds an equivalent in the borderlands of colonialism. In colonial literatures, romance emerges as a way of writing about this border territory, between civilization and wilderness. Romance lends itself to erosions of the distinct self in its preoccupations with *doppelgängers*, split selves and other forms of character linkage: 'orders between characters are strangely abrogated. As in a dream – or nightmare – figures explode, implode, split up, coalesce, fragment, reassemble and defy closure.'[47] For Gaunt, Jamaica lends itself to this kind of romance. She travels around the island and 'looks with the eye of the romance writer', proceeding from the relics of one great house to the next. From the scene of slave rebellions to Morant Bay, she is able to reincarnate the Maroons, planters and slaves which 'haunt' the Jamaican landscapes, and to insert herself into this history. In her self-fashioning as 'the Buckra lady' and 'the white missus', Gaunt is able to undertake an exploration of whiteness at a threshold of difference where white supremacy finds its most thorough and complete articulation, and yet also where it is most haunted and threatened – the plantation. In this way, Africanism is embedded in her construction of herself as a white woman, in the grounds upon which she constructs her difference as an Australian, and in the terms whereby she understands what it means to be 'colonial'.

That romance should feed on the relics of slavery in this way should not surprise us. Although this representation of Jamaica is the extravagance of an Australian woman in reaction to the equally fantastic projections of 'terra nullius' (or absence of past) in representations of her own colonial society, it fed on Jamaican white writing too. In her travels to Jamaica Mary Gaunt became part of a vigorous Jamaican intelligentsia, in particular the writers who gathered around H. G. de Lisser and his journal *Planter's Punch*. Extracts from Gaunt's travel writings appeared in *Punch*, and her comings and goings are recorded in the society pages. She notes her indebtedness to De Lisser in particular in *Reflection – in Jamaica*. H. G. de Lisser was a white Creole writer, whose socially conservative 'Buckra' views have been compared to those of the English writer and traveller J. A. Froude.[48] Mary Gaunt surely found the De Lisser circle congenial for, like her, he championed imperial federation; he was also deeply attached to historical fictions in which Jamaica appeared as a wild, colonial land untouched by civilization or time. For de Lisser, like Gaunt, the figure of Columbus was never far away. Fantasy and romance are grafted on to the facts of recorded history, with slavery as a canvas full of melodrama and adventure. H. G. de Lisser's most successful historical novel, *The White Witch of Rosehall* (1929), was published during Gaunt's last visit to Jamaica.

This fiction is loosely based on the biography of Annie Palmer, a planter's wife notorious as a necromancer and murderer. Here, as in Gaunt's two Jamaica travelogues, the romance writer turns to slavery, and the history of colonization is exploited as a source of violence and rebellion, the lurid and the sensational.[49] Coincident with this, in Trinidad at this very same time, local writers, including C. L. R. James and Alfred Mendes, were using the periodical press to critique colonial romanticism and to explore a different way of writing about the local scene. They focused on the present, turning to the barrack yards and experimenting with the techniques of realism rather than relics and romance. For James, Mendes and the other members of the *Beacon* group, black writing and rhythms in the United States suggested new ways of connecting to Caribbean histories and realities. Through them we begin to see Caribbean writers both shaping and drawing on that pool of energies which Gilroy calls the black Atlantic.[50]

The strange synchronicities and unexpected intimacies I have drawn on in this chapter alert us to the uneven and mixed genealogies of colonial literatures. The histories of these literatures are too often collapsed into a grand narrative of progress to modernism and postmodernism on the one hand, or read in terms of the introspection and singularities of a nationalist history on the other. Mary Gaunt reminds us of some of the 'improper', less familiar processes of creolization and hybridity which proliferate through colonial encounters. For Gaunt, no less than Seacole, writes towards an understanding of what it means to be 'colonial born' through the kind of self-fashioning and recomposition which travel writing facilitates. In the travel writing of both Seacole and Gaunt, the straightforward power relation of dominance of colonizer over colonized is displaced by more intricate processes of cultural contact, intrusion, fusion and disjunction, trespass and impropriety. Creolization and syncretism have long been associated with Caribbean cultures, and recently an Australian critic has argued that grafting and bringing the seemingly incompatible together is a distinctively antipodean activity.[51] Both ways, to articulate what it means to be colonial-born requires complex transactions in the colonial domain.

To ignore the kind of rogue connections, the unexpected colonial encounters between places as remote from each other as Jamaica and Australia, or West Africa and Australia, or the Crimea and Jamaica for that matter, is to suppress peripheral connections which are vital to an understanding of postcolonial autobiographic writing. Familiar as we are with that centre–periphery dynamic which we see explicated so clearly (if momentarily) by English travellers, we miss the volatile circuitries of autobiographic writing, its unexpected exchanges and intersections which emerge in particular in colonial travel writing. We also miss some of the complex ways in which colonial relations feed into fantasy and desire. Plantation slavery, that most violent of colonial encounters, and most schematic and brutal of colonial geographies, connects to articulations of black and white long after relations between master and slave were redundant in law. It continues even as the architecture of the great houses decays into the benign landscapes of the tourist brochure.

Notes

1   Jamaica Kincaid, *A Small Place*. New York: Plume, 1988, p. 30. Further references to this edition in text.
2   Nicholas Thomas, *Colonialism's Culture: Anthropology, Travel and Government*. London: Polity Press, 1994, p. 5.
3   James Morris, *Heaven's Command: An Imperial Progress*. Harmondsworth: Penguin, 1986, p. 19. Further references to this edition in text.
4   Anna Jameson, *Winter Studies and Summer Rambles in Canada, Vol III*. London: Saunders & Otley, 1838, p. 260. Further references to this edition in text.
5   See e.g. Anna Jameson's description of herself as a 'clod' for her inability to respond with adequate aesthetic emotion to the Niagara Falls. See also Deidre David's discussion of Emily Eden's travelogue in *Rule Britannia: Women, Empire and Victorian Writing*. Ithaca, NY: Cornell University Press, 1995, pp. 17–42.
6   Simon Gikandi, *Maps of Englishness: Writing Identity in the Culture of Colonialism*. New York: Columbia University Press, 1996, p. 117. Further references to this edition in text.
7   See e.g. Sara Mills, *Discourses of Difference: An Analysis of Women's Travel Writing and Colonialism*. London: Routledge, 1991, and Vron Ware, *Beyond the Pale: White Women, Racism and History*. London: Verso, 1992.
8   Susan Morgan, *Place Matters: Gendered Geography in Victorian Women's Travel Books about Southeast Asia*. New Brunswick, NJ: Rutgers University Press, 1996, p. 3.
9   Mary Louise Pratt, *Imperial Eyes: Travel Writing and Transculturation*. London: Routledge, 1992, p. 90. Further references to this edition in text.
10 Gikandi, *Maps of Englishness*, discusses this issue at length.
11 Toni Morrison, *Playing in the Dark: Whiteness and the Literary Imagination*. Cambridge, MA: Harvard University Press, 1992, p. 38. Further references to this edition in text.
12 Carl Plasa and Betty J. Ring (eds), *The Discourse of Slavery*. London: Routledge, 1994, p. xiv. See also Ware, *Beyond the Pale*.
13 Paul Gilroy, *The Black Atlantic: Modernity and Double Consciousness*. London: Verso, 1993. Further references to this edition in text.
14 This is in contrast to the extraordinary number of autobiographical narrations by slaves that are the foundation of the African-American literary tradition. See Henry Louis Gates, Jr, 'Introduction', *The Classic Slave Narratives*. New York: Mentor, 1987.

15 James Walvin, *Black Ivory: A History of British Slavery*. London: Fontana, 1992, p. 10.

16 Pratt, p. 6.

17 See Diana Brydon and Helen Tiffin, *Decolonising Fictions*. Sydney: Dangaroo Press, 1993, p. 44, for further discussion of this comparison.

18 Mary Poovey, *Uneven Developments: The Ideological Work of Gender in Mid-Victorian England*. Chicago: University of Chicago Press, 1988, p. 164. Further references to this edition in text.

19 Catherine Hall, *White, Male and Middle-Class: Explorations in Feminism and History*. London: Routledge, 1992, p. 208. Further references to this edition in text.

20 In October 1865 a riot took place outside the court-house in Morant Bay, a small town on the south-eastern side of Jamaica. Crowds had gathered to protest about a disputed fine; the protest turned to violence and a number of people were killed, both by rioters and volunteers. There was already a high level of political tension on the island and the British Governor, Edward John Eyre, fearful of a general rising of the 350,000 blacks against the 13,000 whites, proclaimed martial law and sent in the troops. In the subsequent reprisals, 439 blacks and 'coloureds' were killed, 600 men and women were flogged and over 1,000 huts and houses were burnt. A member of the Jamaican House of Assembly, George William Gordon, was hanged. A Royal Commission was set up to investigate but, despite its doubts as to Eyre's conduct, the government decided not to prosecute him. Debates about Eyre's conduct involved major intellectuals of the day, with Thomas Carlyle leading the committee defending Eyre, while John Stuart Mill led the committee which argued for his prosecution. For a discussion of this debate see Hall, 'Competing masculinities: Thomas Carlyle, John Stuart Mill and the case of Governor Eyre', in *White, Male and Middle-Class*.

21 Thomas Carlyle's 'Occasional discourse on the negro question' was published in *Fraser's Magazine*, Vol. 41, January 1850, p. 672, and republished in a revised version as a pamphlet in 1853. This version, titled 'Occasional discourse on the nigger question' appears in *English and Other Critical Essays* (London: Dent, 1964). The significance of the change in title is discussed by Hall in *White, Male and Middle-Class*, p. 291, fn. 32.

22 Hall, p. 275.

23 Hall, p. 288.

24 Gikandi, p. 142.

25 Ross Chambers, *Room to Maneuver*, p. 2.

26 See A. James Arnold, 'Charting the Caribbean as a literary region', in A. James Arnold (ed.), *A History of Literature in the Caribbean. Volume 3. Cross-Cultural Studies*. Amsterdam/Philadelphia: John Benjamins, 1997, pp. xi–xvii.

27 Pratt, p. 188.

28 Gikandi, p. 90. Gikandi is quoting from Georges van den Abbeele, *Travel as Metaphor: From Montaigne to Rousseau*. Minneapolis: University of Minnesota Press, 1992, p. xviii.

29 Whether mythological points of reference and the concept of *oikos* hold for a Creole traveller is open to question. They certainly held valency for Victorian

travellers out of Europe; J. A. Froude called his book of travels in the Caribbean *The English in the West Indies or the Bow of Ulysses*, a travelogue that deploys the rhetoric of the imperial epic.

30 bell hooks, *Black Looks: Race and Representation*. Boston: South End Press, 1992, p. 173.

31 Toni Morrison, quoted in Gilroy, p. 221.

32 See Leigh Gilmore, 'The mark of autobiography', in Kathleen Ashley *et al.* (eds), *Autobiography and Postmodernism* (Boston: University of Massachusetts Press, 1994) for a discussion of the connections between postmodernism and self-representation.

33 See James Clifford, 'Notes on theory and travel'; Caren Kaplan, *Questions of Travel: Postmodern Discourses of Displacement*. Durham, NC: Duke University Press, 1996; Frances Bartkowski, *Travelers, Immigrants, Inmates: Essays in Estrangement*. Minneapolis: University of Minnesota Press, 1995.

34 See Ros Pesman, *Duty Free: Australian Women Abroad*. Melbourne: Oxford University Press, 1996, p. 13. For a feminist reading of *Kirkham's Find* see Pamela Murray, 'Staking a claim: Mary Gaunt and *Kirkham's Find*', Honours dissertation, Griffith University, 1991.

35 Mary Gaunt, *Alone in West Africa*. London: T. Werner Laurie, 1912, p. 4.

36 Mary Gaunt, *Where the Twain Meet*. London: John Murray, 1922, p. 2.

37 Mary Gaunt, *Reflection – in Jamaica*. London: Ernest Benn Ltd, 1932, p. vii.

38 See Stephen Nicholas and Peter R. Shergold (eds), *Convict Workers: Reinterpreting Australia's Past* (Sydney: Cambridge University Press, 1988) for a comparative analysis of slavery and convictism as forms of transportation and indentured labour in the British colonial system.

39 J. B. Hirst, 'The pioneer legend', in John Carroll (ed.), *Intruders in the Bush: The Australian Quest for Identity*. Melbourne: Oxford University Press, 1989.

40 Patricia Grimshaw *et al.*, *Creating a Nation*. Ringwood: McPhee Gribble, 1994, p. 179.

41 Ros Pesman *et al.* (eds), *The Oxford Book of Australian Travel Writing*. Melbourne: Oxford University Press, 1996, p. xxi.

42 See Cheryl McEwan, 'Encounters with West African women: textual representations of difference by white women abroad', in Alison Blunt and Gillian Rose (eds), *Writing Women and Space: Colonial and Postcolonial Geographics*. London and New York: The Guilford Press, 1994, pp. 73–100.

43 Ali Behdad, *Belated Travellers: Orientalism in the Age of Colonial Dissolution*. Durham, NC: Duke University Press, 1994, p. 16.

44 Mary Gaunt, *Reflection – in Jamaica*, p. 258.

45 Morrison, p. 25. See also Kay Ferres, 'Rosa Praed and the sites of memory: Hornet Bank 1857', unpublished paper.

46 Nathaniel Hawthorne, *The Scarlet Letter*. Boston: Houghton Mifflin, 1960, p. 38.

47 Michael Hurley, *The Borders of Nightmare: The Fiction of John Richardson*. Toronto: University of Toronto Press, 1992, p. 5.

48 Amon Saba Saakana, *The Colonial Legacy in Caribbean Literature*. Trenton, NJ: Africa World Press, Inc, 1987, p. 54.

49 For discussion of de Lisser's historical fictions see Victor Chang, 'The historical novels of H. G. de Lisser', in Mark McWatt (ed.), *West Indian Literature and Its Social Context*. Cave Hill, Barbados: Department of English UWI, 1985, pp. 12–17; Frank Birbalsingh, *Passion and Exile: Essays in Caribbean Literature*. London: Hansib Publishing Ltd, 1988. De Lisser also published more realist or regional fictions, most notably *Jane's Career* (1914), which focuses on Jamaican lower- and middle-class society.

50 Mary Gaunt glimpses these synchronicities when she 'tunes in' to New York on Jamaican radio, one of the moments of instability in her imperial rhetoric.

51 Susan Sheridan (ed.), *Grafts: Feminist Cultural Criticism*. London: Verso–New Left, 1988.

4

Kenya

The land that never was

'Let's have a look at Kenya from a different angle for once,' said John.
'From without, so to speak,' said Bill.
'The explorer's angle,' said John.
'The writer's angle,' I thought.[1]

Finding Karen Blixen

At the very start of *Gorillas, Tea and Coffee* (1996), her travel diary from Africa, the Australian writer Kate Llewellyn is 'for the first time in my life' unable to speak. Arrival in Johannesburg and the minibus tour of Soweto leave her 'sitting in the back of the bus shrinking from what I had seen as a snail sprinkled with salt. I was practically hissing and fizzing'.[2] Day 3: on to Kenya, to Nairobi. Here traffic fumes, street children and enquiries about her sex life produce more hissing and fizzing. Lonely Planet's *Africa on a Shoestring* warns: '[a]t every border, at every turn the woman traveller is under suspicion' (15). In Nairobi two things bring Llewellyn out of her shell to effect an imaginative entry into Africa. One is to find she can buy her favourite earplugs, the same French Quires she had bought in Paris, at a Nairobi chemist. The second discovery is the Karen Blixen Museum. Blixen's memoir *Out of Africa* is one of Llewellyn's favourite books, a twentieth-century masterpiece 'so full of love that it shines and shines' (20). She discovers that the house stands 'as if Karen Blixen had just walked out for a day' (19). The white linen and lace spreads are ready in the guest-room; the dining-room stands 'as if for guests, lace table cloth ... roses embroidered on tapestry-covered straight-backed chairs. Danish blue and white china'(19). Jodhpurs and pith helmet and tiger-skin rug hang in the bedroom; in the dining-room a great lion-skin is on the floor, 'the head snarling or roaring with long white teeth' (19).

For Kuki Gallmann, too, *Out of Africa* is embedded as a template for her recent autobiography *I Dreamed of Africa* (1991). From the very outset this narration of migration from a degenerate postindustrial Europe to a Kenya which represents new possibilities for becoming 'one's true self' draws on tropes and figurations which are fundamental to Blixen's memoir. *Out of Africa* is there in Gallmann's dream of Africa, not just in the epigraphs, or the resemblance suggested in the cover blurb, but in a more extensive borrowing of trope and metaphor. Gallmann, too, will construct a narrative of belonging to Africa, of finding her true self there. She too will find a sensual expression of herself through liaison with a European man who possesses an innate nobility that can find its most authentic expression in Africa. Gallmann's husband and son, contemporary expressions of the white hunter mythography, are buried in the land in a ritual of possession and ownership, which echoes the burial of Finch-Hatton in *Out of Africa*. Through this ritual Kenya becomes 'a land over which he shall reign for ever, and from which he shall never be separated' (179). Gallmann plants a yellow fever tree on each of these graves: 'one day, its roots ... would reach the body, which would nourish the tree and become part of the landscape.' This metaphor of burial as a means of claiming the land is a trope of settler writing. In *I Dreamed of Africa* it takes a distinctive turn in that these two trees, nourished by the bones of these white warriors, become the emblem of the Gallmann Memorial Foundation. This is dedicated to the conservation of threatened species in Kenya, and to the 'harmonious coexistence of man and the environment'. Gallmann's narrative culminates in 'the ivory fire', the highly publicized burning of twelve tons of elephant tusks in Nairobi in 1989 which was organized by Richard Leakey when he became Director of the Wildlife Department. For Gallmann, the blaze summarizes, purifies and makes sense of all that has happened in her life. That the white hunter mythography might serve the interests of conservation seems unlikely, given its genesis. The metamorphoses and uses of this trope in women's autobiography will be of ongoing interest in this chapter. So too is the ongoing use of *Out of Africa* in autobiographic writing.

In imagining a part, Kenya, as representative of the whole continent, the quite uncharacteristic and specific nature of Kenya's recent and relatively short-lived settlement as an élite settler colony in British East Africa is obscured. This colonization did not really get underway until early in the twentieth century, with large grants of land to white settlers. Kenya, in particular the area known as the White Highlands, presents an environment that is ripe for European fantasy. For geographical and historical reasons large populations of animals remained in Kenya long after they had been shot out or displaced in western and southern Africa. The natural environment there is particularly responsive to very different kinds of intellectual and physical uses of Africa for the West:

on the one hand, the plains and the highlands, the vegetation and the variety of animals have been available for romantic visions of the loss or discovery of an essential self in nature. On the other hand, they have been equally available to the requirements of sport hunting, where certain kinds of animals become game and large tracts of land are opened up by the safari. The intersections and collisions between these two appropriations of Kenyan space recur in white autobiographic writing. Both have been important in imagining ways that Western men and women – particularly a semi-aristocratic class fragment – might imagine they belong in Kenya. The idea of Kenya as the essence of Africa, spelt out by Blixen, has remained as a powerful and recurrent metaphor.

Recently, *Out of Africa* resurfaces in a third and quite different writing scene, and one which undoes some of the suturing that is so well hidden in the original. In 1988 the remains of a young white tourist, Julie Ward, were discovered in Masai Mara game reserve. After travelling to Kenya with an overland safari, Ward had remained in Kenya to photograph the wild animals. When left alone in the reserve she disappeared. The story of the search for Ward, the discovery of her remains, and the claims by Kenyan officials that wild animals were responsible in a desperate attempt to preserve the image of game parks like Masai Mara as tourist havens, led to the long campaign for justice organized by Ward's father. This has been presented in John Ward's own account, *The Animals Are Innocent*, and Jeremy Gavron's *Darkness in Eden*. Under these conditions, as we might expect, for Ward and Gavron Kenya emerges as the essence of a different kind of Africa: primordial, savage, only superficially civilized and rational. The Ward case causes the long history of ideas and associations which are released by the association of lustful black men and defenceless white woman to be set loose once again. In the Kenyan instance it opens a path from the 1990s back to representations of Mau Mau in the 1950s.[3]

In the course of Gavron's enquiries he speculates that Julie Ward was killed by park rangers for two reasons. The first is sexual:

> To the men who were to kill her, Julie's body must have been her most attractive possession. It may have been that Julie's killers had initially intended to rescue her, and that at some point temptation had simply grown stronger than common sense. But the inevitable conclusion, whatever else may have happened, was that Julie's rescuers had turned into her assailants and raped her. Far from help, in a remote corner of Africa, Julie was pitched into a terrible nightmare, a heart of darkness.[4]

Gavron also speculates that Julie Ward witnessed the park rangers dealing in ivory. Hence the association between the innocence of the animals and the white woman, over and against the preparedness of black men to slaughter both. The penultimate scene of Gavron's *Darkness in Eden* is Leakey's ivory fire, which he reads as a sign that Kenya's parks and reserves had become safe havens for elephants and tourists. As in Kuki Gallmann's memoir, the ivory fire is a symbolic moment, a ritual of possession, which functions in the same way as the other ceremonial, when the white hunter is buried to become part of the Kenyan landscape. The fire also becomes a symbol of the rightful restoration of a white Kenyan to a position of authority, a man 'not subject to the tribal pressure which had crippled some of his predecessors' and a sign of the leadership of white Kenyan settlers in the conservation movement.[5] The burning of the tusks episode in *Darkness in Eden* also hearkens back to Gavron's graphic reconstruction of the burning of Julie Ward's body in the Masai Mara by her killers, and so develops further the association between the woman and the wildlife as victims. As we might expect, given the 'heart of darkness' imagery which pervades Gavron's presentation of Kenya, the final scene of his book presents an inversion of the burial ritual of the settler mythography in *Out of Africa* and *I Dream of Africa*. The small memorial to Julie Ward is in the forest and green grasses of North Wales rather than in the highlands of Kenya.

Quartet: Blixen, Simpson, Markham and Huxley

Under these conditions, where things fall apart, Blixen's fantasy of belonging in Africa as an independent woman, and her presentation of Kenya as an Edenic place in *Out of Africa*, is juxtaposed quite explicitly against that other narrative, supposedly the reality to her romance, which presents the horror of Africa, figured in the white woman and the wildlife as innocents who are subject to predatory black men. Rather than separating these in terms of romance and realism, we should perhaps begin to constitute both in terms of the powerful social imageries which Kenyan colonists used to construct and authorize settler hegemony. Blixen's achievement is the construction of a memoir which makes the conditions of its being not only natural but also noble. Familiar as we are with the singularity and pre-eminence of *Out of Africa*, which is deservedly lauded as one of the great modern examples of autobiographic writing, we lose sight of the place of *Out of Africa* amidst a series of autobiographies by women settlers in Kenya from that period between 1913 to 1940. Collectively, these texts emerged from British East Africa in the period when it was known as the White Man's Country and captured it with such force that they continue to provide the popular image of Kenya (and Africa) for Western readers. *Out of Africa*, *West With the Night* and *The Flame Trees of Thika* have been republished numerous times since the early

1980s. Dinesen's and Huxley's books have been the basis of adaptations to film and television which have been highly successful. Kuki Gallmann draws on Blixen, Huxley and Markham for her epigraphs in *I Dreamed of Africa*. Jeremy Gavron argues that the writings of Blixen and Huxley led Julie Ward to seek a Shangri-la in Kenya.

This quartet of autobiographies narrates a critical phase of Kenyan colonization when the process of domestication and consolidation of British authority was underway, and Kenya was popularly known as the White Man's Country. By connecting these four texts, and placing them in the context of a particular writing scene, rather than focusing on the pre-eminent *Out of Africa*, it is evident that this quartet draws upon a series of oppositions, tropes, figures and metaphors which are the circuitry of colonialist representations of Kenya. The white hunter, for example, is a recurrent and indicative figure as is the safari a recurrent scene. They suggest the common ground and the different emphases that emerge in these women's autobiographies from White Man's Country. Ironically, white women have represented this country most powerfully. This repertoire or circuitry is paradigmatic; it organizes contemporary and apparently different enunciations, such as Gallmann's dream of Africa and Gavron's nightmare heart of darkness. The tensions between dream and nightmare we find in contemporary white writing about Kenya can be traced back to that earlier writing scene, where they were emergent as different modes of romance.

Blixen's memoir was published in 1937. Coincidentally, this was also the year when Alyse Simpson's *The Land That Never Was*, foil to *Out of Africa*, was published in London. Simpson's book records a failed pioneering effort by a British couple in Kenya during the 1930s and remains obscure, republished only once, in the USA in 1985. Two other autobiographic narratives return to that same period of Kenyan settlement. Beryl Markham's *West with the Night* was originally published in 1942 and republished by Virago in 1984. In her Introduction to the Virago edition, Martha Gellhorn places Markham's book as a companion piece to *Out of Africa*, complementary to it. Blixen and Markham mixed in the same circles, both close to Denys Finch-Hatton and Bror Blixen. Yet, as their narratives suggest, their place in that settler society was different. Blixen worked to establish the coffee plantation and a domestic refuge for Bror Blixen, Finch-Hatton and their aristocratic friends. She put a light by the door to welcome them home from excursions into the wilds. Markham grew up in Kenya, trained horses there and then learned to fly. As a pilot she became an active part of the safari culture as Finch-Hatton and Bror Blixen experimented with the use of aircraft to hunt game. For Markham, like Blixen, Kenyan settler society is represented as a place of freedom for a white woman. In her case it allowed an escape from conventional expectations of femininity and domesticity. The final text of the quartet is Elspeth Huxley's *The Flame Trees of Thika: Memories of an African Childhood.* This narrative focuses on the years between 1913 and 1915 before the family returned to Europe because of the war. Huxley narrates a Kenyan childhood; she would remain to take an active part in Kenyan settler culture in the postwar period, and to undertake the work of inventing a white Kenyan identity for later generations. Huxley's version of migration and settlement was published in 1959 and needs to be read with the struggle for independence and decolonization in mind, for she writes about the period of consolidation of British rule amidst its demise.

By 1913 white settlement in Kenya had reached a watershed. The frontier era was over, domestication was underway, and white settler political and economic hegemony was in place.[6] In 1913 Bror Blixen arrived to establish the coffee farm at Ngong; Karen Blixen arrived soon after. In 1913 Elspeth Huxley and her parents arrived from England and set off in an open ox cart for their 'bit of El Dorado' at Thika, then still a favourite camp for big-game hunters. The Markhams, who arrived in 1906, were already established at Njoro, adjacent to Lord Delamere's 'Equator Ranch'. In each case these establishments were always tenuous and doomed to wither and fail; yet each is preserved in autobiography, where they remain potent. Raymond Williams' notion of the residual element in cultural processes is useful here. The white imaginary is no longer a hegemonic or dominant force in contemporary Kenyan culture; however, it remains active. Williams suggests that the residual is a set of values, practices, relationships which has been effectively formed in the past, but remains a significant element of the present. Certain experiences, meanings and values which are no longer expressed or substantially verified in terms of the dominant culture are nevertheless lived and practised on the basis of the residue – cultural as well as social – of some previous social and cultural formation.[7] In the Kenyan instance, values and meanings, tropes and allegories which were part of the hegemony of settler culture re-emerge, as we have seen at the beginning of this chapter, in interpreting incidents like the Ward affair, in understandings of symbolic events like the ivory fire, and in attempts by Western travellers and settlers (like Llewellyn and Gallmann) to place themselves in Africa.

That autobiographic writing should remain as one of the most potent resources for sustaining the settler imaginary is not surprising. What is distinctive to Kenya, and a mark of the power of autobiographic writing in the politics of postcolonialism, is the *ongoing* valency of their capture of Kenyan space. The resurfacing and currency of *Out of Africa* is the most obvious marker of this. Yet by focusing on a single text we miss the contradictions and confusions which emerge in a master narrative, and the differences among white colonialists. Reading *across* this quartet of autobiographies requires careful attention to who wrote, when, where, why, and to what effect.

Dystopian autobiography: *The Land That Never Was*

Alyse Simpson's book remains little known. As Kathryn Tidrick has pointed out, it stands as one of the rare examples of a woman's eye view of Empire where the colonizing rhetoric is stripped bare.[8] In the same way that Emily Innes' *The Chersonese with the Gilding Off* (1885) is a dystopian reflection of Isabella Bird's *The Golden Chersonese and the Way Thither* (1883), so too *The Land That Never Was* is a foil to *Out of Africa*.[9] There is no suggestion that Simpson had read Blixen's memoir, for the two books appeared in the same year. The resemblances are produced by Simpson's desire to unravel the vision of British East Africa as a lost Eden by pursuing the other term of the oppositions which are the repertoire of the East African dream: regeneration and degeneration, freedom and imprisonment, and eloquence and silence. These oppositions are the ingredients of the vision of White Man's East Africa that emerged in booster literature for the settler colony and in numerous travelogues. In their most compelling and seductive formulation, *Out of Africa*, Kenya is represented as a place of freedom and regeneration, an Edenic place in opposition to the constraints and social, cultural and economic exhaustion of Europe. Simpson targets and reverses these terms quite ruthlessly in *The Land That Never Was*.

In Chapter 3 I discussed the particular uses of romance in colonial literatures, in part following Toni Morrison's observation that romance was deeply implicated in the exploration of anxieties and the representation of border territories. Bringing together *The Land That Never Was* and *Out of Africa* circles back to the issue of how various styles of romance are deployed in the representation of the thresholds of colonial space. The Canadian critic Northrop Frye identifies two worlds of romance: one above the level of ordinary experience, the other below. He associates the first, the idyllic world, with a narrative of ascent. The second, a demonic or night world of adventure, involves humiliation and imprisonment, and is associated with a narrative of descent.[10] Frye's identification of different modes of romance is especially useful in thinking about colonial discourse.

In white autobiographical writing about Kenya we can readily observe the different forms of romance – on the one hand, its strong utopian expressions, on the other, the more dystopian, dark modes. This is not to invoke an opposition between 'romance' and 'realism', for Simpson's 'ungilded' narration about the place that becomes demonic is no more or less 'realistic' or true to life than Blixen's gilded pastoral landscapes. Each text is heavily stylized; there is a strong tendency to representation of character, landscape and event in estranged and fantastic forms. Thus the hopelessness of Simpson's autobiographic narrator Joan is no less fantastic than Blixen's sense of finding herself 'where I ought to be'. Simpson's 'barren, utterly dry, soundless, almost hostile' (63) landscape is the lowlands to Blixen's 'strong and refined essence of a continent' in the Highlands. The parody of the *ngoma* in *The Land That Never Was* is paradigmatically related to the epic version in *Out of Africa* (or Gallmann's *I Dreamed of Africa*). Simpson's parody is generically akin; it shares the same typical oppositions, themes and forms of characterization as the African dream, but they are reversed and taken into nightmare and despair rather than into the pastoral and the Edenic.

As the narrative progresses, the autobiographic narrator Joan loses her senses and reason in a place which is increasingly demonic. Simpson is careful to present this as in some ways a rational response to an irrational situation. The emphasis on the absurdity of colonizing schemes which send young English couples to Kenya, and the yawning gap between the Kenya of the English imaginary and the reality of the pioneer white society, means we are not inclined to interpret Joan's predicament in terms of psychic weakness or individual pathology. Joan's integrity as a narrator is important, for what is sought is a different reference to the empirical environment which she provides. The imperfect Kenya of *The Land That Never Was* is in a kind of dramatic dialogue with that other Kenya of the booster literature and the travelogue, a dialogue which places the reader at a site of ambiguity, irony and difference. By thinking about *The Land That Never Was* and *Out of Africa* as inversions of each other, we can come to understand more of colonizing discourse about Kenya. For example, how particular objects, groups and individuals (such as the white hunter, the noble savage, the kindly missionary, the dedicated white farmer) are invested with meanings that define indigenous peoples as subjects of colonialism, and create colonists with varying degrees of freedom and constraint from the metropolis, the colony, each other, and the indigenous peoples.[11]

The relationship between the experiences of the young couple in *The Land That Never Was*, Joan and John, and those of the Simpsons, who farmed an arid valley for six years in the 1930s and then sold up and went home, is unclear. However the failure of small undercapitalized and underconnected white farmers to prosper in British East Africa was not uncommon. Two political developments need to be kept in mind when assessing what might produce an autobiography of alienation like Alyse Simpson's. Firstly, in the 1930s more small farmers were impoverished as a result of the Depression. Throughout this decade the number of people who left Kenya and Rhodesia was nearly as large as the number who entered them.[12] Secondly, in the 1930s more carefully organized campaigns to conscript emigrants to Kenya and to maintain the immigrant population were underway. The Kenya Association – established in 1932 – produced a series of pamphlets to promote Kenya's climate, scenery, abundant servants, and the polo and thoroughbred horseracing. These assets appealed to the tastes and income of wealthy whites. Warnings that 'the slump in world commodity prices makes it impossible to say that any crops can be farmed at a profit' also indicate that the Kenya Association was eager to exert some control over the social character of immigrants, maintaining strict social, financial and ethnic standards for white settlement in Kenya by deterring small farmers, and encouraging retiring officers and others with an independent income.[13] Ironically, in the very year Simpson's autobiography was published there were plans in Kenya to strengthen white settlement by encouraging young people to emigrate and establish small farms: 'We had left something behind, but we knew not what.... But I know now – it was our youth' (268). Simpson was writing, then, amidst a resurgence of booster literature about Kenya, the high-flown rhetoric which enticed John and Joan to leave a dreary city in the Midlands in the first place:

> 'Come to Kenya,' – thus ran an advertisement which had helped to change our lives and which had held forth new hopes and conjured images of untold happiness and success to our youthful minds. 'Delightful climate, glorious scenery, ideal place for the man with small capital'. (7)

Like Susanna Moodie and Catharine Parr Traill, who wrote about the establishment of English settlement in Upper Canada, Alyse Simpson sets out to write a cautionary tale, to write against the booster literature about the colony.

The Land That Never Was is marketed in the prefatory blurb as 'a true record of first-hand experience that is told in a curiously artless style'. As an experiment in taking a dystopian form of autobiographic writing into colonial discourse it is anything but 'artless'. By transforming her own experiences into those of John and Joan, by using pseudonyms and fictitious places, Simpson is able to mimic and reverse the conventions and tropes of the white settler imaginary quite ruthlessly. She warns of her intentions from the very outset:

> I shall not, I hope, commit the unforgivable sin of encouraging other similar young lunatics with insufficient capital to go out to Kenya in search of wealth or romance. Enough of this sort of bunkum has been written, Kenya is a cruel country, if the truth be told; but alas, men like John do not write books ...
>   The everyday task of the pioneer on the Equator, his Sisyphean labour, will not encourage him to talk about himself; like the soldier back from the war or the sailor back from the sea, he will keep silent. It is not he

who will tell you of this distant Eldorado. Let others write of elephant-hunts, of facing charging lions and rhinoceros, or of the love life of natives and other interesting facts. His concern from day to day is, 'will it rain soon?' 'will the "fly" get the coffee?'; 'will the locusts come this way?' ... John's diary, his only attempt at any kind of writing, was merely a sort of log.

The things nearest at heart were entered, but there was no poetry there ... 'Pigs eaten by sow'; 'mule died of horse sickness'; 'ox blown by new green grass, dead'; 'two more oxen blown, dead'. (6)

John finally speaks his mind after five 'blank and profitless years': 'I'd sell this seventh hell' (223). Like the male figures of *Out of Africa* and *I Dreamed of Africa*, John is silent. It is not the white hunter who has written eloquently of the hunts, it is the lover who observes from aside, reflecting his image at twice its size as it were. Yet in *The Land That Never Was* the female narrator is increasingly silenced, finally reduced to a vegetative state where there is no perception of time or change. As a pioneer farmer John does not achieve the masculine promise of Kenya, the freedom to 'lead a man's life in God's own country'. In fact both John and Joan lose their freedom in Kenya. John becomes, in Joan's view at least, a prisoner, driven by visions of splendid crops of maize: 'the clanking of the plough-chains brought John to my mind – toiling out there for Heaven knew what' (75). Joan feels they are serving a sentence for some unknown crime. The meaning of freedom becomes an important issue. When Joan presses a neighbour, Jim, about 'freedom' in Kenya ' – 'Free for what?' – his answers evoke a masculinist dream that a chap needn't dress, or shave, or be part of institutions like the Church, Rotary or the Chamber of Commerce. The freedom to hunt is part of this. Jim's 'trophies', two eland heads, hang on the verandah rail for the sun and the ants to do their work:

> by tea-time the smell was indescribable, which attracted every fly in the district! The flies swarmed on the food and drowned in the teacups, but the men did not seem to mind either the smell or the flies.... This was Jim's sense of freedom; he could not have indulged in such exciting activities at home! (122)

The culture of the hunt, translated into its distinctively African variant of the safari, is fundamental to the aristocratic romance of freedom in Kenya. In Simpson's story the safari degenerates into a farcical episode. John, Joan and Bill trek into the highlands with half a dozen carriers, a dilapidated tent, and the child in the saddle: 'Ours was a poor sort of outfit, not like those of the professional hunters, Government officials or other rich people who brought along their baths, cane chairs, gramophones and other twentieth-century luxuries' (231). Predictably the land is 'silent', with not a single creature in sight. As they ascend to the Highlands, 'the top of the world and far away from any creeping city', the altitude makes them giddy and nauseous. Again Simpson mocks dreams of freedom: flies swarm, ants bite. There is nothing heroic or noble about this venture: 'for three days we trekked with absolutely nothing of interest happening at all.' In ascending to where 'it was quite possible that no other White man had ever come', the would-be hunters dream of Somerset and Cornwall; even the Midland city they left with such joy just a few years before seems preferable. Only the natives who accompany them seem to belong here. This translation of the safari into the night world of dark romance continues the association between the colony and a demonic world. This world is not Edenic but postlapsarian, drawing on ideas of expulsion and the fall from grace.

In *The Land That Never Was*, like *Out of Africa* and *I Dreamed of Africa*, the couple is at the centre of the narrative, but to very different ends. One of the tropes of Simpson's narrative is degeneration, sterility and the perversity of the natural world in Africa. Both the human and animal worlds are doomed to suffer – like those notes in John's log, nothing survives. Debased images of maternity and mothering accumulate. For example, the birth of Joan's child is represented in a profoundly melancholic fashion. The pregnancy is intimated when she 'feels seedy', and she doesn't tell John until well into the pregnancy in order to save him worry. The baby 'did not seem to want to live at first', and grows into a weedy child. Birth and mothering produce no relief or change into the 'appalling sameness about the days and months' which increasingly overwhelm and paralyse the narrator: 'to me, our life seemed a kind of penal servitude for some vague offence. In such a frame of mind we spent Christmas' (83). There is no change, the tropics are lifeless, an empty world where birth and death are associated: birds abandon their young; on the baby's first outing they come across the body of a Kikuyu woman, the grandmother of one of the 'boys'; the baby is threatened by snakes and 'natives', anaemia, dysentery, sunstroke and ophthalmia; the chicks are taken by mongoose; the cow has to be killed after calving because of a diseased udder; when Joan finally leaves the farm for a dance in Nymba the child in the next room dies. In short, all forms of maternal care are damned to futility. When a neighbouring 'memsahib' has a miscarriage, Joan seeks to comfort her by remarking, 'perhaps it's for the best'.

Rather than 'truth', this emerges as a relentless attack on the propaganda of rearranging the scheme of things by populating the distant places of Empire, 'trying to relieve the pressure at home' and regenerating the race in the settler colonies. Joan is scathing of the blinkered, self-serving ways in which those who remain in England – their family, the public, the government – use the

Empire as a panacea for social and economic problems which need to be addressed in Britain itself. The virulence of Simpson's critique and her depiction of Joan as a pioneer wife and mother are a response to the pressure on those of her class and her generation to leave England and thrive elsewhere. The illusions of prosperity in East Africa serve as an instrument of population management, where the likes of Joan and John are 'ousted from our places on the hearth-rug' by an older generation, regime and class interest which resists the kinds of changes required in Britain itself. The ideology of freedom for the white man that is articulated through Kenya is based on an ideal of aristocratic masculinity unfettered by social and domestic obligations which Simpson contests. The idea that settlers like John and Joan might find freedom there is countered by the relentless presentation of their experience in terms of incarceration, degeneration and metamorphosis into inarticulate creatures that are the victims of fate and chance.

From the outset, Kenya was planned as a settler colony where the immigrant population would be drawn from the British élite. In this it was markedly different to Rhodesia, the neighbouring colony. Dane Kennedy's comparative study of these two colonies suggests numerous ways whereby migration to Kenya was managed in order to attract a migratory élite of large landholders rather than small farmers like John and Joan. Connections established through the British public schools, universities and the Services (both military and colonial) were important. The presentation of Kenya as a rural, hierarchical society sustained by a semi-feudal relationship between European and African was attractive to men educated to the ideals and expectations of gentlemanly status. As Kennedy argues, the attraction to Kenya must be understood in the context of a revulsion against the forces of urbanism, industrialism, democracy and egalitarianism which were emergent in the modern industrial states of Europe.[14] The association of Kenya with regeneration, with finding new ways of self-expression and freedom draws on aristocratic concepts of nobility, taste and discrimination. We find this in Gallmann's contemporary autobiography as well as in *Out of Africa*.

It is no accident, then, that an autobiography centred on the experiences of a young couple who leave a British Midland city with £2000 to become small farmers in Kenya should be so scathing of the relatively limited nature of the freedom and self-expression which are celebrated in dreams of Africa. The preoccupation with degeneration and sterility, the proliferation of images and metaphors of imprisonment and degradation throughout *The Land That Never Was* find their origins in a class-based critique of the Kenyan dream. Simpson's book is important. As a parody it throws into relief those tropes which are so apparently natural or real when they emerge elsewhere. Unfortunately but not coincidentally, this book, a rare occasion where a woman autobiographer reverses the terms of the white hunter mythography which organizes settler inventions of Kenya, remains obscure. This is not to say that *The Land That Never Was* is an unheralded classic of autobiographic writing, or to make claims for it as a literary accomplishment comparable to *Out of Africa*. Nevertheless, by establishing connections between the two, and by exploring a parodic relationship between them, we can see more clearly the kinds of social and cultural assumptions which are naturalized so successfully in the tropes of settler romance. The shaping of the autobiography in terms of a narrative of ascent, where the colony is idyllic, where settlers achieve heroic status and transcendent relations to the natural world, is no less a distortion or illusion, no less of a romance. It is, to return to Frye's typology, a different mode of romance.

Autobiography at Independence: *The Flame Trees of Thika*

In *The Flame Trees of Thika*, too, the white hunter is cut down to size as the romance of *Out of Africa* is reworked and renovated amidst the emergence of African nationalism in the 1950s. Here it is done through the narrative eye of the child rather than the disaffected settler. Elspeth Huxley travelled to Kenya as a child. Although she recalls the pioneering phase between the wars – in fact the narrative begins with the memory of the ox-wagon trek to the newly purchased land – the task for her generation is to invent an identity for the white Kenyan in an independent African nation state; that is, to imagine styles of white indigeneity in Kenya. Huxley's autobiography is frequently placed alongside *Out of Africa* and *West with the Night*, and it does, like them, represent that period of settler domestication in Kenya. There are nevertheless significant differences between these. In light of an understanding of cultural politics which stresses the role of culture in processes of social change and social control, it is important to note that it was written in the 1950s, first published in 1959 and became widely available in Penguin paperback in 1962, much later than the autobiographies by Simpson, Blixen and Markham.

Why did Huxley turn to autobiographical writing at that time? She was already an established author and an eminent member of the settler community in Kenya. Her biography of Lord Delamere – the patriarch of Kenyan colonization – represented the early years of settlement in epic terms. *White Man's Country: Lord Delamere and the Making of Kenya* (1935) became a standard reference for the early history of Kenyan settlement, and established Huxley as a promoter for the cause of a 'benevolent' style of white settlement in Kenya.[15] Her 'documentary novel' *Red Strangers* (1939) presents the coming of the European to Kikuyuland from a Kikuyu point of view. Again the early settlers are depicted as benevolent, and Africans are seen to benefit from colonial rule.[16]

The Flame Trees of Thika was published at the end of the decade when the struggle for decolonization and independence emerged. Mau Mau, a movement to overthrow the colonial government largely waged through guerrilla warfare by Kikuyu, and closely related groups the Meru and Embu, led to armed struggle and a declaration of a state of emergency in Kenya in 1952. Mau Mau was determined to eliminate European domination in Kenya and to attain an African government. It was not the beginnings of resistance to colonization – the first organized African protest movements emerged in the 1920s – yet it was the movement which forced a widespread recognition of African resistance to the existing social order. It transformed the settler map of Kenya, challenging the alienation of lands that had made Ngong, Njoro, Nyeri and Thika (for example) evidently available to settler colonialism, the 'islands of white'. In that decade of struggle Huxley wrote articles and commentaries in support of multiracial government for Kenya in local and international media. This argument sought to achieve a peaceful and profitable transition to independence for the European farmers, and sets the stage for the bargaining over land which took place between 1960 and 1965.[17] The year the autobiography was published, 1959, was also the year the British government abolished the White Highlands as a white settler enclave.

Huxley's memories of an African childhood cannot be abstracted from this context. The re-emergence of the narrative of the white settlers bringing domesticity to 'their' piece of Kenya at the point of the renegotiation of the ownership of African land is important. Land was fundamental to Mau Mau resistance to British authority. The well-known first sentence of *Out of Africa*, 'I had a farm in Africa, at the foot of the Ngong Hills', places Blixen's possession of the farm in the past tense. The loss of the farm in *Out of Africa* is due to failed schemes of settler capitalism. The notion that possession might be forfeited or renegotiated with the indigenous peoples is not on the horizon, although Blixen is aware of herself as an interloper. Much has been made of the fact that Blixen individualizes black Africans; for example, they are named as characters in *Out of Africa*. Yet the operation of racism in Kenyan settler polemics is not to deny the presence of African people but to deny them integrity, authority and agency. The African peoples are 'available' and 'to hand' for the settler project, and in need of white leadership. Enlightened versions of settler polemics suggest that Europeans are benevolent, able to bring to some Africans skills and knowledge that produce extraordinary outcomes – such as Blixen's highly accomplished cook. Alyse Simpson is scathing about the pretensions of British settler colonialism, yet the basis of her critique is a class analysis; this does not include a review of the racial politics of settler capitalism. She is, for example, virulently anti-Semitic as well as immune to the effects of their presence on the African people.

Colonialists created stories to justify their rule, stories by which to rule. Africans had competing narratives and images of themselves; they both accommodated and resisted colonialist narratives in their own construction of colonial society.[18] Colonial hegemony was not uncontested. However, the work of settler autobiographies is to stake the claim and to imagine the terms of a white presence in Africa. For autobiographers like Huxley and Markham, who immigrated to Kenya as children and came to regard it as home rather than a respite from Europe, the task is to invent themselves as white Africans.

In *The Flame Trees of Thika* the child as the focal point of the narrative is fundamental both to the politics and the poetics of the autobiography. Huxley chooses to script herself into the settler epic even as the black nationalist movement is emergent in Kenya, and she does so in a way that attempts to renovate the tropes of the settler narrative to accommodate a different dominant order. By removing the adult as the focal point of the narrative, Huxley is able to place herself as a child *outside* some of the conventions of the settler society which she and her parents inhabit. Thus, for example, the child clearly observes the absurdities of the 'club set'. Not just the excesses of the rich young man who is found stark naked astride the roof of the Norfolk hotel, holding a tin bath over his head and proclaiming himself to be a mushroom, but also the gullibility of Robin, her father, who buys 'a bit of El Dorado' in the bar of the Norfolk Hotel 'from a man wearing an old Etonian tie'.[19] Using the child as a narrative device, Huxley represents the trappings of British settler culture and society in that moment when dominance was established with a clear sense of its absurdity and imposture: the pith helmets and red flannel, the old school tie, the gramophones and sewing machines which bearers carry into the foothills, the bath which is carried on safari, the struggle to transport a piano to the farm. The District Commissioner's authority resides in his topee, 'a kind of magic, like Samson's curls'. Throughout the narrative, forms of dress are a metaphor, representing the tenuousness of the power and authority of the Europeans:

> Those were the days when to lack respect was a more serious crime than to neglect a child, bewitch a man, or steal a cow, and was generally punishable by beating. Indeed respect was the only protection available to Europeans who lived singly, or in scattered families, among thousands of Africans accustomed to constant warfare and armed with spears and poisoned arrows, but had themselves no barricades, and went about unarmed. This respect served them like an invisible coat of mail, or a form of magic, and seldom failed; but it had to be very carefully guarded. The

least rent or puncture might, if not immediately checked and repaired, split the whole garment asunder and expose its wearer in all his human vulnerability. Kept intact, it was a thousand times stronger than all the guns and locks and metal in the world; challenged, it could be brushed aside like a spider's web. (16)

Huxley, writing at a time when this authority was in the process of being challenged through a guerrilla war (it would not be brushed aside) represents herself in the narrative in the unique position of the child who is inside that settler culture and able to observe its fantasies, and yet is not constituted by it. It is her father Robin who believes that the game and the fertile soil are inexhaustible, there for the taking; it is he who regards the landscape with a 'dreamy' look. The ironies of this possession of the land are made clear by the narrator. It is this romantic and deluded patriarch who is puzzled as to why the Kikuyu 'don't seem to realize this is my land and I'm offering ... a chance to work' (33). It is the child's father who can assert 'I have a lot of clearing to do', and the narrator who includes African labour by remarking, 'All the clearing had to be done by hand, by young men with pangas' (17). It is Robin and his generation who buy, literally and figuratively, the agent's claims that any amount of labour is there for the taking: 'You've only got to lift your finger and they come', and that 'thousands of years of untapped fertility are locked up in the soil' (9). These are the romantics who are drawn to Africa by dreams of fortune, freedom and danger.

The work of *The Flame Trees of Thika* is to establish a position for the later generation by modifying the rhetoric of that first generation of colonizers. Huxley, as we have seen, advocated a multiracial government for an independent Kenya; however, the terms for constructing a white Kenyan identity as a component of this needed to be spelt out. The issue of what is discarded and what is retained of that earlier settler rhetoric is therefore pertinent. The child's view represents the relations between the settler and African societies in the following way:

it was like living in one world while another co-existed, but the two scarcely ever meshed. Sometimes, when Tilly made a cake, she let me use the beater, which had a red handle that you turned. The two arms of the beater whirled around independently and never touched, so that perhaps one arm never knew that the other was there; yet they were together, turned by the same handle, and the cake was mixed by both. I did not think of it at the time, but afterwards it struck me that this was rather how our two worlds revolved side by side. (154)

This metaphor draws on the innocence of the child to represent the settler and indigenous societies as separate yet equal, each necessary to the making of Kenya. There is no controlling adult focal point introduced to alert the reader to the illusion of racial equality in this metaphor. We can see here the work that Huxley's re-creation of the earlier settler culture in *The Flame Trees of Thika* is trying to accomplish. Like Markham, she makes much of being a child in Kenya, and suggests that the innocence and openness of the child allows it to find a place in both indigenous and settler societies. Each uses her autobiography to stake a claim to a style of white indigeneity, a claim based on an affinity with the land and the animals, an affinity which is learned from African carers and from immersion in the landscapes around the farm. The child is free to find a space between the two worlds, black and white. Most importantly, the child in Huxley's narrative ultimately perceives that the binary opposition of two worlds, black and white, savage and civilized, fails to account for a third world, inside and intermingled with the other two:

> a world of snakes and rainbows, of ghosts and spirits ... a world that had its own laws and for most part led its own life, but now and again, like a rock jutting up through earth and vegetation, protruded into ours, and was there all the time under the surface. It was a world in which I was a foreigner, but the Kikuyu were at home. (192)

The child learns this other knowledge from the Kikuyu and Masai peoples around the farm, and ultimately it affects how she represents the human and animal life around her, so the reader too glimpses a logic that the first-generation settlers cannot perceive. In this way the child comes to represent a different way of being part of both European and indigenous cultures, uniquely placed to draw upon the knowledge of both. From Huxley's humanist perspective, the topee and the pith helmet and heavy felt which encase them as they set off for Thika are emblematic of a settler dis-ease with the land and its peoples. They can be cast aside by her generation to allow a more equal relationship to emerge between black and white Africans.

In *The Flame Trees of Thika*, like *The Land That Never Was*, the safari emerges as an important scene in the narrative, a way of measuring the relationships between the settlers, the indigenous peoples, the landscapes and the animal world. For Huxley, like Simpson, the safari is a symbol of that aristocratic, feudal imposture, the pomp and circumstance expression of colonial authority. The child observes that her parents, Robin and Tilly, 'believed as firmly as their friends did that to shoot animals was one of life's richest pleasures, [yet] I do not believe their hearts were ever wholly in it' (46). Their passion is planning irrigation works, dams and furrows, and ways to process the coffee, citrus and other crops they had not yet planted. This distinction between leisure and industry is an important one. Hereward Palmer, the white hunter figure in the narrative, who brings five different kinds of gun and animal trophies from shooting expeditions in Kashmir to Kenya, is mocked quite explicitly. As his wife infers, the size of the trophies of the hunt is a measure of Hereward's masculinity, at least in his mind. The opposition between sport and industry, safari and settlement is quite explicit. Again Huxley uses the child as the focal point of narration in a way which places a distance between herself and a romantic view of Africa which is organized around the safari. As we see in the following passage, the distancing effect is achieved by focusing the depiction of the safari on the child, who can see only the departure and the return and must stay home to memorize the Kings of England and *The Lady of Shalott*:

> They were gone, marching to far romantic places beyond the last farm, the ultimate shamba, where the wild game of Africa had their wide plains and secret reeded water-holes all to themselves, and when you camped among the thorns beside a dry sand-river, and dug for moisture in the hot sand it might be you were treading where no man, white or black, had ever set foot before. It was a moment to lift the heart, but also to fill the mind with anguish because the others were going, and I was left behind, and would never see those far imagination-torturing places, or taste the solitudes where nature keeps her pure and intricate balance free from the crass destructiveness of man. (182)

The imperial epic style is almost always parodied in *The Flame Trees of Thika*. As we learn from the very first page, Thika is renowned as a favourite camping ground for big-game hunters. It is now being domesticated and the site of a different kind of European presence. The child's view of the environment is very different. She sees the microscopic detail and intricacy of the plant and animal life there, and learns the interconnections and spiritual meanings that are perceived by the indigenous people. Significantly when the child comes to leave the farm, a growing thing torn up by the roots, she leaves a world where the human and animal elements – horses, chameleons, Masai, Kikuyu and settlers – are indistinguishable: Moyale and Mohammed, George and Mary, Alec and Mrs. Nimmo, Njombo and Sammy and Andrew, Kupanya and old Rohio.

In this way, some elements of the rhetoric of settler colonialism as it emerged in Kenya in the interwar period are presented ironically, and discarded. The child's view is important in this process of discerning what is false and what is true, what is valuable and what is sham and pretence. The settlers took with them notions of improvement and cultivation that remain important, and function as a centre of gravity by which other ideas and behaviours can be measured. For example, although the father, Robin, is a man in search of the romance of Africa, the mother, Tilly, frequently embodies a much more practical and workmanlike approach to their life in Kenya. It is Tilly who mocks associations between Kenya and Edenic fruitfulness and plenty, not least because they obscure the need for Europeans to labour for their living. It is Tilly who disapproves of the leisured memsahib style embodied in Lettice Palmer. The sexual intrigue and leisured feminine style, the 'spicy scent' that surrounds Lettice, fascinate the child, yet are contrasted to the reason and diligence of Tilly. Questions about why the settlers are in Africa, and how they might best occupy themselves and the land, are addressed quite specifically among the characters themselves. The ideas of escaping from 'slavery' in England, and building a new colony under the Crown, are rehearsed by various characters, but it is Tilly's notion of improvement, of bettering the self, of raising the condition of indigenous peoples and making the land fertile and productive through practical work, which captures the moral and ethical centre of the narrative. In the mother the child observes the intention to find a place in Africa not by reproducing a feudal order which placed the Europeans in a remote position of aristocratic authority, but by establishing a benevolent rule which aspires to establish 'joy and happiness for all creatures' (40). As the child takes up this idea, it is extended to include a perception of that 'third world' of African knowledge and belief, which allows the invention of a form of white indigeneity.

In the world which Huxley creates there is no contradiction in the fact that as the family leave for Europe the African people assume stewardship of the farm and keep a place in anticipation of their return, as if it were a shared enterprise. The emphasis is on a partnership between settler and indigenous populations rather than the dependency that emerges as Blixen leaves her farm workers at the end of *Out of Africa*. Huxley's child leaves as a creature of the different worlds that come together at Thika. For her, Europe is an interlude, and not a home. Aunt Mildred's house in Porchester Terrace is the unknown. Kenya is where roots have been established and where she will grow. The child embarks on the ship for Europe laden with tokens, treasures, eggs and cocoons, some grenadillas, a Kikuyu sword, and a Dorobo bow and arrows. These relics mark the distinctive style of belonging to Thika which has been created around the child and through her eyes. Somewhat like the young version of the self in Markham's narrative, here too the child occupies a unique intermediate space between gendered, racial and ethnic identities. For both Markham and Huxley, this creation of a childhood in Kenya assures an ongoing presence and place in Africa. They invent styles of white indigeneity which cast aside the flannels and topees of that first generation of settlers, yet which remain deeply invested in Africa as a place of freedom, expansiveness and nobility. Most importantly, it constructs a white African identity drawing on African settler culture, and it imagines that race relations in Kenya are structured in terms of consent rather than conflict. As *Thika* was published in the wake of Mau Mau and on the eve of Kenyan independence, the strategic importance of Huxley's subtitle 'Memories of an African Childhood' needs to be kept in view.

Out of Africa: the biography of the white hunter

That *Out of Africa*, rather than *The Flame Trees of Thika*, or *The Land That Never Was* enables Kate Llewellyn's entry into African space should not surprise us. Blixen presents Africa as a transcendent empowering space for women, and the autobiography is a superb rendition of Africa in the pastoral mode. Since its first publication in 1937, Blixen's memoir stands as the most powerful and seductive capture of Kenya, and arguably the most influential invention of African space for Western readers: 'Africa distilled up through six thousand feet, like the strong and refined essence of a continent.'[20] Llewellyn's recollection of the museum display of Blixen's house draws out the components of this seduction, and why the house might initiate the entry into African space which she desires. Readers of *Out of Africa* know the dining-room well. It is where Kamante, the Kikuyu houseboy whom Blixen transformed into a royal cook, served *omelette à la chasseur*. The china and linen were part of what Berkeley Cole called his sylvan retreat, where he and Denys Finch-Hatton could listen to the latest gramophone records from Europe. Here Blixen, against all probability, induced peonies to grow (but not propagate) in her African garden. What is captured in the museum is the aristocratic plenitude which is depicted so graphically in the book, and it needs to be associated with the supremacist vision attached to that domestic setting. The author tells us that as she and Finch-Hatton linger at the table, their talk is so incandescent that they imagine 'the wild Masai tribe, in their manyatta under the hills, would see the house all afire, like a star in the night, as the peasants of Umbria saw the house wherein Saint Francis and Saint Clare were entertaining one another upon theology'. This 'bringing of light' metaphor is parodied in *The Flame Trees of Thika*, where a quite different kind of relationship between the racial groups which occupy the land at Thika is envisaged.

The incandescence and the illusion of Blixen's presence remain not with the Masai but with her fellow travellers. This is despite the fact that the house is progressively stripped bare in the final stories in *Out of Africa*, hollowed out like a skull; the grass grows up to the doorstep, and the narrator returns to

Europe. In dismantling the place which she occupied on the farm she also dismembers herself and a precarious identity which belonged in Africa for a relatively short time: 'I no longer existed.' Like the peonies, the vision of establishing a viable coffee plantation and a semi-aristocratic retreat in the Ngong Hills would be a brief flowering that would completely disappear. The viability and sustainability of the elitist version of settler colonialism that was planned for Kenya was always a problem.[21] *Out of Africa* presents not only one of the most stunning and seductive visions of how a European woman might declare 'This is where I belong', 'This is where I ought to be', but also the failure and dissolution of that fantasy, and her return to Europe. Like the peony, her identity there is a single brilliant flowering.

The case has been well made that Blixen was involved in a colonialist project that she simultaneously participated in, benefited from, despised and repeatedly sought to subvert.[22] What Llewellyn views at the museum are the trappings of an élite settler society, a fragment which relished the opportunity to turn away from industrialized metropolitan Europe and establish a pre-industrial quasi-feudal order. This is a fantasy world which *Out of Africa* not only constructs, but also dismantles. The book moves from the pastoral plenitude of the first three sections to the fragmentary narratives of the last two, 'From an Immigrant's Notebook' and 'Farewell to the Farm'. That Llewellyn fails to connect the artefacts she views in the museum to a classed, gendered and racial organization of settler culture in Kenya connects back to points I made in Chapter 3 about the uses of Africa in Australian travel writing, and to the strategic forgetting produced by the mirage which Blixen's tapestry animals inhabit. Beset as she is by a struggle to enter Africa imaginatively, to become a writer there, what Llewellyn responds to is a place for her as that absent guest. The display is designed to suggest that the house still awaits occupation, and that some may enter Blixen's magic circle and find their place at that table, in that bedroom where the jodhpurs and pith helmet and tiger-skin rug hang.

In this display is a synecdoche of the memoir. Few texts signal a place for the narratee to enter and listen as brilliantly as *Out of Africa*. Ross Chambers points out that the ongoing readability of texts is crucially dependent on recruiting the narratee, and the ongoing authority of the narrator depends upon this.[23] Again, the politics and the poetics of autobiographical writing need to be brought together. The autobiographic narrator of *Out of Africa* is a brilliant storyteller; her house is not only a repository for books but also a place designed for the telling and hearing of stories. Recent rereadings of *Out of Africa* as an oppositional text draw on feminist and psychoanalytic literary theories to authorize this narrator anew. From these perspectives Dinesen's stories and memoirs are read as more complex, self-reflexive texts, anticipating not only feminist concerns with women's experience in androcentric societies but also conceptions of language and subjectivity associated with the writings of Cixous, Kristeva and Irigaray.[24] This rebirth of Blixen's texts as oppositional narratives authorizes her quite differently and brings a new recruitment of narratees to the feast. Here they must jostle aside an intra-diegesic narratee for whom the place was set, the object of seduction, Denys Finch-Hatton. They must also come to terms with the relationship between the fine china and linen on the table, the great lion-skin beneath their feet and the apparently supplicant Masai in the hills.

Familiar as we are with the figure of the white hunter in the masculinist imperial creations of Rider Haggard and Ernest Hemingway, we miss the significance of his appearance in autobiographical writing by Blixen, Huxley, Markham, and in Kuki Gallmann's more recent memoir. The desire to please the white hunter as an intra-diegesic narratee is fundamental to the writing of *Out of Africa*, which sets before the reader an extravagant and diverse feast of stories, fables and characters. The logic of the memoir and its ongoing power to seduce and capture readers is in part produced by the shape of this writing scene and the profoundly sensual and mythic invention of African space which it produces to satisfy the aristocratic taste of Denys, a listener of discrimination. This narratee tutors the narrator in Latin, the Bible and the Greek poets, and makes sure the farm is stocked with the best in wine and tobacco. On his return the farm becomes a metonym for the narrator: 'it gave out what was in it; it spoke.... When I was expecting Denys back, and heard his car coming up the drive, I heard at the same time, the things of the farm all telling what they really were' (194).

This is fundamental to the work of figuration in the text. I have argued earlier, in Chapters 1 and 2, that colonial encounters foreground processes of scripting the self through connections and unexpected interdependencies. For both Blixen and Beryl Markham, the production of the self in the autobiographic text is critically dependent upon their figuration of Finch-Hatton. The invention of Finch-Hatton as the archetype of the hunter is dependent not upon his own writings, nor those passing references to him as the guide of choice for the élite hunting parties which set out from Nairobi. Others who made his acquaintance find these textual magnifications of him idiosyncratic. He is nevertheless a vital component in the way that both Blixen and Markham authorize themselves. The incorporation of Finch-Hatton into *Out of Africa* as the narratee makes the nature of the exchange very clear. A kind of symbolic economy is at work in the text between narrator and narratee. The hunter brings to the farm the trophies of the hunt: 'leopard and cheetah skins, to be made into fur coats in Paris, snake and lizard skins for shoes, and marabout feathers', and in return Blixen experiments with many curious recipes out of old cookery books, and works to make European flowers grow in the garden (179). For Finch-Hatton the exchange includes stories, and the transformation of the narrator into Scheherazade, the woman who tells stories for her life, for their mutual pleasure. It should not surprise us that the death of the narratee produces the symbolic death of the narrator. As the house is emptied and the ambience dissipates the narrator herself is dismembered, expelled from the nobility of Africa to the degradations of Europe, just like the giraffes in the little sketch 'The Giraffes go to Hamburg'. The white hunter, on the other hand, attains immortality and indigeneity through one of the tropes of settler writing: the burial where he becomes part of Africa and leaves his own mark upon it. His place as a natural aristocrat is confirmed when the lions habitually come to the grave 'and make him an African monument' (308). He also, of course, has a small memorial at Eton. Gallmann's return to this scenario in *I Dreamed of Africa* is evident. Although the narrator abandons the farm in the hills, the place and significance of the narratee remain assured.

The transmutation of the relationship between Blixen and Finch-Hatton into a liaison between two quite different ways of occupying Kenyan space in that period of early settlement *and* into the textual apparatus of narrator and narratee is a brilliant innovation which is fundamental to the work of smoke and mirrors in *Out of Africa*. By smoke and mirrors I mean the processes of erasure and figuration which occur to naturalize the colonial relation which is being established here, which produce the effects of truth, authenticity and inevitability.

Blixen is quite specific that the safari and the farm are two mutually exclusive domains. Her own passion for safari and the kill is superseded by the domestic relation to space and place on the farm. As in *The Flame Trees of Thika*, industry and domestication supersede sport. In *Out of Africa* we see little of the quite different economy and relation between colonization and environment of which Finch-Hatton was a part: the safari. Even as the establishment of settler colonization based on small-scale farms was proving difficult to establish, this quite different and distinctively modern management of land and animals was emerging in Kenya. Finch-Hatton was a big-game hunter, pioneering the use of the aeroplane to spot game. Tourism, in particular catering for the European élite in search of game, was to become vitally important to the ongoing viability of white settlement in Kenya. As it turned out, this was to be an industry where they would prosper.

The new pioneer: *West with the Night*

West with the Night, Beryl Markham's memoir, is no rival to *Out of Africa's* status as a classic text, but it does open up a slightly different angle on how a new economy was emerging around the white hunter in this period. For Markham, the new technology allows her to script herself into the 'monarch of all I survey' tradition of writing. Mary Louise Pratt argues that the imperial frontier was coded in terms of two 'eternally clashing and complementary languages of bourgeois subjectivity'.[25] This is useful in understanding the differences between *Out of Africa* and *West with the Night*. Blixen draws on the tradition which Pratt associates with the sentimental experiential subject that inhabits the self-defined 'other' section of the bourgeois world, the private sphere – home of desire, sex, spirituality and the individual. The sentimental subject is inclined to present a spiritual (rather than a scientific) understanding of nature as image of the divine. On the other hand, there is an alternative figure, associated with technology-based paradigms of progress and develop-ment, and with the panoptic apparatus of the bureaucratic state. Pratt stresses that these two discourses could not be more different because they are so much defined in terms of each other; they are complementary, and in their complementarity they stake out the grounds of bourgeois hegemony. Both of these figures are innocent; as 'non-heroes of anti-conquest' they sanitize and mystify European expansionism.[26] Differences between representations of Kenya in *Out of Africa* and *West with the Night* can be understood in part because they draw on these different discursive frameworks and figurations of the self.

The aeroplane has from the very start been associated with Kenya, where it rapidly became a preferred mode of transport for the European population. Both *West with the Night* and *Out of Africa* record the transformation of perception which this produced, a sense of a new frontier opening, and the inauguration of a new phase of territorial expansion inland. This 'new frontier' meant very different things to these autobiographic subjects. Blixen describes the expeditions in Finch-Hatton's plane as 'the most transporting pleasure of my life on the farm', in which she feels the pilot carries her upon the outstretched palms of his hands, taking her 'into the heart of the Ngong Hills by a secret unknown road' (208). For Blixen, flying, like the safari, is translated into a private and intimate pleasure with her lover, where they become birds. For Markham, on the other hand, the world of aviation allows her to become an epic hero on a new pioneering frontier. The plane is a machine to escape the bounds of female embodiment and domesticity. This technology allows Markham to present herself as an unencumbered subject, solitary and singular; the plane becomes a topographic machine, extending the borders of Empire, including the empire of the Western subject.[27] From the sky she attains a panoptic view of the landscapes below, monarch of all she surveys, able to interpret the signs of human and animal life she sees below. For Markham, this view is not aestheticized but commercialized. Her flights with Finch-Hatton are very different to the passive experience described by Blixen, and they lead to a different partnership:

> [Denys] asked me to fly to Voi, one day, and of course I said I would ...
> Denys said he wanted to try something that had never been done before.
> He said he wanted to see if elephant could be scouted by plane; if they
> could, he thought, hunters would be willing to pay very well for the
> service.
>   It seemed a good idea to me, even a thrilling idea.[28]

Markham was an important part of Finch-Hatton's project to use the latest technology to deliver what his clients desired: tusks. His intention was to modernize the management of the hunt, to spot elephants 'efficiently' from the air and offer his clients a new service: keeping a hunting party in touch with a moving herd. Ironically, Finch-Hatton's death means that it is Blix, Baron von Blixen, 'to my knowledge, the toughest, most durable White Hunter ever to snicker at the fanfare of safari' (201), who works with Markham to establish a new frontier between hunting and tourism in Kenya, and a quite different relationship between the human and the animal in the hunt. The practicalities are clear, in Markham's words: 'As a White Hunter, his job was to produce the game desired and to point it out to his employer of the moment' (213). There is nothing noble about this enterprise, which inaugurated a different version of the traditional safari. It was the size and pace of the elephant that made it available to a kind of commodification which Markham and Finch-Hatton envisage from the air. The desire to capitalize on this is a perspective that is distinctively modern.

There is no place for this in *Out of Africa*. The skins which Llewellyn sees in the museum, on the floor and on the wall beside the pith helmet in the reconstruction of Blixen's house are the trophies of the élite hunt. The orgasmic pleasure of the kill for Blixen is produced by the purer, more aristocratic hunt for lions with Finch-Hatton that becomes a carefully choreographed elaborate metaphor of intercourse and metamorphosis between the narrator and narratee. The safari emerges as part of an intimate courtship, remote from the commercialization of the hunt elsewhere. Like the flight in Finch-Hatton's plane, the experience is translated into a spiritual, mystical domain. Blixen's fantasy of belonging in Africa, and establishing a house which is 'one with the landscape, so that nobody could tell where the one stopped and the other began' (74), lends itself to another emergent modern sensibility, one which establishes a quite different relationship between the human and animal worlds.

The associations between Romanticism, hunting and conservation go back to the nineteenth century, well before Blixen. The Romantic movement effected a revolutionary transformation in the relationship between humans and animals; in glorifying the natural world, Romanticism fostered the preservation of animal populations rather than the commercialization of the hunt. By the end of the nineteenth century humane feelings towards animals were associated with an enlightened view, and a revolution in perceptions of relations between human and animal worlds.[29] Nevertheless, the era of new sensibilities coincided with the creation of more effective ways to pursue the aristocratic enthusiasm for the hunt — such as Finch-Hatton's scheme for tracking the moving herds of elephant. John MacKenzie suggests that conservation and the gentleman's code for hunting behaviour (which defined hunting as an aristocratic European pursuit) developed apace. Autobiographical writing confirms this view. For, as Markham associates herself with that commercialization of the hunt, so the supremely self-centred insertion of the self into Africa that is performed in *Out of Africa* leads to a highly aestheticized and quite different capture of the animal world.

Animals are vital to the Edenic aestheticized style of *Out of Africa*. Giraffe are long-stemmed gigantic flowers. Rhinos like big angular stones rollick in the long valley. Leopards sit on the roads like tapestry animals. The fawn has a nose like a truffle. Gazelles are like toy animals on a billiard table. The nearness of the animals in Blixen's view, the illusion of oneness with the natural world, represents a kind of intellectual and emotional use of Kenyan landscapes, and leads to a different type of commodification of African space. Blixen captures the animal world for the pleasure of the European gaze. In *Out of Africa* the animals seen on safari become available sights, their proximity is ennobling: 'the big game was out there still, in their own country; I could go and look them up once more if I liked. Their nearness gave a shine and play to the atmosphere of the farm' (23). Blixen is one of the first to translate the new technology of the camera into a modern version of the hunt:

> The civilized people have lost the aptitude of stillness, and must take lessons in silence from the wild before they are accepted by it. The art of moving gently, without suddenness, is the first to be studied by the hunter, and more so by the hunter with the camera. (24)

In this way Blixen is a harbinger of tastes and sensibilities which we recognize still, and which produce the Kenya that was to be so attractive for modern mass tourism, and seductive to the likes of a young British woman like Julie Ward. The desire here is not to dominate in the 'monarch of all I survey' tradition but to enter the wilderness and become part of it. In a distinctively modern fashion, Blixen associates this capacity to enter the African world and become one with it with a certain kind of subjectivity. This is not simply 'enlightened', but a mark of a spiritual, mystical capacity and transcendence. In this Blixen becomes an important precursor of, for example, Gallmann's presentation of herself in terms of the emergence of a conservation movement in east Africa.

Smoke and mirrors

It is tempting to see the white hunter as a masculinist anachronism, superseded by a modern, feminized consciousness where the only trophy of the hunt is a photograph. The lesson of the quartet of autobiographies which are read together in this chapter is that the invention of Kenya in colonial discourse has been a complex intersection of very different fantasies, and the opposition between masculine and feminine, past and present and, I would suggest, exploitative and enlightened inventions of Kenya are called into question. Rather they operate as coordinates within the same discursive web, one which remains deeply implicated in the ongoing fantasy of white supremacism in black Africa, and the interests of that small settler fragment. Gavron's narrative of the Ward murder, which radically calls into question fantasies about white women in particular 'belonging' in Kenya, operates within the same discursive frame in that invocation of the wildlife and the tourist, the shared rights of both elephants and Julie Ward to roam free as innocents in the Masai Mara. In this web, as Kuki Gallmann reminds us, a passion for hunting 'might logically evolve into pure conservationism' (56). Both Gallmann and Blixen literally and figuratively bury the white hunter and ensure that white writing about Kenya will continue to feed on his bones.

How do white women imagine their place in Africa? What are the effects of their fantasies of belonging there? Defeated by the 'complexity, the vastness, the entire universal rave that is Africa', Kate Llewellyn returns home to her kitchen in Leura, New South Wales to cut up tomatoes and think about it, 'the smell of Gay Bilson's adaptation of Philip Searle's roast tomato chutney fills the house' (215). Llewellyn feels more at home as a traveller in India, but that is another story. The record of her ongoing struggle to enter Africa imaginatively and to write about it compares favourably with Gallmann's wholesale appropriation of settler mythographies.

There are other stories of white women in Kenya, and they unravel some of the skeins of that discursive web which has been the subject of this chapter. The Irish writer Dervla Murphy gets off the plane in Nairobi with her sixtieth birthday present, a Dawes Ascent mountain bike, the cyclist's equivalent of a Rolls-Royce, named Lear. Lear and Murphy make their way to a Christian guest-house on Bishop's Road, where Lear is locked to the bed and Murphy spends the day ambling around Nairobi, getting beaten up by paramilitaries on the way. That night she watches television:

> Julie Ward's father was being interviewed outside Nairobi's imposing courthouse. On that flickering screen the poor fellow seemed to have St Vitus's Dance. The Luo teacher beside me muttered angrily, 'Why so much fuss about this one murder? Only because she was White and killing her is bad for the tourist trade. Everyday Kenyan people are murdered in Kenya and there is no fuss!'[30]

Murphy comes to Africa from Northern Ireland; she recognizes the smoke and mirrors of colonial discourse, and cycles out of Nairobi the next day without visiting the Karen Blixen Museum. As she later points out, the settlers' view of the African, absorbed from Blixen, renewed by Kuki Gallmann, focuses on the land and its animals and remains well within the comfort zone of white readers with a taste for African romance. What gets left out, or at best cast in very limited ways, are the African peoples themselves. Murphy, who writes about Kenya in the midst of the AIDS crisis, observes that this kind of Africanism has real effects: 'this endangers the Africans who, as I write these words, are being indirectly killed, in considerable numbers, by relentless First World profiteering' (38). The animals may be innocent, but as Murphy infers, the writers and readers who continue to produce and consume white dreams of Kenya are not.

Notes

1   Alyse Simpson, *The Land That Never Was*. London: Selwyn & Blount, 1937, p. 230. All further references to this edition in text.
2   Kate Llewellyn, *Gorillas, Tea and Coffee: An African Sketchbook*. Hawthorn, Victoria: Hudson Publishing, 1996, p. 4. All further references to this edition in text.
3   Kathryn Tidrick also suggests that around Mau Mau relations between black and white were represented in figures of the white woman and the black rapist. Fears of the thin veneer of civilization in Kenya were accentuated following the murder of a white woman and her family in their lonely farmhouse in 1952. In 1992, as in 1952, the discovery of a lock of blonde hair from the victim is axiomatic; this piece of evidence becomes metonymic of the femininity, whiteness and innocence of the victim and the violence and depravity of black men. Dane Kennedy argues that 'the black peril' was an important element in reminding settlers of their shared interests as a race, reminding them of their common needs and fears. In her study of rape as a highly charged trope that is implicated in the management of rebellion, Jenny Sharpe suggests that European fear of inter-racial rape does not exist so long as

there is a belief that colonial structures are firmly in place. She uses Mau Mau as an example of a rebellion which is not sexually coded. In the writings about the Ward case the spectre of the dark-skinned rapist emerges very clearly, with the essentialized racial and sexual meanings that the stereotype articulates about both black and white. See Kathryn Tidrick, *Empire and the English Character* (London: I. B. Tauris, 1992), p. 158; Dane Kennedy, *Islands of White: Settler Society and Culture in Kenya and Southern Rhodesia, 1890–1939* (Durham, NC: Duke University Press, 1987), p. 146; Jenny Sharpe, *Allegories of Empire: The Figure of Woman in the Colonial Text* (Minneapolis: University of Minnesota Press, 1993), pp. 2–3; and David Maugham-Brown, *Land, Freedom and Fiction: History and Ideology in Kenya* (London: Zed Books, 1985), p. 55, 124.

4   Jeremy Gavron, *Darkness in Eden: The Murder of Julie Ward*. London: HarperCollins, 1991, p. 183.

5   *Ibid.*, p. 205.

6   By 1913 indigenous resistance had been crushed, a strong institutional authority had been established through the Kenyan Civil Service and the first coercive controls over African labour had been introduced. Pass and registration ordinances were introduced in 1915.

7   Raymond Williams, *Marxism and Literature*. Oxford: Oxford University Press, 1977, p. 122.

8   Tidrick, p. 149.

9   Another referent is Susanna Moodie's *Roughing It in the Bush*, also an autobiographical narration of pioneering failure and the experience of crushing poverty.

10 Northrop Frye, *The Secular Scripture: A Study of the Structure of Romance*. Cambridge, MA: Harvard University Press, 1976, p. 40.

11 Carolyn Martin Shaw, *Colonial Inscriptions: Race, Sex and Class in Kenya*. Minneapolis: University of Minnesota Press, 1995.

12 Kennedy, *Islands of White*, p. 91.

13 *Ibid.*, p. 86.

14 *Ibid.*, p. 46.

15 See Tidrick (pp. 142–146) for a more extensive discussion of Huxley's biography and also her debate with the English academic Margery Perham about the ethics and politics of white settlement in Kenya.

16 Martin Shaw, p. 196.

17 Tidrick, p. 171.

18 Martin Shaw, p. 180.

19 Elspeth Huxley, *The Flame Trees of Thika: Memories of an African Childhood* (London: Penguin, 1962), p. 7. All further references to this edition in text.

20 Karen Blixen, *Out of Africa* (Harmondsworth: Penguin, 1982, p. 13). All further references to this edition in text.

21 Kennedy, *Islands of White*, p. 44.

22 Susan Hardy Aiken, *Isak Dinesen and the Engendering of Narrative*. Chicago: University of Chicago Press, 1990, p. 213. All further references in text.

23 Ross Chambers, *Room for Maneuver: Reading Oppositional Narrative*. Chicago: University of Chicago Press, 1991, p. 11. All further references in text.

24 Hardy Aiken, p. 8.

25 Mary Louise Pratt, *Imperial Eyes: Travel Writing and Transculturation*. London: Routledge 1992, p. 39.

26 *Ibid.*, p. 78. By 'anti-conquest' Pratt refers to the strategies of representation whereby European bourgeois subjects seek to secure their innocence at the same time as they assert European hegemony.

27 Sidonie Smith, 'The other woman and the racial politics of gender: Isak Dinesen and Beryl Markham in Kenya', in Smith and Watson (eds), *De/Colonizing the Subject: The Politics of Gender in Women's Autobiography*. Minneapolis: University of Minnesota Press, 1992, p. 417.

28 Beryl Markham, *West with the Night*. London: Virago, 1992, p. 193.

29 John M. MacKenzie, *The Empire of Nature: Hunting, Conservation and British Imperialism*. Manchester: Manchester University Press, 1988, p. 26.

30 Dervla Murphy, *The Ukimwi Road: From Kenya to Zimbabwe*. London: Flamingo, 1994, p. 6.

5

Autobiography and resistance

In short, the autobiographical quandary after poststructuralism requires that reader and writer are both recognized to be subject predicaments rather than fixed positions that occupy known spaces within history and culture.[1]

What is an autobiography compared to a dreaming track? Then I realised the obvious. But it didn't increase my respect for books, at the time. The pen is mightier than the sword but the finger in the sand is mightier than that, in its own way.[2]

Reading across the South

In May 1990, a few months after Nelson Mandela was freed from prison, the South African activist Mamphela Ramphele visited Australia. She found a mix of the familiar and the strange. The landscape seems similar to her native country. The '1960s Australian activists' who are professionals and bureaucrats in the 1990s are dealing with the same tensions as Ramphele herself. What she sees of indigenous community organizations reminds her of the stifling male leadership in her own country. The approach of some Aboriginal leaders disappoints this anti-apartheid campaigner. For example, the land rights campaigns seem akin to a 'homelands' strategy, 'some of the leaders had difficulty understanding why South African blacks were clamouring for the dismantling of homelands'. To Ramphele, the turning away from integrationist approaches and glorification of indigenous culture of which she sees signs in Australia suggest a failure to come to terms constructively with modernity.[3]

Eight years later, and in a different epoch, in December 1998 Ramphele's son, Hlumelo Biko, visited Aboriginal communities in north Queensland. He described what he saw there as 'the most appalling living conditions being experienced by any black people', worse than the poorest street dweller in Soweto:

Soweto is a vibrant community ... the people have work and feed their children, and everything is clean ... they see that there is progress and a government that is responsive to their demands. Here there is nothing. My father's Black Consciousness Movement is applicable here.[4]

Unlike Mamphela Rampele, Hlumelo Biko does not comment upon the 'stifling male leadership' at home – or away.

The contradictions and complications between these two moments are rich, and not easily resolved. As we have seen in Chapter 4, for the Australian traveller Kate Llewellyn, Soweto and Johannesburg were the antithesis of 'home'. Biko's 'vibrant community' is Llewellyn's hell.[5] Whether Queensland Aboriginal communities such as Doomadgee and Burketown enter into Llewellyn's idea of 'home' is open to question. The differences between mother and son can be read back into the different discursive frameworks of these comments. The first is an extract from an autobiography by a woman who is a seasoned campaigner, who visited Australia as a guest of the federal government when the emergence of a 'new' South Africa was by no means assured. The second is from a series of newspaper articles highlighting alcohol abuse and violence in Aboriginal communities, and Hlumelo Biko speaks with moral authority about human rights 'as the son of the murdered freedom fighter Steven Biko', with Mandela's ANC government firmly established in the new South Africa. This is a different epoch. South Africa no longer stands as the place of ultimate racism, where the colonized black and the settler white eternally confront each other. It is now, post-apartheid, in the revolutionary process of coming to terms with the past in a process of reconciliation and healing. In Australia, on the other hand, potentially symbolic moments loom – the centenary of Federation, progress towards a republic – with no clear agreement on processes of reconciliation.

What South Africans find in Australia tells us a good deal about what they have left behind – both in knowledge and in denial – at home. And the reverse is, of course, true. Both Llewellyn and Biko choose to locate the nadir of race relations elsewhere, to think in terms of oppositions. The legacies of settler colonization in the white dominions of the south make South Africa and Australia akin, yet there are fundamental differences. Australian 'land rights' and 'Aboriginality' are not equivalent to South African 'homelands' and 'Black Consciousness'. Aboriginal Australians are a minority group in terms of numbers and influence. In South Africa white settlers have always had minority status numerically, but not in terms of power and authority. On the other hand, the politics of reconciliation organize political, cultural and social affairs in both contexts in the late 1990s, and Aboriginal activists such as Murrandoo Yanner look to South Africa in thinking about race relations in Australia. Issues of race and indigeneity are at the heart of both similarities and differences, produced by the shared settler myths of the 'empty land' and policies of white racial domination which are the legacies of Empire in these southern white dominions. Ramphele, Biko and Llewellyn are reminders that these southern spaces have been available for very different ends. Working across them requires a critique which does not begin from the given grounds of opposition, where each finds its antithesis in the other and so brings about closure, but rather an approach which begins with exchange and opens up a space of translation which alters how we recognize and understand politics and writing in the new South Africa and contemporary Australia.[6]

The focus of this chapter is contemporary and antipodean. It will read across selected contemporary autobiographic writing by black African and Australian indigenous women to consider the place of autobiography in contemporary campaigns for decolonization. What is the work of this writing? How, where and why? In both Australia and South Africa these autobiographies have been a distinctive feature of contemporary writing for the past decade. What are we to make of this? How can we read back from these to the politics of identity in contemporary Australia and South Africa? What conditions created the enunciative space that these autobiographies occupy? What is their readership? How do they relate to existing and emergent regimes of truth and authority? By reading black and indigenous autobiographic writing by women we can explore how it relates to the work of creating new narratives about national identities, but we must always be careful to ask what had to be in place in order for this writing to appear at all.

These questions organize a series of discussions in this chapter. Firstly, a consideration of 'thresholds', the grounds for the emergence of black women's autobiographic writing in Australia and South Africa. In these autobiographies various discourses of truth, authority and power become available to black women at what is in each context a critical conjuncture in debates about politics and identity. However, the 'fit' between discourses of racial and gendered identities is by no means secure. Secondly, a review of the role of 'foreign agents' — white collaborators and readers — who have been a constitutive part of this writing and reading scene suggests the politics of production are always important in reading these autobiographies. As we saw in *The History of Mary Prince*, these agents both interrupt and facilitate unauthorized autobiographers, both at the time of writing and in the ongoing processes of reception and critique. They are fundamental to the making of the text, and yet remain implicated in the always complex and ambivalent relations between black and white women. Finally, and with these issues in mind, questions about how subjectivity and the body of the self figure in these autobiographies as a *combinatoire*, a discursive arrangement which holds together in tension different lines of race, gender and sexuality will be discussed in a reading which foregrounds the predicaments of the autobiographic narrator and her reader.[7]

To date, work on Australian and South African literatures has been organized in terms of national frameworks. The best work on contemporary writing requires a close working knowledge of the particular and local conditions. For example, Dorothy Driver's work on African women's autobiography draws on a detailed knowledge of political, cultural and social formations which cannot be generated in bursts of scholarly tourism from the northern hemisphere, or from across the South. However, comparative work does not seek to reproduce this kind of detailed local knowledge. As I have argued elsewhere, it has different strengths.[8] In his review of a collection of essays which compare settler societies, Robert Wilson playfully (yet usefully) conceptualizes the need for the comparative view to model 'the fly's eye':

> Seeing with a fly's eye requires that the individual facets focus clearly and that they are functionally co-ordinated. A co-ordinated set of perspectives, constituting a compound structure for analysis and explanation, works effectively in proportion to the extent that its principles of structuration make sense, are arguable and coherent ... What does seem to work ... is a perspective grounded in either the socio-cultural history of the two (or more) national literatures ... in a recognizable theoretical model ... [and] a conceptual archive with sufficient depth and sophistication.[9]

Only a comparative, 'fly's eye' view can answer those large questions about the ways in which black women's autobiography can emerge and function politically in two very different national formations. Even when the kind of chronological synchronicity that has occurred in women's autobiography across 'southern spaces' in the past decade seems to invite a more expansive approach, it is important to remain attuned to the local and contingent. There can be no collapsing of the very different locations and discourses of South African and Australian black and indigenous consciousness or the politics of white supremacy. Nor does postcolonial theory construct a stable platform for comparative work across these two locations.[10] However, the point remains that these two societies are contact zones where African and indigenous populations have been dispossessed, eradicated, managed, incarcerated and 'civilized' over a long period of time, and, in turn, have engaged in entrenched, strategic and sometimes violent resistance.

Autobiography after Soweto

When does autobiography become active in the politics of identity? A discursive threshold must be reached before autobiographic writing appears as an agent. This is clearly not the case for each individual autobiographic act. It is a requirement for the kind of phenomenon I am interested in here – an episode where quantities of autobiographic work, oral and written, by black and indigenous women find an editor, a publisher and a readership, and become active in identity politics. In both South Africa and Australia in the past decade black women's autobiographical writing is emergent. Publication has frequently required the services of the white amanuensis, editor, patron or collaborator. These autobiographies are hostages to publishers, the tastes of the reading public, and shifts in the political, cultural and social life of the nation. Sometimes there is a windfall – the Bicentennial in Australia in 1988, for example. Sometimes a catalyst – such as the recent Truth and Reconciliation Commission in South Africa and the 'Bringing Them Home' Inquiry in Australia – which invite testimony and narration specifically about racial oppression. Sometimes things fall apart, and contestation within the African and Aboriginal communities erupts around and through autobiographic writing, for example, the debates about race and gender relations spurred by Ruby Langford Ginibi's *Don't Take Your Love to Town* and Sally Morgan's *My Place*, or the gendered tensions between township and prison writing in South Africa; or when the right of the autobiographer to speak as an indigenous subject is called into question, for example, the controversy surrounding Roberta Sykes' *Snake Dreaming* autobiographies during 1998.[11]

Contemporary South African autobiography is extraordinary, unmistakably a world of its own. Tattooed across its surface is a series of political events that configure and invade the private domain.[12] As Sindiwe Magona suggests, in South Africa seemingly disparate events – in her case having to apply for a passbook, the death of two students, and South Africa becoming a Republic in 1961 – are irretrievably linked in her memory, in part because they are 'strands of the same hideous whole. In them, terribly articulated, was our voicelessness.'[13] It is the work of autobiography to make these links between the public and private. The politics of race *and* gender work to produce this threshold. Arguably it was the renewed interest in women that made room for Elsa Joubert's *Poppie Nongena* (1980). First published in Afrikaans in 1978, the book was widely read. Since it could be read as a simple story about a black woman and her life, the problems of her children and how the family was affected by apartheid, as seen through the eyes of an Afrikaaner woman, it was acceptable even to National Party supporters: 'there was room for it'.[14] There was less room for the cocktail of anti-apartheid and woman-centred politics in autobiographies in English authored by black women activists which began to emerge to an international readership five years later: Ellen Kuzwayo's *Call Me Woman* (1985), Caesarina Kona Makhoere's *No Child's Play* (1988), Emma Mashinini's *Strikes Have Followed Me All My Life* (1989) and Sindiwe Magona's *To My Children's Children* (1991) and *Forced to Grow* (1992) were all published in London by the Women's Press. More recent autobiographies, such as Mamphela Ramphele's *A Life* (1995), are being published for the first time in South Africa.[15] The links between black women's autobiographical writing in the 1980s, woman-centred campaigns, the anti-apartheid movement both within and outside of South Africa and the beginnings of the reform movement, are constitutive of this threshold moment. For Magona, Ramphele and Kuzwayo, communities of women – local, European and American – were vital to the anti-apartheid movement, and to their own survival and sense of agency, although writing *across* such a diverse readership could be problematic. Sindiwe Magona suggests there is a danger that resistance to apartheid will become identified symbolically with the experience of incarceration at Robben Island, strategically forgetting the experiences of wives, mothers and daughters in the townships.[16] To write autobiographically about the potent and visceral impact of apartheid and the anti-apartheid struggles upon women's bodies in townships and bantustans required deft and ongoing negotiations across the politics of race and gender.

These autobiographies are associated with a critical process in the articulation and deconstruction of apartheid. The discourse of non-racialism expressed in the Freedom Charter and in the tradition of the Congress resistance movement began to emerge as the dominant political language of the black communities in South Africa in the early 1980s. At this stage of the anti-apartheid movement, non-racialism as a way of thinking began to supplant the language of Black Consciousness, which had been the emergent language of resistance following the unrest at Soweto in 1976. As the 1980s progressed, non-racialism increasingly succeeded in articulating a vision for those disaffected with the apartheid regime, a vision that incorporated black, coloured and white resistance. This incorporation was a requirement for an inclusive and effective anti-apartheid movement that could change the order of things. It subsequently became the basis of a new anti-apartheid regime of truth in the 1990s and the cornerstone of the social imaginary of post-apartheid South Africa.[17] As Aletta Norval suggests, the discourse of non-racialism engaged simultaneously in a process of *articulation* and *disarticulation*. *Articulation* in that it was an effective resistance strategy, underwriting the goals of the democratic movement as it progressed through a series of different resistance groups and organizations, both black and white, in the 1960s, 1970s and 1980s. *Disarticulation* in that it had to challenge and unravel the apartheid imaginary by presenting alternative principles of order and identification.[18] The core principles of apartheid, which defined social groups according to race and colour and envisaged separate territories and development for each, are fundamentally challenged by visions of a non-racial unitary state, where race, tribe and ethnicity are not the defining features of identity politics and social organization. Black Consciousness and non-racialism interpellated women as subjects and connected to the politics of gender in quite different ways. The grounds of resistance in African women's autobiography are thus deeply conflicted and the texts themselves are embedded within the shifting possibilities and constraints in the last decade of apartheid and the first years of freedom.

Call Me Woman

This is evident in African women's autobiographic writing as it emerged in the 1980s. Ellen Kuzwayo's *Call Me Woman* was germinal, both chronologically and conceptually. Emma Mashinini refers to it as the text that induced in her a sense of selfhood and autonomy amidst the strife and terror of the last years of apartheid. What 'Woman' might mean at that stage of the anti-apartheid campaigns is an open question, and Kuwayo's title suggests an intertextual relation. It was chosen specifically in relation to Mtutuzeli's book *Call Me Not a Man*. Kuzwayo's book shapes a discourse of militant maternalism by inserting woman-centred concerns into discourses of Black Consciousness. In the wake of Soweto in 1976 resistance movements increasingly focused on the formation of unity on the basis of a black identity although, as we will see, the synchronicity between gendered and racial issues was somewhat precarious. The book was published in 1985, when there was as yet no light at the end of the tunnel and the events in 1976 in Soweto had led to a radicalized youth movement at the forefront of anti-apartheid campaigns within South Africa: 1985 is both five years and light years before Mandela's walk to freedom signalled the ending of organized apartheid. As we can see elsewhere, for example Sindiwe Magona's *Forced to Grow* and Elsa Joubert's *Poppie Nongena*, the radicalization of schoolchildren brought the violence home in ways that were profoundly unsettling for women in South Africa. *Call Me Woman* is, in part, a response to this decisive stage in the resistance too, creating a place for African women to speak as activists and as mothers. It authors a distinctively different autobiographic voice, and circulated in very different networks, to *Poppie Nongena*. Soweto was one of the triggers that shaped women's autobiographic expression, although the outcomes took various forms.

This is clearly evident in Kuzwayo's autobiography, which is divided into three parts: 'Soweto', 'My road to Soweto' and 'Patterns behind the struggle'. *Call Me Woman* opens with a Preface by Nadine Gordimer, followed by a Foreword by Bessie Head, and then chronologies of Ellen Kuzwayo's career and 'Principal legislation and major events affecting the black community in South Africa'. The autobiography proper begins with another deferral in the form of a letter to Kuzwayo from Debra Nikiwe Matshoba, held in detention in 1978 at the Johannesburg Fort. Kuzwayo is introduced to us intimately, as 'Darling Mama': 'Thank you Mama for the message, so soothing, so inspiring.' Matshoba's letter introduces the autobiographical 'I' as she cannot introduce herself, in her inspirational and heroic characterization as the Mother of Soweto. It also establishes her credentials to write, for Kuzwayo has experienced detention herself: 'I don't have to tell you how life is at the Fort. You've been here.' When Kuzwayo's narrator enters the text it is as an ironic interpreter of the vernacular in Matshoba's letter:

> 'I'm now a Plural' — a strange sentence, I'm sure to anyone unfamiliar with South African society, but it made me laugh.... Over a century, black people have had at least three different labels: 'Natives', 'Bantu' and even 'Plurals'. Does it make sense to you? I hope it does.[19]

The autobiography is written directly to the reader *outside* the closed world made by the legislative and linguistic constructions of the apartheid system, and works to pull the reader into the world which the narrator inhabits: 'Some call it a ghetto. Is it a ghetto? You can size it up for yourself' (6). We 'see' it through the eyes of a narrator who is a witness: 'I have seen ...', 'I have lived here ...' and who constructs an intimate relationship with the reader: 'Just stop and think ...', 'Contrast at this point ...', 'Let me go back in history a little ...' The book addresses the foreign reader, and offers a history of how Soweto and what happened there in the student protest movement in 1976 was produced by influx control legislation and the Native Land Acts many years before. This history is strategic; it is gender-based and written against the stereotypes of black women in the townships as passive victims. It focuses in particular on the history of women following the departure of men to become migrant labourers in the urban workforce, which left women and children to survive in a society where gendered and familial roles had been transformed. In this narration, which culminates with a first-person account of the Soweto uprisings in 1976, these women survive because they are articulate, strategic and active.

When the narration turns to Kuzwayo's particular history in Part Two, beginning with her birth on the farm of her maternal grandfather in the Orange Free State in 1914, the reader is already familiar with a narrator who is empowered by Steven Biko's concept of Black Consciousness – 'a concept which has created awareness among blacks about who they are and were, and helped to build up the determination to regain their strength and personality as a nation' (47) – and a particularly South African history of black womanhood and 'women's presence'. The shift from the streets of Soweto in 1976 to the farm in Thaba Patchoa in the early 1920s, when the narrator 'first becomes aware of myself', sets up the framework for a presentation of childhood as a time of prelapsarian innocence. The presentation of a utopian childhood, despite significant breakdowns in familial relations, is strategic rather than historic. It suggests, for example, that within living memory the black community possessed a 'moral coherence', an integrity which it was to lose in the 1930s and 1940s. Like Sindiwe Magona, Kuzwayo's representation of childhood is shaped to highlight the trauma of the recent past for black Africans under apartheid.

The suturing of the private and the public from the very start in the related chronologies of Kuzwayo's career and the major public events during her lifetime is indicative of the work of *Call Me Woman*. Through Kuzwayo's own life story a history of black resistance and women's particular place in the African communities is established. The narrator recounts her own experiences, but the drive of the autobiography is always towards the collective – both in the sense that her own identity is traced back to African rural communal and familial formations fractured by apartheid legislation, and the sense that her suffering is shared by many black women. *Call Me Woman* makes a claim to a gendered and racial identity. It is the work of the text to suggest and define what this claim of African womanhood in fact might mean in this context.

The Foreword and Preface are important in this respect. As we have seen throughout this study of postcolonial autobiography, the marginal texts are always important. In this case Nadine Gordimer's Preface stresses the achievement of the 'wholeness of the transitional woman': '[Kuzwayo] is history in the person of one woman.... [She] is not Westernized; she is one of those who have Africanized the Western concept of woman and in herself achieved a synthesis with meaning for all who experience cultural conflict.' This individual life bears the burden of documenting many lives, both explicitly and metaphorically. As the title suggests, Kuzwayo's autobiography represents South African black women to themselves and to outsiders as activists and gendered subjects at a quite specific historical juncture. Here identity is not commensurate with individuality. Nevertheless, identity is represented in terms of wholeness and authenticity.

Gordimer's desire to find a whole subject in black autobiography, like Moira Ferguson's search for the truth in *The History of Mary Prince*, is constantly contradicted by the autobiographical text we have before us. In reading *Call*

Me Woman it is the contingent and historical nature of gendered and racial identities which are brought into view, rather than their continuities. In her Foreword to *Call Me Woman*, the African writer Bessie Head stresses a different aspect of the autobiography. She is interested not in gender so much as drawing on humanist discourses to suggest that Kuzwayo reveals the bodies under the black skins, the triumph out of suffering in South Africa: 'Books like these will be the Bible one day for the younger generations.' Again autobiography is yoked to a desire which is strategic and political for a whole and essential subject, in this case an essence defined by race.

The balance being sought here is tricky. As an autobiographic subject Kuzwayo is typical and exceptional, representative and yet heroic. The narrative techniques characteristically define its autobiographical subject as a self among others. As Judith Couille points out, *Call Me Woman* draws on traditional South African notions of selfhood where the individual is never 'self-made' to depersonalize the narrative.[20] Yet we cannot assume that these traditional notions of subjectivity are any more appropriate, authentic or strategically useful than the other identifications which circulate through the autobiography, and which draw on other discourses, such as Black Consciousness or feminism. Appropriately, in her analysis of *Call Me Woman*, Dorothy Driver draws attention to the apparently incompatible codes which comprise Kuzwayo's self-projection. The text advocates the kind of female empowerment and separatism which is characteristic of some forms of Western feminism; however, as Driver points out, Kuzwayo honours the refusal by black South African women to assume a position largely formulated by, and for, white Western middle-class women. Nor is Kuzwayo's maternalist discourse as critical of feminine stereotypes as we might expect from a Western feminist perspective.[21] She identifies primarily with black separatism as promulgated by Steven Biko: 'to me Black Consciousness was an institution, a process whereby blacks in South Africa were beginning to take a serious look at themselves ... and to find a way of redeeming themselves ... I believe in Black Consciousness.'[22] *Call Me Woman*, first published in 1985, suggests some of the tensions in this work of articulating a resistance strategy while disarticulating the core principles of apartheid at that point in time. Black Consciousness gives Kuzwayo a discourse for resisting apartheid, but does it accommodate the expression of her experiences as a woman? For example, fractures and stresses are evident in one of the last chapters, 'Finding our strength'. Here Kuzwayo testifies in public that she believes in Black Consciousness as an institution, gaining the high praise 'You are not an ordinary woman, you pleaded like a man, only a man could speak the way you did' (227). Kuzwayo is, in turn, immobilized: 'I sat huddled in my seat as if nailed to it.'

As Driver argues, to speak in terms of Black Consciousness was to accept a discourse based upon binary oppositions, not just black and white but also masculinity and femininity. These polarities are, as we have seen in earlier chapters, almost always fragile in postcolonial autobiographics. They deconstruct in *Call Me Woman* not only when Kuzwayo testifies to her belief in Biko's Black Consciousness Movement and so is understood to speak 'as a man', but also, shortly afterwards, when she recoils from a delegation of English women who appeal to her on behalf of a shared identity as women across the boundaries of race. Kuzwayo initially responds to them militantly, seeing 'whites' not 'women'. In fact, non-racial and gender-based international links will be an important part of her campaigns for women in Soweto, and integral to her autobiography through the implied 'foreign' readership.

In this way, a series of quite different gendered and racial codes and identifications coexist and to some extent compete in the autobiography. There are personal and political experiences in *Call Me Woman* that cannot be accounted for in terms of the Black Consciousness Movement, with its assumptions of a selfsame and continuous racial identity, nor the more collective notions of subjectivity which Couille identifies. Most particularly, Kuzwayo's account (and reticence) about her experiences as a wife and a mother, and those of black African women more generally, are problematic because these experiences of the sexed body are neither ahistorical nor, primarily, a matter of racial identity. The text works to envisage a wholeness and continuity in terms of Black Consciousness, and yet a more divided and decentred self emerges in the course of the narrative.

Nevertheless, Black Consciousness played a major role in allowing Kuzwayo, and other women such as Mashinini, to shape an authoritative speaking position.[23] Some of the differences it makes are evident if we compare *Call Me Woman* with *Poppie Nongena*. Both take the schoolchildren's uprisings in Soweto in 1976 as a generative moment to present an autobiographic narrator as a maternal figure, yet they achieve very different kinds of strategic presence and authorization, almost mutually exclusive readerships, and they were published in two quite different networks: one through the feminist Women's Press in the United Kingdom in 1985, the other first published in Afrikaans in Cape Town in 1978. The comparison is instructive as a reminder of how *Call Me Woman* addresses the silences of *Poppie Nongena*. Kuzwayo claims outright 'I am the author of this book'; there is no collaborative or obviously fictional artifice here. As a black African woman she is fluent and comfortable in a number of South African languages, but Afrikaans is not one of them, for it is the language of the oppressor. The work of her autobiography is to suture the private life to a public history of women's resistance and activism, it is a life *in* the community. *Poppie Nongena*, on the other hand, preserves the separation between the politics and the family, the public and private worlds. 'Poppie Nongena' is a witness but not an activist; what she sees does not lead to a political consciousness of herself as a woman or an African. Whereas 'Poppie' buries her grandchild who is killed in the Soweto uprising and asks 'For what ... all this for what?', Kuzwayo's women's organizations mourn, and then regroup, renegotiate and extend their networks. It is inconceivable that an Afrikaaner woman could in any way articulate or broker this narrative, or that it would be welcomed by the Afrikaaner intelligentsia in the last decade of apartheid.

Yet the events of that decade were such that the place to speak was constantly shifting and in transformation. Sindiwe Magona, like Kuzwayo, suggests that the events of 1976 produced a 'sieving year'; however, the ideological and discursive registers, and institutional locations, of Magona's activism were rather different to the Black Consciousness sympathies and association with the YWCA in Kuzwayo's resistance. Three organizations shape what Magona calls her intellectual and political awakening to becoming 'truly South African': the South African Committee for Higher Education (SACHED), which campaigned against the effects of the segregation of higher education, is the place where for the first time Magona mixes with people of different classifications: 'Suddenly I was part of a brilliant rainbow, partaking of the wealth of human diversity that is South Africa's' (102). SACHED is a 'melting-pot' where Magona is 'awakened' to the racial identification of South African whites. This continues in Church Women Concerned (CWC), an inclusive organization where white, black and coloured women campaigned together against apartheid to effect reconciliation. Finally as a result of that 'sieving year', she is a foundation member of the Women's Movement, linking the colonization of women in South Africa to experiences of women elsewhere: 'Men made policies the world over. Women suffered consequences' (141). There are intersections between Kuzwayo's and Magona's experiences as African women – each begins her autobiography by representing childhood as a time of wholeness and integrity in the African community. Furthermore, for both Kuzwayo and Magona the stressful and ambiguous experiences of marriage and motherhood in an oppressive state are a precursor to activism, for violence permeates even the most intimate relationships. Their experiences as mother and wife bring to the forefront a questioning of subjectivity and identity. However, in *Forced to Grow* the activist identity, which is shaped from more inclusive and recognizably post-apartheid ways of thinking about what it means to be South African, falls apart. The autobiography is shaped in terms of a series of rebirths, and an ongoing process of growth and enlightenment. Yet for Magona (as for Mamphela Ramphele) this finally requires that the severing of public and private, the shaping of personal voice in terms of

communal and representative expression, be put aside. Magona begins to arrange
to leave South Africa in 1980:

> I had disengaged from organizations working for peaceful change or any
> kind of change ... I drew little consolation from being proved right. The
> violence I had predicted had come, all right. What I had not foreseen was
> its blindness, its lack of discrimination and its openness to exploitation.
> (185)

The grounds of Magona's activism, and her interpretation of anti-apartheid
resistance, are not able to withstand what follows Soweto, for the children
reject what is always for Magona the means of liberation: education.

Poppie Nongena (1978), *Call Me Woman* (1985), *Forced to Grow* (1992) and
Ramphele's *A Life* (1995) were published across the period between the events
of 1976 and the establishment of an ANC government. Sequentially they
indicate that process of deconstructing the apartheid imaginary through
resistance discourses which, in the first instance, immediately after the events
of 1976, focused on the formation of unity on the grounds of black identity.
Later the Congress tradition of non-racialism, where the boundaries of the
apartheid imaginary were crossed, emerged. Apartheid worked by instituting a
system of rigid, fixed identities based on race. However, autobiographical
writing reveals that these identities are fractured and discontinuous, closely
linked to various institutional and ideological locations. The struggle against
apartheid has involved a process of articulating different ways of thinking
about the self in terms of intersections of gendered, racial and classed
identities. These autobiographies suggest what this has meant for one group in
the South African community – black African women. Gillian Slovo's *Every
Secret Thing*, AnnMarie Wolpe's *The Long Way Home*, Helen Suzman's *In No
Uncertain Terms* and Zoë Wicomb's *You Can't Get Lost in Cape Town* present
other perspectives. Autobiographic writing proliferated during this period, and
yet, at the same time, the grounds for creating the self in autobiography were
shifting and turbulent in unprecedented ways. Autobiographic writing was
both necessary and yet impossible in the sense that discourses of truth, identity
and power were in crisis and open conflict. Under these conditions, the work of
stabilizing truth and a subject who may utter it is on display.

Black Australian autobiography

In Australia too, the 1980s was a phase of critical change and realignment in
identity politics. As in South Africa, autobiographic writing by black women

was constitutive in these processes of change, and caught up in its stresses and fractures. In both South Africa and Australia a series of legislative changes *within living memory* (that is, within the reach of contemporary autobiography) produced an ongoing process of government interventions on the basis of race. By 1911 most state governments and the Northern Territory had legislated for state control of indigenous people by establishing either white 'Protectors' or an 'Aborigines Protection Board' to manage indigenous affairs. Land was made available for reserves and missions, and these were managed by local police or government managers, or missionaries. In these institutions indigenous people were subjected to highly restrictive controls and management. As Aileen Moreton-Robinson suggests, this shift in policy from extermination to protection has been associated with the activity of the anti-slavery and humanitarian movements in Britain; however, it was also the case that the shift marked the establishment and dominance of white social structures following the pioneering phase of settlement and frontier wars.[24] From 1940, policies of assimilation, in theory at least seemingly antithetical to apartheid's notion of separate development, organized the management of indigenous populations across Australia:

> Miscegenation was again the catalyst for this new policy because it disrupted racial purity and offered white society a pool of cheap labour. Mothers and children from such unions were usually removed from the indigenous community. Indigenous women's sexuality had to be policed and contained and their children removed from the influence of kin and community.[25]

At the heart of social memory in indigenous women's autobiographical writing is the systemic invasion and destruction of black communities and kinship structures that were licensed by these policies.

In the 1980s, Aboriginal resistance to assimilation had reached a critical point. There was a vigorous Aboriginal intelligentsia with access to mainstream media, and to processes of decision-making at federal and state levels. This was the product of two decades of organized resistance work, during which Aboriginal people developed a sense of common interest and group solidarity and, a critical point, a strategic sense of united identity which subsumed tribal and regional identifications. This Aboriginality became fundamental to the development of an effective counter-discourse, which could challenge the principles of white nationalism. Two features of this Aboriginality need to be stressed: firstly, it is formulated in terms of past Aboriginal culture and in terms of their current placement as a minority group in white Australian society. That is, Aboriginality arises from the intersubjective relationship between black and white Australians: '"Aboriginality" ... [is] a field of subjectivity in that it is remade over and over again in a process of dialogue, of imagination, of representation and interpretation' by successive generations of indigenes and settler/migrants.[26] Secondly, concepts of Aboriginality are increasingly presented as contingent and tactical, responsive to changing political contexts and agendas.[27]

These contingencies are evident in black autobiography. Aboriginal women's autobiographical narrative has been associated with two different processes. To return to Norval's discussion of the deconstruction of apartheid, this is the work of articulation and disarticulation, of identity formation and critique, which is the heart of resistance to colonialism. Autobiographical writing has been fundamental to this process of resistance in Australia and South Africa. Autobiographic narratives by Aboriginal women began to appear in the late 1970s: Monica Clare's *Karobran: The Story of an Aboriginal Girl* (1978), Ella Simon's *Through My Eyes* (1978), Shirley Smith and Bobbi (Roberta) Sykes' *Mum Shirl* (1981) and Elsie Roughsey's *An Aboriginal Mother Tells of the Old and the New* (1984) are representative of this 'first wave'.[28] Two books which came out within a year of each other, Sally Morgan's *My Place* (1987) and Ruby Langford Ginibi's *Don't Take Your Love to Town* (1988), are the most widely read and discussed. Although *My Place* wasn't the first autobiographic narrative it was, in Ruby Langford Ginibi's words, 'the first to open this country up' , an act of 'intercultural brokerage' which for many Australians was their first meaningful picture of contemporary urban Aborigines.[29] As the sheer volume and diversity of this writing in the past decade suggests, it has been at the forefront of cultural work, both within Aboriginal cultures and across the Australian community. The work of 'articulation' here is not singular. The importance of tribal, regional, familial and generational affiliations emerges strongly. The idea of 'the' Aboriginal, fixed and singular, is a fantasy which this writing has superseded, turning to more mobile and plural notions of subjectivity and identity. In fact it is around and about this writing that notions of Aboriginality and racial identity, what Bain Attwood calls the *making* of the Aborigines, have been discussed in public and controversial ways.

As the South African case suggests, effective discursive intervention requires two strategies: articulation and disarticulation. In terms of disarticulation or critique, Australian women's autobiography engaged with Aboriginalism on a number of fronts.[30] Aboriginalism makes Aborigines into an object of knowledge over which European Australians, as the dispensers of truth about their needs and requirements, gain control. This effectively silences Aborigines, disallows Aborigines' self-representation, and is fundamental to colonial structures of power. Yet, as reading these autobiographies and discussions of them make clear, there is no clear discursive break between

'Aboriginalism' and the preferred alternative, a more open-ended and historically sensitive notion of 'Aboriginality'. Moving from 'Aboriginalism' to 'Aboriginality' is notoriously hard to do, and even the indigenous writers' ability to 'vault ethically' over political difficulty is open to question.

Sally Morgan and Ruby Langford Ginibi: the making of Aboriginality

Sally Morgan's *My Place* uses the resources of autobiographical narrative brilliantly to present the *making* of Aboriginality, specifically of an Aboriginal identity which is available to urban Aboriginal Australians of mixed descent, and grounded in cultural and spiritual identification. The autobiographic narrator's own story finally fades into the background to make way for the autobiographical narratives of preceding generations: Arthur, Gladys and Daisy Corunna. One narrative begets the next, one narrator initiates the next, and the making of the text becomes both explicit and in its own way a determining force. Conventions of Western popular fiction – the detective story and quest narratives, where there is a mystery, a destiny and search for 'truth', all of which require resolution – ensures that *My Place* appeals to a wide popular readership. By focalizing these issues through the child in the first instance, the text is seductive. It also allows for the projection of an Aboriginal identity which is apparent through inexplicable intuitive and spiritual events and cultural difference unmediated by an adult consciousness. For example, the way the child draws, perceives nature, and feels threatened by institutional spaces such as the school, the hospital and the orphanage are all 'signs'. The naiveté of the autobiographic narrator, her constant questioning, is an important part of the narrative technique, suggesting a growing sense of difference and 'the feeling that a very vital part of me was missing and that I'd never belong anywhere'.[31] The narrator is a university student and married before her mother, 'without thinking', confirms that 'We're Aboriginal' and so gives her 'a new heritage' and 'a beginning'. Shortly afterwards the project of writing a book about the family history, 'My Place', begins. Two processes are involved in this: solving the mystery of what happened in the past, and reading this past in terms of a politics of identity.

Why did this autobiography open up the country of identity politics and Aboriginality? This is due in part to timing: the book was published immediately prior to the Bicentennial, a time when Australians were encouraged to focus on their personal, communal and national histories. In addition, the address of this autobiography is designed to accommodate the foreign reader. *My Place* allows quite specific questions about Aboriginality to be voiced by the 'naive' narrator:

What did it mean to be Aboriginal? I'd never lived off the land and been a hunter and gatherer. I'd never participated in corroborees or heard stories of the Dreamtime. I'd lived all my life in suburbia and told everyone I was Indian. I hardly knew any Aboriginal people. What did it mean for someone like me? (141)

These questions are produced by the phenomenon of an urbanized mixed-race Aboriginal population which swelled as a result of assimilation. They were also acutely relevant to black and white Australians at a time of national reckoning and the 'celebration of a nation' organized around the Bicentennial in 1988. *My Place* both raises these questions and suggests an answer through the writing of the family history. Autobiography is presented as an authentic mode for the recording of 'talkin' history'. As the narrator begins library-based research into Aboriginal affairs and records the stories of Arthur and Gladys, her relationship to the implied reader changes to a more didactic, authoritative tone. The trip north, to Corunna Downs, concludes the quest trope of the narrative; here the narrator finds completion as they are 'owned' by the Aboriginals remaining on the land: 'What had begun as a tentative search for knowledge had grown into a spiritual and emotional pilgrimage. We had an Aboriginal consciousness now, and were proud of it' (233). *My Place* unseated long-held notions that wholeness and authenticity in Aboriginal identity reside in colour, 'blood' and physical characteristics. It has replaced these with more contemporary and flexible notions of identification, and an autobiographical enactment of Aboriginal heritage as a spiritual tie with the land, which passes on, undiminished, through generations. *My Place* opened up debates about Aboriginality, and deconstructed Aboriginalist discourses. It stands as the most accessible and familiar 'making' or 'articulation' of Aboriginality for non-Aboriginal Australians, and much of this is due, as I have suggested above, to its use of the technologies of autobiography to generate truth and authority for Sally Morgan's autobiographic narrator.

The ongoing sales of the book, now fuelled by its status as a classic text for secondary and tertiary curricula, and the publication of pictorial and easy-to-read versions, suggests an 'ease of acceptance' which has made critics like Stephen Muecke, Bain Attwood, Jackie Huggins and others uneasy.[32] As we saw in reading across a series of South African autobiographies, we need not turn to critical writing to look for different perspectives. We can do this by making connections to different autobiographical texts. This is easily done in the case of *My Place* because two quite different presentations of Aboriginality in autobiography were published within the year: Ruby Langford Ginibi's *Don't Take Your Love to Town* and Glenyse Ward's *Wandering Girl*. Neither Langford Ginibi nor Ward has ever been in any doubt as to her Aboriginality;

'passing' has not been an option for them, and there is no explicit process of making Aboriginal identity through the process of autobiographic writing such as we find in *My Place*. In fact, Langford Ginibi's autobiographic narrator turns aside from any apocalyptic expressions of Aboriginality, for example, on her visit to Uluru, near the end of the book. This is not to say that the book rejects spiritual affirmations of Aboriginality; the narrator remains 'connected' to the land of the Bundjalung people, and yet as an urban Aboriginal of mixed descent, identity is presented as syncretic rather than authentic. The writing of her autobiography is considered within the text itself, but this is in order to problematize notions of Aboriginality rather than to make them accessible to a non-Aboriginal readership. *Don't Take Your Love to Town* has outraged white middle-class notions of morality and propriety, and yet on the other hand the narrator points out that 'plenty of people lived like that, poor whites as well as blacks'.[33] There is a more complex sense of community at work here, organized not just in terms of race but through intersections of classed, gendered and racial experience.

Whereas *My Place* presents autobiography as part of a process of liberation, *Don't Take Your Love to Town* presents more complex negotiations and intersubjectivity. As Tim Rowse has pointed out, there is a comfortable position for the non-Aboriginal reader in Morgan's text, where life is ultimately seen in terms of an intelligible pattern that is understood by the narrating subject. Langford Ginibi's character, on the other hand, is much more complex, frustrated by her attraction to weak men, battling against obesity, often unable to understand her motivations and sometimes expressing grief through violence and drink. The autobiographic narrator cannot shape this life in terms of a growth towards prosperity or enlightenment, and cyclical rather than lineal patterns shape the narrative:

> We have to work harder to see the coherence of Langford's book than we do to get what Sally Morgan has to show us, and the effort delivers a more innovative and uncomfortable knowledge of the gendered contingencies of Koori experience.[34]

In both Australian and South African contemporary writing there have been clear thresholds where black women negotiated the authority to speak autobiographically. Who they were speaking *to* is of critical importance. Autobiographic narratives have staged in the most compelling and diverse fashion new ways of thinking about black and indigenous identity, presenting various constructions of the racial and gendered self. Autobiographic narratives like *My Place* and *Call Me Woman* draw on the technologies of autobiography to make claims to truth, wholeness and authenticity at a historical moment when deeply personal and individual histories of racism and resistance do important ideological work. On the other hand, *Forced to Grow* and *Don't Take Your Love To Town* present more opaque and conflicted versions of the autobiographic self, turning aside from liberatory rhetoric and authentic racial identity. The strategic importance of autobiographic writing is evident, for it is a way of reclaiming history, and presenting hitherto 'invisible' histories of oppression and poverty. It is also a means whereby different discourses of race, gender and identity – black and white – are characterized and circulated. However, in contemporary autobiography, as in the past, black women become autobiographic subjects through contextual inter-racial relations which are negotiated in and around the text, and which must be engaged with in the process of critical reading.

Black writers/white readers

These autobiographies circulate through and around a series of different constituencies and interests. Although we know little of the reading practices of African and Aboriginal women, it is evident that these autobiographic narrations are influential in their communities, not only because they narrate experiences which are often shared, but also because the act of writing and publication is in itself significant.[35] These autobiographies have didactic power. Rita Huggins tells her daughter to make the story of her life accessible to her family and the Aboriginal community: 'This means no big words, little (conscious) politics and my story.'[36] Yet, as black women's autobiography emerged in Australia and South Africa in the 1980s, the presence of the 'foreign' reader is omnipresent.

Some critics suggest these should not be labelled 'autobiography' at all, for they do not present the self in terms of the classic autobiographic narrative of individualism. As we have seen in earlier chapters, the 'classic' autobiography is derived from a Euroamerican canon that has strict racial, classed and gendered boundaries. The traditional notions of autobiography are grounded in the idea of the single authoritative life being defined in and through the text, written in splendid isolation and eloquence by the autobiographer him/herself. This is, of course, almost always an illusion. Most Western literary (and other) autobiographies are the products of extensive editorial work. The illusion is not sustainable at all in the postcolonial domain. In particular, as we saw in the case of Mary Prince, inter-racial collaboration is frequently constitutive of black women's autobiographical writing, and this transforms the politics of production and consumption. To label these in terms of variants of autobiography – such as 'life writing', 'life history writing', 'slave narrative', 'testimony' – is useful to the extent that it introduces cultural and historical specificity. It is risky to the extent that it reinforces the xenophobia in the uses of the term 'autobiography'. Leigh Gilmore's use of the term 'autobiographic' is helpful here in that it steps aside from terminal questions of genre and delimitation in thinking about autobiography and looks to autobiographics, 'those changing elements in the contradictory discourses of truth and identity which represent the subject of autobiography'. This sets up a different set of questions: Where is the autobiographical? What constitutes its representation? In what cultural institutions and forms does self-representation occur?[37] Given the technologies of postcolonial women's autobiography, this shift in emphasis is a useful strategy.

The issue of where and how black and white women might meet in the production and reception of autobiographic writing remains an issue. We are back at that 'traffic jam', the 'critical intersection' which occurs around and about *The History of Mary Prince* in Chapter 1. But not quite. For both the subjects and the collaborators in contemporary work install traffic-lights – or 'robots' – to direct the flow of reading to some extent. For example, a number of the autobiographers bring the production of the text into view, as we have seen in discussion of *The History of Mary Prince* and *The Wonderful Adventures of Mrs. Seacole* in earlier chapters. This is sometimes in the form of an outright claim to authorship. For example, Ellen Kuzwayo dramatizes the writing self: 'As I write this chapter in 1983, I am sitting in full view of the Atlantic Ocean, at a point where I can raise my eyes and catch a glimpse of Robben Island' (198). Kuzwayo acknowledges the role of the editor and the Women's Press in bringing the book to completion, but this makes it no less her autobiography. Likewise, Emma Mashinini clearly establishes the production work in Britain, and the work with an editor who 'lovingly nurtured' the text following Mashinini's completion of a final draft:

> I finished writing my final chapter today at 5am. The radio was playing Frank Sinatra singing 'Come Fly With Me', and for that moment I remembered my youthful optimism and excitement, and my romantic expectations of the future, and my spirit soared. I close the manuscript with a surge of elation, hope and happiness. (xvi)

Mashinini acknowledges 'without embarrassment' that she is a speaker, not a writer, that language differences and her level of education have made her 'hastily scribbled thoughts' difficult for an editor to understand, yet this remains her autobiography.

Both Ruby Langford Ginibi's *Don't Take Your Love to Town* and Sally Morgan's *My Place* are extensively edited – Langford Ginibi shared copyright with her collaborator Susan Hampton. This has led to criticisms that as a result they lack legitimacy and authenticity, and yet in both instances the writing of the text is openly embraced as part of a process of 'making' Aboriginality.[38] There is nothing covert about this. In fact in each case the autobiography becomes self-referential. For example, Langford points out:

> I was working with my editor on rewrites of the book, and keeping my eyes open for anything related to Kooris and writing. I'd read Charles Perkins' autobiography *A Bastard Like Me*, and James Miller's *Koori, a Will to Win*. Now I read Mum Shirl's biography, a book by Margaret Tucker called *If Everyone Cared*, and then *My Place*, by Sally Morgan. (259)

Langford Ginibi's autobiography is richly intertextual: the title is from a Kenny Rogers song, she has a Land Rights poster next to her typewriter and sings along to Peggy Lee. Authorship becomes explicit: the autobiographic narrator becomes aware of language as 'a glass door we walked into BANG all the time' (231). She muses openly about cliché – how can she describe Uluru? She begins to think of herself as a writer and to understand her own experiences in terms of the larger debates about Aboriginal identity and rights as they emerged in the 1980s, for example, the deaths in custody campaigns. Most importantly, the narrator's growing sense of herself as a writer supersedes her sense of herself as first and foremost a mother. Yet there is no pristine or authentic identity, indigenous or otherwise, as a point of arrival in the autobiography. How could there be for an urban Aboriginal of mixed descent? This is nowhere more evident than in her trip to Uluru towards the end of the autobiography. This is not a liberatory moment; on the contrary, it is embedded in text. Her movements around Uluru are choreographed and recorded by a film crew as she returns home: 'I was writing up my notes for this book, and I wished at that moment I'd been born fullblood instead of the degree of caste that I was' (236). In fact Langford Ginibi lives in an urban half-black half-white world; the role of the editor is merely one of a series of indications within the text of a self-conscious negotiation of meanings among texts of all kinds.

Moments when the construction of the autobiography through inter-racial collaboration is brought into view are strategic. They are not an escape from textuality into truth, as I have argued in preceding chapters.[39] Rather it is a point where the stage lights come up, and the apparatus around the production of the autobiographic self are brought into view. The editor, author, implied readers, autobiographic subject or narrators emerge, however briefly, to foreground textuality and difference. This reminds us that the text is not a place where the desire to speak is liberated unconditionally, but rather a site of multiple constraints and negotiations of meaning, where there is room to manoeuvre, for oppositionality to arise, and change to occur. Too often the assumption is made that speaking in terms of subjectivity and constraints denies 'the other' a place to speak. In fact, the opposite is the case. It should not surprise us that the writings by people who are violently and forcibly 'othered' in an oppressive society will most readily encourage a reconsideration of the literary and social conventions of selfhood within which autobiographers are expected to work.[40] The humanist notion of authentic singular subjectivity is no less oppressive to 'others' than the poststructuralist preoccupation with discursive complexities and negotiations.

Foregrounding collaboration and the making of identities is to bring into view processes which colonialist thinking obscures. For example, Shula Marks' biographical project *Not Either an Experimental Doll: The Separate Worlds of Three South African Women*, while not a biography in any conventional sense, takes full advantage of the fragmentary and dispersed nature of the correspondence between Lily Moya, a young Xhosa schoolgirl, Mabel Palmer, a 'liberal' British expatriate working at the University of Natal, and Subusisiwe Makhanya, one of the first Black social workers in South Africa, to create a biographic narrative which explores inter-racial collaborations in Natal between 1949 and 1951. Marks' precise study of how each of these women understood racial and sexual identifications in terms of such different registers as Makhanya's ethnic, cultural nationalism, Moya's Christian Xhosa upbringing in the Eastern Cape, and Palmer's Fabianism and feminism is a brilliant analysis of the 'delicate chemistry' of individual psychology, social context and historical process. It is also a very explicit analysis of the problems of collaborative work, for Lily Moya's final letter to Mabel Palmer from Sophiatown in 1951 is a sharp reminder of her autonomy and resistance: 'I was never meant to be a stone but a human being with feelings, not either an experimental doll.'[41] This is as much a problem for Marks in 1981 as it was for Palmer in 1951, for Marks is a foreigner telling Lily Moya's story: 'was I after all another Mabel Palmer, a "misguided do-gooder"?' (196).

There is always the danger that black women will emerge from collaborative inter-racial work as 'the experimental doll'. The origins of the Aboriginal and African life story are not in literature or history but in social anthropology, a discipline which frequently erased indigenous women's experiences of colonization and its impact on their subjectivity.[42] Although feminism led to a deepening interest in African and indigenous women in the 1980s, it did not necessarily promote the self-reflective sense of race-privilege or position we find in Marks' work. Jackie Huggins' methodology in her mother's biography, published in 1994 as *Auntie Rita*, pursues intra-racial mutual articulation in a 'mothering/daughtering tongue'. Huggins draws on matriarchy and the power of listening to the mother's voice, a connection made through blood and bone:

> I remember all of my mother's stories, probably much better than she realises ... I too have lived through every one of those feelings as she relates them to me ... It goes without saying that by virtue of being Rita's daughter (and a close one at that), I possess many of her experiences.[43]

Inter-racial collaboration is, in Huggins' view, contaminated by the investigations, surveillance and intrusions which were characteristic of the period of 'protection' and 'assimilation'; it remains caught in the force field of colonial relations.

White women are also scripted as racial subjects in this field. As we have seen in earlier chapters, readers are not incidental. In its first (and subsequent) publications the autobiography must manoeuvre to capture this foreigner. These readers are not disembodied, but are pulled into the narrative in an intimate way and required to think through their own racialized sense of self. Margaret Somerville characterizes her role as a 'white ghost' in the production of *Ingelba and the Five Black Matriarchs*. This 'life (hi)story' as a hybrid form was developed in collaboration between Somerville and an Aboriginal woman, Patsy Cohen:

> Hers is the Aboriginal story, the story of her life and the place and the people that go to making her sense of that life. Mine is the process of constructing a written text ... I feel it is important not to create another silence for women and that white women need to address the issues involved in this sort of work; to own that particular input into such endeavours.[44]

The way Somerville attempts to 'own' her part in this text is deeply problematic, and foregrounds two issues: firstly, the use of feminist methodologies in working across racial boundaries; secondly, how Australian settler women might pursue their own racial and gendered identities in biographic writing. Feminist methodology and commitment drive Somerville's sense that she is engaged in a deconstructive project from which new narratives and new forms will be created, enabling 'us' to 're-evaluate the telling of all our lives'. In this sense the stories of 'Patsy' and 'Margaret' are produced in a collaborative relationship, where two selves interact. Given that these 'two selves' are an Aboriginal and a settler woman, Somerville's sense that the interaction is essential to both identities is potentially a radical one.

However, the use of feminist methodology here constructs a bridge which takes Somerville home free, across the chasm of race and colonial relations.

How can Australian settler women 'own' a place here? Somerville's work with Aboriginal women makes her profoundly aware of her own alienation in the Australian landscape, and so her need of collaboration grows from her sense that 'I could only achieve a sense of belonging through my relationship with Aboriginal women' (97). Again this is potentially radical, and yet Somerville continues to elide gender and race:

> The problem of subjectivity is compounded for *Australian* women where there is a special and added meaning to the fact that 'patriarchal discourse situates women outside representation as absence, negativity, the dark continent, or at best a lesser man' (Smith 1987, 76). The dark continent is doubly dark because of our relationship with its original inhabitants and the complex silences that we have to overcome. This is again resonant of my original question about myself in the Australian landscape, a question that cannot be addressed in any immediate and direct sense. A beginning to approaching this question was made in creating separate but interdependent voices for Patsy and myself through our collaboration. (107; my emphasis)

Patsy Cohen is doubly silenced here: firstly, in Somerville's creation of her voice in the text; secondly, in the assumption that the category 'Australian' women does not include indigenous women. Clearly the colonial power relations between black and white women and men in Australia are not suspended in 'life (hi)story writing'. Somerville's argument that it 'was easier to overcome the silences imposed by the written form in the case of finding a voice for Patsy than it was in finding a voice for myself' is the dilemma of a 'white ghost'. Her project illustrates precisely why moving from 'Aboriginalism' to 'Aboriginality' is notoriously hard to do; the place of 'foreign agents' remains contentious. It is incumbent upon white ghosts to be uneasy in their skins.

Bodiless women

The opportunities and constraints which autobiographic narrative offers black women are apparent now, as they were in very different circumstances in the production of *The History of Mary Prince* a long time ago. As the preceding discussion of 'thresholds' and 'foreign agents' demonstrates, these autobiographic texts are all negotiation and compromise, caught in the tangles of representation and referentiality that involve writer, reader and those in between. For black women autobiographers it was ever thus. And so too for 'white ghosts'.

Autobiography is a poor tool for the task of representing the experiences of contemporary African and Aboriginal women in the aftermath of colonialism – at least to the extent that it seems to offer access to liberation, autonomy and interpretations of experience in terms of truth, wholeness and authenticity. Hence Ruby Langford Ginibi's rhetorical question: What is autobiography compared to a dreaming track? And yet autobiographic writing can offer black women access to authoritative discourses and to a public that, in certain times and in certain places, allows their histories to perform important political work and to engage with social change. So it was with Mary Prince, and so it has been at a time in South Africa and Australia when the effects of colonization on the African and indigenous populations has been brought to light with unprecedented force. In both places the current politics of reconciliation works to bring the nation into contact with the demons of its past in what is beginning to unfold in each place as a precarious and different phase of decolonization.

The question of what 'white ghosts' do – as editors, readers, critics, teachers – with black women's autobiographies is an important one. This is not for one moment to displace the work of readers and critics who read these autobiographies as black women with the capacity to identify. The readings enabled by this intra-racial relation are also subject to debate, and a number of critics address this specifically and imaginatively.[45] For Mary Prince, Mary Seacole and, more recently, Ruby Langford Ginibi, Ellen Kuzwayo, Sindiwe Magona and others, the autobiography must both cross and reveal the boundaries of race. They must engage readers with whom they do not identify, and who may not in the first instance recognize and take responsibility for their own implication in colonialism's culture, given the transparency of whiteness as a racial identity. From its initial point of presentation, in *The History of Mary Prince*, the work of inter-racial politics around black women's autobiography has been fundamental to thinking about 'the intimate empire'. I have argued that this 'intimacy' can only be understood in terms of quite precise understandings of institutional and historical locations. This argument has frequently drawn on the idea of performance in and around the text, which is useful as a way of stressing the shifting qualities of discourses, embodiments and subjectivity. It also suggests a way of stepping outside of readings, of performing different scripts quite self-consciously. Given that the discussions in this chapter are 'close to home', and involve inter-racial criticism which is problematized in the script of the 'white ghost', I want to look at several different ways of 'performing' a conclusion to the comparative work of this chapter. This is in order to critically reflect on methodology and pedagogy, ethics and subjectivity, in inter-racial reading, criticism and teaching about black women's autobiography.

The issue here is how a comparative reading connects these texts to contexts and to each other. Ethico-formalist readings, the mode of much postcolonial and feminist criticism, use discourse analysis to create a relationship between text, culture and society and – in the instance of postcolonial criticism – colonialism's culture. In this way, the aesthetics of the text are linked to social context. In what follows, this method will be used to read across a number of the autobiographies which have featured in this chapter, using the figure of 'The bodiless woman'.

The image of 'the bodiless woman' comes from Ruby Langford Ginibi's *Don't Take Your Love to Town*. It is in fact the title of the chapter where she begins dating Sam and which concludes, 'I realised I was pregnant but I didn't know the facts of life' (54). Earlier in the chapter, Ruby and her friend Gwen go to the Royal Easter Show in Sydney. There they see the bodiless woman – alone, in an empty tent. Ruby speaks to the head displayed on a box: 'The head smiled. I couldn't see how her body could have fitted into the little box under the cushion, but I didn't dare ask where the body was' (50). Later Ruby will look at her own body after surgery to cut thirteen kilos of fat from her belly: 'I looked like I'd been sliced in half, and I thought of the Bodiless Woman at the sideshow ... I lay on the bed wishing I could send my spirit somewhere so my body could heal' (264). The problem of making connections between the body and the spirit, the body and the mind, and different desires and needs – sexual, spiritual, intellectual, emotional – recurs throughout *Don't Take Your Love to Town*, although not in the confessional, introspective soul-searching fashion of Western autobiography. Langford Ginibi's autobiographic narrator does not attribute this kind of plenitude and consistency to the autobiographic 'I', and it is the act of writing which links relationships, employment and habitations in a series which is chronological but not necessarily logical and certainly not linked to knowledge, reason and volition. The idea of her body as alien is recurrent:

This town was a Mecca of civilisation to me, look, here was a dress shop – I went right in. I needed a new dress. Halfway into the shop I saw myself in the long mirror, close up. Here was a pregnant woman with blistered hands like a man's, her face peeling like flaky pastry and black, she started black, but her arms were BLACK and the hair ginger. I stared at myself for a long time. (93)

In this disembodiment the narrator's body confuses male/female, human/object and black/BLACK; it bears marks of her class, race and gender, but all confused, and she is unknown and unknowable to herself. In *Don't Take Your Love to Town* the body does not anchor gendered and sexual identity and self-consciousness in any stable or consistent way; rather it becomes symptomatic of dislocation and disorientation, unavailable to a rhetoric of liberation. As we have seen, Langford's autobiography at several points explicitly rejects epiphanic or authentic experiences of Aboriginality.

Versions of the bodiless woman recur in these autobiographies, one way and another, to signal difficulties in placing the body in the autobiographic text in any stable or consistent way. For example, in the discursive repertoire of *Call Me Woman*, as we have seen, Ellen Kuzwayo is unable to express the trauma of her experiences as an abused wife and her separation from her sons in Rustenburg. Although she suggests the writing of the autobiography is therapeutic, Kuzwayo's own intimate experiences as a daughter, wife and mother remain unaddressed: 'Even now I find I cannot write in detail about it' (124). Kuzwayo's silence could be read as strategic, but she apparently desires to speak. Here her experiences of family breakdown as a daughter and then as a wife cannot be understood in terms of racial oppression in the first instance; a more nuanced and gendered explanation in terms of race and masculinity is required, and yet this is not available to her. In *My Place* an autobiographic subject might be seen to withhold personal details as a gesture of power – the refusal of Daisy Corunna to confirm the truth about her own likely experience of miscegenation and incest as daughter and mother in *My Place* can be understood positively in this way. Even so, Daisy Corunna's long-held suspicion of institutions – the school, the hospital – is confirmed as her body is made an object, stripped, probed and analysed without her consent, for the knowledge of young white male doctors before she is allowed to leave.

In Mamphela Ramphele's *A Life* there is also a struggle to come to terms with a tremulous and private female body. Ramphele's autobiography is one of the rare examples where sexual pleasure is a part of the presentation of self. For Ruby Langford and Sindiwe Magona sexual activity is registered, autobiographically at least, only in consequences – when it results in pregnancy. Ramphele, on the other hand, presents sexual desire and sexual desirability as closely linked to her Black Consciousness activism and liberation:

At the University of Natal the circle of friends centred on Steve Biko coalesced into a tight-knit community as the activism intensified. I was drawn closer into this circle and began to adopt some of the behaviour of the group ... The 'black is beautiful' slogan of the time had its desired impact on all of us. Some of us switched over to the use of our African names instead of the 'slave names' we had hitherto used. I also became more daring in my outfits, taking advantage of my figure and the fashion trends of the time ... hotpants became my specialty. Hot pants were exceedingly short pants which fitted snugly around one's body, hovering tantalisingly around the limits of modesty. (57–58)

This accords with Driver's remark that Black Consciousness thinking highlights racial and gendered difference in its rhetoric of liberation. On the other hand, for Ramphele pregnancy, birth and motherhood are more difficult to accommodate into her self-portrait as a transgressor. She uses a Sesotho saying, *tswala e bolaile tsie* (birth has killed a locust) to refer to the indignity and humiliation of birth as she experienced it, the 'necessarily sacrificial action to give birth to children and to raise them' and, later, the tension between the demands of political activism and parenting. Her response to the release of Nelson Mandela in 1990 is a 'serious metaphorical post-natal depression'. Liberated psychologically by black consciousness, Ramphele is throughout her narration subject to the frail and fragile female body, which houses the transgressive 'I'.

The trope of the bodiless woman can be read as a figure where personal and collective histories connect in these autobiographies. At the heart of apartheid and assimilation was the surveillance and management of the sexuality and reproduction of black women:

And remember, at the same that the government was encouraging us to curb our wombs, our black wombs, the same government stepped up its immigration recruitment drive. The people who were being lured here had to have one criterion, and one only. They had to be white.[46]

There is one narrative thread which strings together these African and Australian autobiographies: the loss of traditional formulations of what it means to be a black woman – mother, daughter and wife – in the space of little more than a generation. The symptoms of this are abundant: absent and estranged husbands and impotent fathers; stolen children; death due to disease, violence and poverty; communities of women in abject poverty in townships, reserves, locations, homelands, suburbs and missions. These grow from the destruction of indigenous kinship structures which was a planned outcome of settler colonialism in Australia and South Africa, the results of twentieth-century race-based legislation such as the Aborigines Protection Acts, the Group Areas Act, the Bantu Authorities Act, among others. At the centre of these autobiographies is the need to reconstruct black womanhood, to reformulate mothering and domestic life, masculinity and femininity in new urban circumstances.

This is the work of imagining what Nadine Gordimer in her Preface to *Call Me Woman* calls 'the wholeness of the transitional woman'. This 'wholeness' in transition is, as we have seen, a contradiction in terms, a wish for an authentic, independent subject free of the text that cannot be met. As I argued earlier, the strategies of decolonization in autobiographical writing are most likely to occur in terms of recognition of multiple identification, and the explicit making and unravelling of identities. Neither the truthful informant of traditional anthropological enquiry, nor the authentic female body of some Western feminist discourses, nor the idealized mother of nationalist and Africanist discourses will serve in these circumstances. These 'transitional' subjects reveal and conceal, give and withhold her identity and body. This is necessarily so, given the particular operations of apartheid and assimilation on the familial and sexed bodies of black women. Whereas in a stable society gender constitutes the invisible, seamless wrapping of the self, binding sexual and social identity, in unstable social conditions these bindings fall apart.[47] The connections between femininity and the body, subjectivity and experience, and writing and memory are not in place:

> Suddenly, I felt that even memory would be impossible if I did not turn my attention to the violence very close at hand, attendant, in fact, upon the procedures of my own writing. This awareness fused with the need to voice the truths of the female body, precisely that which had been torn away, cast out from the linguistic awareness I had refined.[48]

Reading 'the bodiless woman' produces familiar feminist and postcolonial figures at two levels: on the one hand, 'black bodies' emerge as transitional, transgressive, hybrid subjects and, on the other, the 'white ghost' operates as the postcolonial and feminist reader. To review this reading critically is, to some extent, to be rendered 'uneasy in my skin'. This defamiliarizes a speaking position and reading strategy. One set of problems raised by this reading goes back to the scene where Mary Prince's body was 'read' by disembodied white women, read for truth. In this case the black body is read not in terms of truth and authenticity but, on the contrary, in terms of the volatile bodies and intersubjectivity of recent feminist theory drawing on the thinking of, for example, Denise Riley and Teresa de Lauretis. Here the authentic body is displaced by a sense of the complications between experiences, identities and subjectivity. Identity is seen as multiple, shifting and contradictory, made up of heterogeneous and heteronomous representations of gender, race and class.[49] And yet, as Jackie Huggins suggests, colonialism contaminates inter-racial writing and reading. This is no less the case when volatility replaces truth and discontinuity displaces wholeness as the markings on black women's bodies and texts.

How can autobiographies and critical work on autobiography function to emancipatory effect?

[P]ostcolonial criticism can be a significant mode of self-fashioning and work on texts, of self-knowledge (a way of knowing the self as an effect of certain techniques of reading): it produces new readings and new readers ... [however] it is in danger of repeating that over-generalisation and over-estimation of the realm of (literary) culture which is constitutive of the rise of English as a discipline. It is even in danger, in spite of everything it knows, of mistaking the text for the culture and the culture for the society in a series of oversimplified homologies.[50]

Autobiographic writing is not quite 'literary', and so its critics can be insulated from some of the excesses which Carter describes. As we have seen throughout this book, one way and another we are so often reminded of, if not directed to, the operations of history and institutions of textual production in autobiographic writing. Yet the point remains that readings which locate volatile bodies and transitional subjects in texts and connect them to larger social and historical contexts, such as processes of colonization and emancipation, are in danger of being 'really useless knowledge'. As Carter suggests, we need to know something about the production and consumption of the texts, the circulation of literary and critical discourses in postcolonial societies, and their colonizing and decolonizing effects. Rosemary Jolly makes a similar point about postcolonial discourses in post-apartheid South Africa: 'Resistance ... is not a quality inherent in a cultural product but rather an effect of the process of the product's creation and reception.'[51] We need to add to this the ways that texts circulate and, subject to manoeuvre, re-emerge with oppositional potential for different readerships.

To return to 'The bodiless woman' with these two sets of problems in mind, this reading has been a performance where the reader remains transparent, where the bindings of her own identity remain intact and hidden from view. This is the invisible racialized subject position which is almost always available as a choice to the 'white ghost', and from which she is likely to perceive black bodies as other than herself. What must occur here is an equivalent of those moments when the autobiographers turn on the lights to reveal the staging of their performance. For white ghosts, this taking responsibility is difficult to do: How and what is to be done?

Recently, both the Truth and Reconciliation process in South Africa and the 'Bringing Them Home' report in Australia have surrounded Australians and South Africans with testimony about the worst excesses of apartheid and assimilation. The question of what are appropriate responses hangs in the balance here. Guilt? Emotion? Confession? Responsibility? Apology? For literary intellectuals working in institutions of liberal education, the links between everyday practice and all that surrounds Doomadgee and Soweto are easily obscured, especially given that 'literary intellectuals' with institutional power in both Australia and South Africa are a racially homogenous fragment.

Annamaria Carusi has pointed out that grassroots activists in townships do not need Foucault to explain strategies and counter-strategies of power, or that no one is without power, but academics working in tertiary institutions perhaps do. For Carusi, like Carter, the usefulness of a discipline lies in its knowledge of the institutions in (and with) which it works, and in its willingness to assume the power that goes with it.[52] The intimate empire extends into the politics of everyday life and institutional work in quite fundamental and practical ways: what is taught and said, how, and to whom in the classroom, convention and the scholarly article. Anti-racist practice in these domains will mean not just an intellectual engagement and compassion, but an understanding of the intimacies of racism as part of our subjectivity. Aileen Moreton-Robinson's discussion of the work of white female academics in Australian universities reveals that, although we frequently position ourselves as classed and gendered subjects, white women are rarely represented to themselves as white. Nor is there widespread awareness of how whiteness shapes the theory and practice of their academic work.[53] White women are rarely made to feel uncomfortable in their skins. Here again, we find 'the bodiless woman', a head on a box in a circus.

This is to intimate that autobiographical work of various kinds needs to go on in the study of decolonization in Australia and South Africa. At several points in this chapter I have suggested that the threshold which enabled these autobiographies may have changed. This is, in part, to look to the quite different dynamics between autobiographic expression in the form of testimony and the officially sanctioned processes of reconciliation which have been set up around the Truth and Reconciliation Commission and the 'Bringing Them Home' Inquiry. The Land Rights debates around Mabo and Wik in Australia, a new Constitution in South Africa and debates about republicanism and constitutional change in Australia, changes of government in Australia and South Africa and the work of these Commissions are part of a different moment in the politics — social, cultural and intellectual — of these postcolonial nations. Sarah Nuttall argues that autobiographical narratives written in response to the new, more inclusive political moment in South Africa reveal the pressure to tell a 'redemptive' story. For example, one typical mode of autobiographical writing at the moment is to write life stories that proclaim one's liberation from the bonds of the past — Nuttall reads Ramphele's *A Life* in this way.[54] Earlier autobiographic writings, associated with the struggle against apartheid, move towards death or exile, for example, Sindiwe Magona's *Forced to Grow*, or to commitment to a cause, such as *Call Me Woman*. This raises the issue of *how* autobiography connects to social and political contexts. Thus, for example, the silence about the body and the most intimate experiences of violence and loss which haunt black women's autobiographies in the period *before* the politics of reconciliation in Australia and South Africa is in some ways addressed in the genre of the testimony which surrounds us now. This genre is characteristically an expression of violence upon the body, and many of the testimonies before the Truth and Reconciliation Commission and the 'Bringing Them Home' Inquiry reveal intimate, painful histories of this kind, spoken by both women and men.[55]

Reconciliation is a policy which sets out to bring the nation into contact with the ghosts of its past, restructuring the nation's sense of itself by returning the grim truths of apartheid and invasion to the story of South Africa and Australia's being-in-the-world. In both cases these ghosts set a whole range of things into motion.[56] New modes and styles of authority, truth and choice are among these for all South African and Australian subjects who remain at a conjuncture where there is intense self-consciousness, collectively and individually, about subjectivity and identity in the wake of colonialism: 'To worry or to smile, such is the choice when we are assailed by the strange; our decision depends on how familiar we are with our own ghosts.'[57]

Notes

1   Felicity Nussbaum, 'Autobiography and postcolonialism', *Current Writing: Text and Reception in Southern Africa*, 3 (October 1991): 24–30.

2   Ruby Langford Ginibi, *Don't Take Your Love to Town*. Ringwood, Victoria: Penguin Books, 1998, p. 255. Further references to this edition in text.

3   Mamphela Ramphele, *Mamphela Ramphele: A Life*. Cape Town: David Philips, 1995, p. 194. Further references to this edition in text.

4   *The Courier Mail*, 5 December 1998, pp. 1, 4. In supporting Yanner, Hlumelo Biko is legitimating a radical separatist activism which stands apart from the politics of reconciliation accepted by other Aboriginal leaders, or senior members of the ANC government, to the extent that they comment upon Australian indigenous politics.

5   Kate Llewellyn, *Gorillas, Tea and Coffee: An African Sketchbook*. Hawthorn, Victoria: Hudson, 1996.

6   Homi K. Bhabha, *The Location of Culture*, p. 25. Jackie Huggins prefers to think in terms of juxtaposition rather than translation, suggesting that translation can be detrimental to the integrity of one or the other historical tradition, or both. Jackie Huggins, *Sister Girl*. St Lucia: University of Queensland Press, 1998, p. 100.

7   Elspeth Probyn, *Sexing the Self: Gendered Positions in Cultural Studies*. London: Routledge, 1993, p. 1.

8   'A "white-souled state": across the "South" with Lady Barker', in Kate Darian-Smith *et al.* (eds), *Text, Theory, Space: Land, Literature and History in South Africa and Australia*. London: Routledge, 1996, pp. 65–82.

9   Robert R. Wilson, 'Seeing with a fly's eye: comparative perspectives in Commonwealth literature', *Open Letter*, 8th Series, 2 (winter 1992): 23. Wilson is reviewing Russell McDougall and Gillian Whitlock (eds), *Australian/Canadian Literatures in English: Comparative Perspectives* (Sydney: Methuen, 1987) and discusses a series of approaches to postcolonial writing.

10 For debates about the strengths and weaknesses of relating Australia and South Africa as settler colonies, see Rosemary Jolly, 'Rehearsals of liberation: contemporary postcolonial discourse and the New South Africa', *PMLA*, 110 (1995): 17–29; Bill Ashcroft *et al.*, *The Empire Writes Back: Theory and Practice in Post-Colonial Literatures*. London: Routledge, 1989; Christy Collis, 'Siting the second world in South African literary culture', *New Literatures Review*, 27 (summer 1995): 1–15.

11 See e.g. *The Australian*, 21 October 1998; *The Weekend Australian*, 24–25 October 1998 and 7–8 November 1998.

12 A brief summary includes: the formation of the African National Congress (ANC) (1912); the Native Land and Trust Act which fixed the distribution of land and allocated 13 per cent to the African majority (1936); the election of the Nationalist Government (1948); the Group Areas Act, which extended racial segregation (1950); the Bantu Authorities Act which set up Bantustan structures as African 'homelands' (1951); the Bantu Education Act which limited education available to black Africans (1953); the Freedom Charter, which set out the non-racial objectives of the anti-apartheid movement (1955); the Sharpeville massacre and banning of the ANC (1960); the Rivonia Trial and imprisonment of the ANC leadership (1964); the Soweto uprisings (1976); unbanning of the ANC, Pan African Congress and South African Communist Party, release of Nelson Mandela (1990); the first non-racial elections, producing an ANC-led government (1994); the Truth and Reconciliation Commission (1996–98).

13 Sindiwe Magona, *To My Children's Children: An Autobiography*. London: Women's Press, 1991, p. 87.

14 June Goodwin and Ben Schiff, *Heart of Whiteness*. New York: Scribner, 1995, p. 304. There is an extensive and excellent analysis of *Poppie Nongena* in Anne McClintock, *Imperial Leather: Race, Gender and Sexuality in the Colonial Contest*. New York: Routledge, 1995.

15 For bibliographical information about South African autobiographical writing to 1990, see the special issue of *Current Writing: Text and Reception in Southern Africa*, 3 (October 1991). Magona's *Forced to Grow* was published simultaneously in London and Cape Town in 1992.

16 Sindiwe Magona, *Forced to Grow*. London: Women's Press, 1992, p. 134.

17 Aletta J. Norval, *Deconstructing Apartheid Discourse*. London: Verso, 1996, p. 273. The association between the Congress, the Freedom Charter which emerged from Kliptown in 1955 and an inclusive racial perspective is made in Emma Mashinini's recollection of the event:

    The ANC had a uniform then, and these women were wearing black skirts and green blouses ... I was not a card-carrying member, but at that meeting I was a member in body, spirit and soul. It was so good to be there, just to hear them speaking. Every race was there, everybody, intermingling. I would sit under the shade of a tree and listen to everything, and it was as though everything I heard was going to happen in the next few days. I feel the same when I listen to the Freedom Charter now ... Kliptown was the right place for this meeting to be held. It was a non-racial area. There were very many Indian people, and it was almost like a coloured area, but we were there as well. And there must have been some whites and so forth.... It was total racial harmony. (Emma Mashinini, *Strikes Have Followed Me All My Life*. London: Women's Press, 1989, pp. 23–24)

Further references to this edition in text.

18 Norval, p. 270.

19 Ellen Kuzwayo, *Call Me Woman*. Randburg: Ravan Press, 1996, p. 5. Further references to this edition in text.

20 Judith Lütge Couille, '(In)continent I-lands: blurring the boundaries between self and other in South African women's autobiographies', *Ariel*, 27(1) (January 1996): 133–148.

21 Dorothy Driver, 'M'a-Ngoana O Tšoare Thipa ka Bohaleng – The child's mother grabs the sharp end of the knife: women as mothers, women as writers', in Martin Trump (ed.), *Rendering Things Visible: Essays on South African Literary Culture*. Johannesburg: Ravan Press, 1990, pp. 225–255.

22 Kuzwayo, p. 227. For a discussion of the absence of a critique of gender relations in *Call Me Woman*, see Desiree Lewis, 'Myths of motherhood and power: the construction of "black woman" in literature', *English in Africa*, 19(1) (May 1992): 35–51.

23 It also recurs in the extensive prison writings of the period. See J. U. Jacobs, 'The discourses of detention', *Current Writing: Text and Reception in South Africa*, 3 (October 1991): 193–199.

24 Aileen Moreton-Robinson, *Talkin' up to the White Woman: Indigenous Women and Feminism in Australia*. St Lucia: University of Queensland Press, in press. For a detailed analysis of the management of Aboriginal affairs in Queensland, see Rosalind Kidd, *The Way We Civilise: Aboriginal Affairs – The Untold Story*. St Lucia: University of Queensland Press, 1997. Aboriginal Affairs became a federal jurisdiction after the referendum in 1967; until then it was the province of state legislatures and bureaucracies.

25 Moreton-Robinson, in press.

26 Marcia Langton, 'Aboriginal art and film: the politics of representation', *Race and Class*, 35(4) (April–June 1994): 89–106.

27 Anne Brewster, *Reading Aboriginal Women's Autobiography*. Sydney: Sydney University Press, 1996, p. 4.

28 See Brewster for a useful recent list of Aboriginal autobiographical narratives by women.

29 Brewster, p. 7.

30 Bain Attwood identifies three interdependent forms of 'Aboriginalism': (1) the
    display of scholarly knowledge by European scholars who claim that indigenous
    peoples cannot represent themselves; (2) the style of thought based on the
    epistemological and ontological distinction between 'them' and 'us'; and (3) the
    exercising of authority over Aborigines by authorizing views of them and ruling
    over them. Bain Attwood and John Arnold (eds), *Power, Knowledge and Aborigines.*
    Melbourne: La Trobe University Press, 1992, p. i. See also B. Hodge and V. Mishra,
    Dark Side of the Dream. Sydney: Allen & Unwin, 1991.

31 Sally Morgan, *My Place.* Fremantle: Fremantle Arts Centre Press, 1987, p. 106.
    Further references to this edition in text.

32 See the debate in *Australian Historical Studies*, 25 (April 1993): 458–469, triggered
    by Bain Attwood's article in *ibid.*, 25 (October 1992): 302–318.

33 Ruby Langford Ginibi, *Don't Take Your Love to Town*, p. 84. See Mary Rose
    Liverani, 'From outside, without insight', *Weekend Australian*, 28–29 March 1992,
    p. 6, as an example of hostile responses to Langford Ginibi's presentation of the
    Aboriginal community.

34 Tim Rowse, *After Mabo: Interpreting Indigenous Traditions.* Melbourne: Melbourne
    University Press, 1994, p. 103.

35 Margaret Daymond, 'On retaining and on recognising changes in the genre
    "autobiography" ', *Current Writing: Text and Reception in Southern Africa*, 3(1) (1991):
    32. See also Sarah Nuttall, 'Reading in the lives and writing of black women',
    Journal of Southern African Studies, 20(1) (March 1994): 85–98.

36 Huggins, p. 47.

37 Leigh Gilmore, *Autobiographics: A Feminist Theory of Women's Self-Representation.*
    Ithaca, NY: Cornell University Press, 1994, p. 13.

38 Some of these issues are canvassed in Mudrooroo's discussion of the politics of
    literary production in his two books of literary criticism, *Writing from the Fringe: A
    Study of Modern Aboriginal Literature.* South Yarra: Hyland House, 1990, and
    Indigenous Literature of Australia: Milli Milli Wangka. South Yarra: Hyland House,
    1997. Although Mudrooroo's critique of Sally Morgan's *My Place* is notorious, his
    discussion in these books raises a number of important issues about writing and
    reading indigenous literature in Australia.

39 See e.g. the discussion of Mary Prince's reference to the amanuensis, and Moira
    Ferguson's interpretation of this in Chapter 1, and the reading of the discussion
    between Mary Seacole and her editor in Chapter 3.

40 Daymond, p. 32.

41 Shula Marks (ed.), *Not Either an Experimental Doll: The Separate Worlds of Three South
    African Women.* Bloomington: Indiana University Press, 1987, p. 186. Further
    references to this edition included in text.

42 Mudrooroo, *Writing from the Fringe*, p. 150. See Moreton-Robinson for an extensive
    discussion of this issue.

43 Jackie Huggins, 'Writing my mother's life', *Hecate*, 17(1) (1991): 88–94. Republished
    in *Sister Girl*, pp. 37–48.

44 Margaret Somerville, 'Life (hi)story writing: the relationship between talk and text', *Hecate*, 17(1) (1991): 95. Further references included in text.

45 See e.g. Carolyn Cooper's 'bilingual' discussion of Sistren's edition of autobiographies, *Lionheart Gal*, where she strategically shifts into Creole, 'Writing oral history: Sistren Theatre Collective's *Lionheart Gal*', in Stephen Slemon and Helen Tiffin (eds), *After Europe*. Sydney: Dangaroo Press, 1989, pp. 49–57; Ann duCille, 'The occult of true black womanhood: critical demeanour and black feminist studies', *Signs*, 19(3) (spring 1994); Rafia Zafar, 'Over-exposed and under-exposed. Harriet Jacobs and "*Incidents in the Life of a Slave Girl*"', in Deborah M. Garfield and Rafia Zafar (eds), *Harriet Jacobs and 'Incidents in the Life of a Slave Girl'*. New York: Cambridge University Press, 1996, pp. 1–10; Aileen Moreton-Robinson, *Talkin' up to the White Woman*. Occasionally a critic will identify across the boundaries of race; for example, in her reading of Aboriginal women's autobiographies Kateryna Olijnyk Longley draws attention to her own status as a member of a colonized and marginalized group as an immigrant Ukrainian as well as a white middle-class academic ('Storytelling by Aboriginal women', in Sidonie Smith and Julia Watson (eds), *De/Colonizing the Subject: The Politics of Gender in Women's Autobiography*. Minneapolis: University of Minnesota Press, 1992, pp. 370–386).

46 Sindiwe Magona, *To My Children's Children: An Autobiography*. London: Women's Press, 1991, p. 164.

47 Elizabeth Fox-Genovese, 'To write myself: the autobiographies of Afro-American women', in Sheri Benstock (ed.), *Feminist Issues in Literary Scholarship*. Bloomington: Indiana University Press, 1987, pp. 161–180.

48 Meena Alexander, *The Shock of Arrival: Reflections on Postcolonial Experience*. Boston: South End Press, 1996, p. 4.

49 Teresa de Lauretis, 'Feminist studies/critical studies: issues terms and contexts', in de Lauretis (ed.), *Feminist Studies/Critical Studies*. Bloomington: Indiana University Press, 1986, p. 9.

50 David Carter, 'Tasteless subjects: postcolonial literary criticism, realism, and the subject of taste', *Southern Review*, 25(3) (November 1992): 294.

51 Rosemary Jolly, 'Rehearsals of liberation: contemporary postcolonial discourse and the New South Africa', *PMLA*, 110 (1995): 17–29: 19.

52 Annamaria Carusi, 'Post, post and post: or, where is South African literature in all this?', *Ariel*, 20(4) (October 1989): 94.

53 In her pioneering study of the effects of whiteness in the academy, Moreton-Robinson's thesis uses a close study of a selected group of academic women to examine the intersections of racial, gendered and class privilege. This thesis has been germinal in my thinking about the subject of academia and whiteness in this chapter.

54 Sarah Nuttall, 'Telling "free" stories? Memory and democracy in South African autobiography since 1994', in Sarah Nuttall and Carli Coetzee (eds), *Negotiating the Past: The Making of Memory in South Africa*. Cape Town: Oxford University Press, 1998, pp. 75–88.

55 Testimonies are available in *Bringing Them Home: The Report of the National Inquiry into the Separation of Aboriginal and Torres Strait Islander Children from Their Families*.

Canberra: Commonwealth of Australia, 1997. Extracts are included in Carmel Bird (ed.), *The Stolen Children: Their Stories*. Sydney: Random House Australia, 1998. See also Quentin Beresford and Paul Omaji, *Our State of Mind: Racial Planning and the Stolen Generations*. Fremantle: Fremantle Arts Centre Press, 1998. Readily available discussions of the Truth and Reconciliation Commission in South Africa include Antjie Krog, *Country of My Skull*. Johannesburg: Random House South Africa Pty, 1998; Kader Asmal *et al.*, *Reconciliation Through Truth: A Reckoning of Apartheid's Criminal Governance*. Cape Town: David Phillip Publishers and Mayibuye Books, 1996, and the aforementioned Nuttall and Coetzee edition, *Negotiating the Past*.

56 Ken Gelder and Jane M. Jacobs, *Uncanny Australia: Sacredness and Identity in a Postcolonial Nation*. Melbourne: Melbourne University Press, 1998, p. 30.

57 Julia Kristeva, *Strangers to Ourselves*, quoted in Gelder and Jacobs, p. 30.

6

In memory of the colonial child

How can I make a durable past in art, a past that is not merely nostalgic, but stands in vibrant relation to the present? This is the question that haunts me.[1]

Autobiography and utopia

In her biomythography *Zami*, Audre Lorde points out that she was 26 years old and deep into a library science degree before she found a map that included the Caribbean island of Carriacou. She had come to believe that her mother's geography was either fantasy or just plain wrong. Perhaps she came from Curaçao:

> But underneath it all as I was growing up, home was still a sweet place somewhere else which they had not managed to capture yet on paper, nor to throttle and bind up between the pages of a school book. It was our own, my truly private paradise of blugoe and breadfruit hanging from the trees, of nutmeg and lime and sapadilla, of tonka beans and red and yellow Paradise Plums.[2]

The figuring of the Caribbean in particular as a 'sweet place' that is shaped in terms of the imagination of the child recurs in autobiographical writing. It places the Caribbean as a kind of mythic space, shaped by the forms of longing, memory and identification that are frequent markers of diasporic writing.

As I have argued elsewhere, this nostalgic celebration of 'Caribbeanness' is part of a tradition of autobiographic writing in which, as James Clifford observes, the memory, vision or myth-making about colonial spaces represents them as sites of longing and ambivalence, held in a utopic/dystopic tension.[3]

The dystopic mode is evident; for example, when Jamaica Kincaid writes autobiographically of her childhood in the West Indies island of Antigua, recollections which are stirred as her brother dies of AIDS. Lorde's 'sweet place' finds its dystopian counterpart in Kincaid's 'small place'.[4] Kincaid abandons her childhood and mother–daughter relations which are seen as traumatic, and stages her own rebirth through migration out of the colony to an American metropolis.

In the postcolonial domain, the question of how the estrangement of the child's eye is used to write of the colonial condition, and the ongoing implications of colonialism, is at issue here. As a style of estrangement, utopian writing is a threshold genre that is about reality on the boundary,[5] and so it can be used to particular effect to represent the ambivalence of postcolonial subjectivity. 'Utopia' contains two different references. The first is the sweet and good place we find in *Zami*, which is correctly labelled a 'eutopia'. The second is the dark vision of the suppressed and totalitarian small space of the 'dystopia', such as we find in Kincaid's *My Brother*. Memories of colonial childhoods draw on each of these modes and exist in the tension between them. Through the child-self the autobiographer can access estranged styles of writing, that is to say a narrative which pursues a transformative rather than a realistic reference to the empirical environment. Utopian writing (like fantasy, folk-tale and science fiction) sits uneasily on the boundaries between fact and fiction. Autobiography draws on utopian modes to represent liminal, threshold states and perceptions. Childhood is one of these states and illness is another.[6] Although estranged genres may seem to be 'escapist', utopian writing informs the present and refers to it, for the estranged and the present are framed by each other, each gaining meaning from the other. Thus, for example, in Chapter 5 the authentic tribal childhoods presented in Kuzwayo's *Call Me Woman*, and Magona's *To My Children's Children* are not historic but strategic. They reflect on the present rather than the past. So too does Elspeth Huxley's use of the child narrator in *The Flame Trees of Thika*.

The work of memory – remembering, commemoration, nostalgia, invention – is at the heart of contemporary postcolonial autobiography. This is, in part, to return to the issues of knowing the ghosts of the past which concluded Chapter 5, and the work of autobiography in bringing versions of the colonial past into the present. Vron Ware suggests that the continuous reconstruction and recycling of memories of colonialism happen at two levels. The first refers to the recycling of cultural material which came directly out of the colonial experience, but which continues to be absorbed and/or reconfigured in the present – such as the autobiographic texts which were discussed in the first four chapters of this book. The second level is the reconstruction of historical memory in contemporary representations of colonialism.[7] At this second level

Ware is particularly interested in how films such as *A Passage to India* and *Out of Africa*, and television series such as *The Flame Trees of Thika* and *Jewel in the Crown* fictionalize and romanticize the colonial past in versions of 'sweet places'. My concern in this chapter is with the role of contemporary autobiography in this production of social memory about colonialism and colonized spaces. As the examples from Kincaid and Lorde suggest, the connections between estrangement, nostalgia and memoirs of childhood are fundamental to this.

Autobiographic writings are among the most powerful forms which contribute to the social production of memory, the consensus view of the past and personal experiences which are significant and memorable. As Sarah Nuttall argues, appropriate styles of commemoration are open to change and rearrangement. The past is negotiated continuously, and memories are made — and remade.[8] Social memory is not just the property of individuals, although their life stories contribute to it; rather it is a complex cultural and historical phenomenon which is constantly subject to revision, amplification and 'forgetting'.[9] The personal, social, cultural and intellectual histories that surface in autobiography are constantly on the move, for example, in the emergence of previously non-authoritative autobiographers; or in the ways that political moments 'invite' certain styles of commemoration and make others redundant; or through the renegotiations of readership which Ross Chambers discusses in *Room for Maneuver*. Both writers and readers of autobiography must always be aware of the 'forgetting', the invention and reinvention of memory.

It has been suggested that autobiographies of childhood and adolescence are an autonomous subgenre.[10] David McCooey remarks that first memories are not signs of historical understanding, but metaphors for the ahistorical nature of childhood: 'early memories are more poetical than historical.'[11] The eutopian idea of childhood represents it as a mythic, autonomous world, apart from history, which implies the knowledge of difference, desire and danger. And yet as autobiographical writing is used by those who have not been authoritative or dominant, the more likely it is that the narration of childhood will be dystopian and include the incursions of history and conflict rather than a pre-adolescent idyll. Mary Prince, for example, realized she was 'owned' in infancy; Rita Huggins describes the forced removal of her family to a reserve at an early age. African and Aboriginal autobiographers either reject the trope of innocent childhood entirely, or present childhood in terms of a mythic tribal past which is lost not through adolescence but through totalitarian state intervention. Generic and archetypal constructions of childhood are brought into question if we read widely across postcolonial autobiography. There are many childhoods.

For writers whose childhood was, one way or another, implicated in the pink spaces of the maps of Empire, the connections between time and place are critical. Recollections of a colonial childhood are likely to incorporate (sometimes imperfectly) two dimensions of selfhood. Firstly, a retrospective understanding of the self as formed by a historicized world, in historical time, a world where difference and desire are taken into account. This is an understanding which usually escapes the child herself. Thus, for example, in *Zami* the narrator turns away from her mother's sense of exile from Carriacou and her child's acceptance of it and uses the vision to invent a more 'fruitful' way of identifying herself in the present, and in terms of a series of historically produced connections and differences: poet, lesbian, Afro-American, Caribbean. Secondly, the familiar post-Romantic idea of the child as an emblem of the self that remains deep within the individual recurs, and so the autobiographic narration of childhood becomes a 'complex way of revealing and giving meaning to the self'. How a childhood in postcolonial spaces can be connected to the subjectivity and identity of the adult writer is open to question. In *Zami*, Carriacou is the eutopian space from which Lorde's biomythography can arise, and it connects to the present as a source of power and transformation. The translation of the sweet places of childhood into history and the present is fraught with difficulty for many autobiographers.

The tension between history and myth, between colonized spaces and sweet places, tells us less about childhood subjectivity than the use of the idea of childhood in remembrances of things past in autobiography, and ways in which this stands 'in vibrant relation' to the present. Here, as before, 'place matters', not just in terms of geography and chronology but also the connections between 'place' and 'colonial relation', and as an element in the construction of the narrating subject. What kind of colonial encounters and contacts, fantasies and infusions are produced in the narration of a colonial childhood? What are the effects of these remembrances of a Eurocolonial past? Arjun Appadurai argues that the past is not a land to return to in a simple politics of memory. It is rather 'a synchronic warehouse of cultural scenarios, a kind of temporal central casting'.[12] The 'window' of memory for contemporary autobiographies of childhood is approximately the 1920s to the end of the 1960s. At the beginning of this period Bartholomew's maps signified large slabs of territory 'in the pink', or at least striped with pink, to mark the domain of British authority. By the end of this period just a few small islands of pink remained. So what does it mean to return to this cultural scenario and cast oneself as a child within it? What scripts are available for this casting of the self? And what are the effects of these autobiographies as they circulate as commodities in what Appadurai calls the 'ideoscapes' 'ethnoscapes' and 'mediascapes' of global cultural politics? How is the past revived in eutopian and dystopian styles for new, very different and rapidly changing readerships? These are the questions which recur in this chapter.

A Childhood Perceived: Penelope Lively

In 1994, two new 'African childhood' autobiographies were published in Britain: Penelope Lively's *Oleander, Jacaranda: A Childhood Perceived* and Doris Lessing's *Under My Skin*, the first volume of her autobiography. The second volume, *Walking in the Shade*, was published in 1997. These autobiographies are, of course, very different. Lessing's construction of childhood draws on dystopian traditions, and Lively's is a reflection upon the making of the eutopian childhood and the nature of childhood perception. Whereas Lessing's parents were settlers in southern Rhodesia, Penelope Lively spent her childhood in the expatriate community of Cairo in the 1930s and 1940s – she returned to England in 1945 when her parents divorced.

The 'I' who is the adult narrator of Lively's autobiography explains that this childhood was distinguished by two things: she was the product of one society learning to perceive the world in the ambience of a quite different culture. The second distinction is that she was cared for by her nanny, tutor and companion Lucy, not her mother. As the subtitle suggests, Lively is deeply interested in the nature of childhood perception, and the relationship between the child and the older 'I': 'She is myself, but a self which is unreachable except by means of ... miraculously surviving moments of being: the alien within.'[13] Expatriatism takes classic features of the autobiography of childhood into overdrive, for the anarchy, innocence and brilliance which Lively, like many other writers, presents as characteristic of the child's perception is here performed in a condition of cultural estrangement. What is seen in innocence here are landscapes of colonialism. Autobiographies of childhood can dramatize with particular force the memory of these places as exotic, mythic, a private eutopia. The work of retrieving this vision not just from the distance of adulthood but also in the very different physical, political and cultural landscapes of the present is apparent in *Oleander, Jacaranda*, where the extra-diegesic narrator becomes preoccupied with the idea of the child as 'the alien within'.

The narrative begins with the autobiographic narrator's return to Egypt for the first time since she left in 1945. She returns as a tourist, 'packaged up the Nile'. The lush and exotic enclave of her childhood at Bulaq el Dakhrur is now hard to find, buried in the suburbs of Cairo. The journey to find the house becomes a metaphor for the work of retrieving the child in the colonial past; vague recollections are tenuously confirmed by present evidence. The white-dappled clover fields and waving sugar cane of childhood landscapes have been replaced by 'a sea of shabbily built apartment blocks ... balconies festooned with washing, the street strewn with rubble, people everywhere, children running around like puppies' (5). The remnants of the house are finally found, 'battered but alive': the grounds are much diminished, and the house itself is part of a technical college. And yet, even in this much degraded and alienated form, Bulaq el Dakhrur still revives for Lively the child embedded in herself, a form in which she will always inhabit what remains of the British enclave in Egypt:

> I felt as though a piece of myself were there, and that I had come back to fetch it. A wave of happiness; a sense of completion. And there was also the powerful feeling that on some other plane of existence the Ur-house was still there also, with the eucalyptus avenue and the lawns and the flower beds, and I with it, a ghost-child ... And there was also a response to this dramatic metamorphosis which was more detached − a perception of the battered house as an expression of a world which was utterly extinguished − the Egypt of foreign administration and also an England of assumptions that are now unthinkable. Half of me was preoccupied with a contorted nostalgia; the other half was asking about the landscape of resurrection all around. (8)

The problems of relating the colonial past to the present, and the child to the adult recurs throughout *Oleander, Jacaranda*. Lively returns to Egypt as a tourist, typically a consumer with no claims of belonging or attachment to the foreign. Yet expatriatism is different, and through her expatriate childhood she does make claim to a kind of belonging in Egypt − as we see in the fantasy of the ghost of herself which remains. This is to go back to the predicaments of belatedness discussed in an earlier chapter, what Ali Bedhad describes as the work of orientalist epistemology amidst late colonial relations of power.[14] Two issues come together here: the loss of childhood, and the implications in this loss of the demise of Empire. Together these produce a 'contorted nostalgia', and a state of ambivalence and introspection.

Lively's autobiographic narrator is forced to confront the ghost raised by her childhood quite explicitly. A series of childhood photographs is included in *Oleander, Jacaranda*. Photographs are always important in autobiographic writing, for they are exposures from the past that can disturb the prose recollections of the narrator. This occurs graphically in a photograph where 'PL' (as Lively calls herself as a child in the photographs) is pictured with other children, and beyond the domain of the lush gardens which surround their house, Bulaq el Dakhrur. The commentary beneath the photograph suggests the narrator's own perception of it as a troubling image: 'PL with *fellaheen* children near Bulaq Dakhrur. A deeply disquieting photo in its brutal contrasts, with the baby donkey as the cosy feature of interest.'[15] In the foreground of the photograph 'PL' strokes the donkey. She has the blonde bobbed and clipped hair, the white socks and T-bar shoes and neat double-breasted coat which was the standard garb for young English girls throughout the 1940s and 1950s. On the other side of the donkey in the background are the fellaheen children, largely hidden by the 'cosy feature of interest', but we glimpse bare feet, assorted long garments and, on the girl, a black scarf which hides most of her face. Where else but in mutual childish pleasure in the photogenic donkey would these children come into contact? The baby donkey is the focal point of the photograph, and its presence alone unites two vastly different images of a childhood in Egypt.

One reading of 'PL', the fellaheen and the donkey would remark on this photograph as an exemplar for colonial discourse analysis, in particular that most elementary trope of the 'self' and 'other', with the British child being defined in and through the fellaheen. The reasons why the narrator might be 'deeply disturbed' by this image is that her own place in a binary organization of identity is so clearly captured here. The photograph produces a 'double exposure' and makes explicit a connection and interdependency which is suppressed in the narrative text. It captures distinctions which the child does not see then, and yet these are fundamental to her own identity, growing up 'English in Egypt': 'Then, I saw simply what I had always seen, with the impervious accepting eye of childhood. This was the world. How could it be otherwise?' (11). The autobiographic narrator now inhabits an 'otherwise' some fifty years later, and in looking at this image of literal contiguity from the past is forced to recognize how the Empire has been implicated in her own sense of selfhood, and how this identity and history is made through relationship rather than essence. She engages with these issues explicitly and mediates between the consciousness of the child-self and the reader:

England was pink. I knew that from Bartholomew's atlas. Pink was good. And there was plenty of it, too, a global rash ... I look back in dismay. There has been a lot of unlearning to do. And can it all be unlearned? Is there perhaps deep within me some unreconstructed layer which believes pink is best. (19)

This is, again, a 'contorted nostalgia'.

The status of these autobiographies of colonial childhood which continue to appear in this last decade of the twentieth century is complex, and they need to mediate their relationship to their readers specifically and with care. How do they touch the present? One reading of *Oleander, Jacaranda* might identify the marks of the 'Raj revival'. That nostalgia for Empire (usually India) is a powerful residue, an 'unreconstructed layer' which emerged anew in Britain in the 1980s. However, this explanation is too domestic. It privileges one colonial relation, and underestimates the complex circuitries of readership both in and beyond the Home Counties. The racial and ethnic formulations of Englishness are not contained by England, or any single colonial relation. They never are and never were. They are produced and consumed in more widespread and heterogenous networks, through the rogue connections and relationships which recur throughout postcolonial autobiography – although perhaps these are clearer if one buys *Oleander, Jacaranda* in Brisbane rather than Bristol; or if one has never been situated in Englishness in the manner of 'PL'. This is to return to Appadurai's discussion of the complex ideoscapes, ethnoscapes and mediascapes which have been produced by the unpredictable passages of people, ideas and images in contemporary culture. A 'Raj revival' reading is both too domestic and too limited in its understanding of how representations of the colonial past can infect the present. *Oleander, Jacaranda* revives and recycles the tropes of romantic orientalism, yet it also attempts to encounter Lively's ghost. Neither Lively nor Doris Lessing have any desire to naturalize past power relations, and to reproduce the nostalgic 'I'. They are aware of the stereotypes of Africanism and the potential for eutopian constructions of childhood to connect to imperialist nostalgia, and the fact that the states of their childhood have been displaced both personally and politically. Here the return to the scenes of a colonial childhood makes the narrator uneasy in her skin. To write autobiographically about it requires a complex understanding of how volatility, ambivalence and inconsistency enter within the frame of the single life, and to understand how the self is encumbered by history. As Lively suggests, her autobiography represents a self which is inconstant.

Lively's narrator historicizes this self in various ways. As she points out, when it comes to the huge manipulations of history, children, like nostalgia, are silent. And so the extra-diegesic narrator is used strategically, to induce an oppositional reading by placing the child in context:

My childhood reaction to the Beit el Kritiliya smacks of romantic orientalism, it now seems to me. This would have been inspired by the *Arabian Nights* ... It did not occur to me at the time that it had any relevance to the real Middle East in which we lived – as indeed it did not. (83)

The narrator foregrounds the making of Englishness in childhood. This is the work of the governess, Lucy, who is confidently and unambiguously an English patriot, and the fountain of knowledge and speaker of gospel truth for the child. The two features which Lively suggests are distinctive to her childhood – being raised English in Egypt, and being raised by a governess rather than her mother – coalesce. For Lively's mother, a shadowy presence in the autobiography, is an ambiguous figure in another sense, in that she is part of the multicultural expatriate community. Lively's childhood ends with the divorce of her parents and her return to England; however her mother remains as an expatriate in Cairo, and remarries. The attachment to England is through Lucy and what she teaches. Education is fundamental: Bartholomew's atlas, the rigid timetable of learning, the flora and fauna of the English pond and stream, the 'telling-back' method of learning 'by heart': Macaulay's *Lays of Ancient Rome*, Rupert Brooke, Oscar Wilde, *Our Island Story*. As Helen Tiffin has argued, reading and recitation, the library and the classroom, were fundamental to an imperial education system which interpellated a colonialist subjectivity not just through syllabus content but through memorizing the English script, taking it into the body and absorbing with the heart and the mind.[16] Englishness is also a set of attitudes about order and disorder, cleanliness and disease – the child assumes that entering the local village will produce instant death by contamination. These are embodiments that are foregrounded by the narrator, technologies which produce both body and soul. *Oleander, Jacaranda* engages in a process of 'unlearning' and undoing that earlier work which racialized and ethnicized the child.

Although, as Simon Gikandi points out, the far reaches of the Empire were sites where sublime affirmations of Englishness could produce an enunciative authority, Lively's autobiography attempts to reflect back on this authority and to question its origins, tastes, competencies and qualities. She does this in part by making the child an unauthorized narrator and putting in place other perspectives. Although Lively remains attracted to the 'child's eye', that surreal and anarchic vision 'before knowledge' depicted by Wordsworth and Woolf, to leave this view in place untethered by an authorized narrator, who introduces history and context, is to invoke the strategic forgetting of imperialist nostalgia. As I suggested in Chapter 4, we see an example of this use of the child narrator in Huxley's *The Flame Trees of Thika*. Carolyn Steedman has argued that the modern idea of history grew to pre-eminence at the same time as the modern idea of childhood. Thus there is a general familiarity with the idea of each and every individual's childhood as the buried past, the place that is *there*, within us, but never to be obtained.[17] Childhood has become an imaginative structure that allows the individual to make exploration of the self in connection to larger social, cultural and historical organizations. This act of self-cognition and self-revelation in the writing of childhood autobiography is altered profoundly by colonialism, and the questioning of what this past means 'within us'. All childhood autobiographies rework past time to give current events meaning, and that reworking provides an understanding that the child at the time cannot possess.[18] This takes on different dimensions when that earlier self was produced in and through colonial relations, and it can lead to ambivalence towards what Lively refers to as 'the alien within'.

Ultimately, Lively's autobiographic narrator suggests that, despite Lucy's best efforts, the child remains unincorporated and uneasy in Englishness. In this respect the expatriate enclave is presented as a site of transculturation rather than affirmation, a place where a different style of Englishness emerges. When she returns to England in 1945, 'poised for adolescence', the child is immediately struck by a dystopian world of the unnatural and the monstrous: 'I knew that I had arrived in another world' (164). Whereas Lucy revels in the camaraderie of 'her own language, her own country', the child is stupified: 'In my mind I had created a place ... all soft-focus landscape, immutable good weather, gambolling animals and happy laughing folk ... I suspect the image was based on Mabel Lucie Attwell illustrations spiced with Arthur Rackham and Beatrix Potter' (174). Like Lessing in 1949, Lively returned to a metropolis devastated by war, with shells and facades of buildings, wastelands of dirt and rubble, ghostly staircases going nowhere. She was, she recalls, like a refugee, an immigrant, a displaced person, cut off in space and time, and severed from her own past: 'If you cannot revisit your own origins – reach out and touch them from time to time – you are for ever in some crucial sense untethered' (175). In this way Lively presents herself as part of the influx of immigrants to Britain after the war and, most importantly, she presents an estranged vision of England as not only alien to her and full of monstrosities but open for reconstruction and reinvention by this new population. It is not uncommon for expatriates, travellers and immigrants to remark on the gap between the real and the imagined metropolis of British imperialism; however, Lively, like Mary Seacole a century before, and Mary Prince before that, uses her autobiographic narrator to suggest that the distinctions of colonialist discourses come undone at this centre. So *Oleander, Jacaranda* concludes with the adolescent exploring the wasteland of rubble around St Paul's Cathedral, in decay 'like some ruined site of antiquity'. What she can glimpse there is the remnants of the medieval wall, and then part of the original Roman wall. For the child who learned British history through the 'patriotic rantings' of *Our Island Story*, these relics suggest histories previously unknown, the presence of other empires and other ways of making connections between England and Egypt: 'What I do remember, with a clarity that is still exhilarating, is the sudden sense of relevances and connections which were mysterious, intriguing, and could perhaps be exposed' (180).

By concluding with this reminder that England was itself once a colony, and by imagining her adolescent self as a displaced person moving into a wasteland, Lively is moving beyond the bounds of Lucy and of Bartholomew's atlas. *Oleander, Jacaranda* refuses closure in a nostalgic dream of going home; rather it suggests links between the hollowing out of the metropolis during the war, and the migrations and regroupings which have reconstituted British

culture and society, and 'Britishness', in the period since then. Lessing and
Lively arrive as immigrant and expatriate respectively in London and represent
what they see in terms of the surreal and the grotesque:

> That London of the late 1940s, the early 1950s, has vanished, and now it
> is hard to believe it existed. It was unpainted, buildings were stained and
> cracked and dull and grey; it was war-damaged, some areas all ruins ...
> and it was subject to sudden dark fogs.[19]

This is 'the end of the Raj ... the end of the British Empire' (15). Lessing and
Lively write from and to a *fin de siècle* in which identity is characterized in
terms of transits and deterritorialization, rather than narratives of originary and
initial subjectivities. Both trace the origins of these contemporary modes of
cultural identification back to the social and cultural displacements produced
by war and decolonization. In this way they place themselves at the beginning
of the mass movement in from the periphery, and come 'home' as strangers, to
a dead heart, and with the power to invent new connections. It is the
expatriates, immigrants and travellers who will write of the ambiguities of
'English' and the mythical constructions of England in a process of
transculturation.

Colonial memory is in a process of continuous reconstruction and recycling,
and available to various and quite contradictory uses. It is a site of ongoing
conflict, contestation and symbolic struggle, equally available to the nostalgia
of 'Raj revival' episodes (as we have seen in *Out of Africa* and Mary Gaunt's
travel writings), and to uses which resist the classifications and categorizations
of colonialism's culture (as in *The History of Mary Prince* and *The Wonderful
Adventures of Mrs. Seacole*). Autobiographic writing is at the heart of both
eutopian and dystopian uses of colonial memory for two reasons. Firstly,
colonialism impacts at the point where our very sense of the possibilities for
self-definition are constituted. Secondly, autobiographic writing is in a state of
tension, for (as we have seen throughout this book) autobiographic subjects are
both agents and victims within colonialism, and postcolonial autobiography
always bears the traces of its origins in specific historical relations of power,
rule and domination. For these reasons, it is uniquely placed to suggest and
reflect back upon how individuals are categorized and attached to identities,
and how identities are invariably produced within the social, political and
cultural domain. It is at this point that autobiographies of childhood are of
particular interest for, as we see in *Oleander, Jacaranda*, these have the potential
to engage both uses of colonial memory: the sweet place of nostalgia, and the
hard place of resistance. They can also bring to crisis that modern construction
of the child as a 'buried self', embedded within the adult. In this way

representations of a colonial childhood can suggest struggles within and between subjects as they engage with the 'unreconstructed layer which believes pink is best', for it is in childhood that identity is attached in and through the body via the creation of desires and norms by which we understand and police ourselves. In colonialism's culture, this attachment and policing always begins with the skin.

Under My Skin: Doris Lessing

These 'attachments' are, as we have seen elsewhere, both volatile and historical. If freedom lies in our capacity to discover the links between certain modes of self-understanding and domination, and to resist the ways in which we have already been classified and identified by dominant discourses, autobiographical writing is a means of recognizing that identities are historically constructed in specific ways, and contingent.[20] This contingency and volatility is apparent between subjects, and within the individual life. In Chapter 1 I suggested that for some autobiographic subjects who write out of colonialism there are extremes and crises of authority and representation. The subject was Mary Prince; here it is Doris Lessing, who was a child in southern Rhodesia, 'and Rhodesia was never anything but the modern version of a slave state'.[21] Lessing's writing is a long process of understanding the meanings of her colonial childhood, with a series of quite different returns to the past. Her two volumes of autobiography are the latest rather than the definitive episode in this process.

Doris Lessing, like Lively, was born the daughter of a bank official in a sphere of British influence – Persia in her case. Her first memories are from the expatriate community in Kermanshah. Following this, seduced by the promise of southern Africa as presented at the Empire Exhibition of 1924 (which coincided with renewed attempts to attract settlers to Rhodesia through the Empire Settlement Scheme), Lessing's parents commit themselves to farming in Africa. In *Under My Skin* Doris Lessing recalls travelling on an ox wagon from Salisbury to her parents' farm near Banket. As we have seen in the discussion of white Kenyan autobiography, this is one of the archetypal scenarios of settler mythology in Africa, and a recollection which indicates the remarkable span of living social memory. Reading Lessing's childhood memoir alongside Elspeth Huxley's *Flame Trees of Thika*, which begins with the ox wagon trek to the farm that promises much and delivers little, demonstrates nicely the point which Dane Kennedy makes throughout his analysis of colonization in Rhodesia and Kenya: these colonies, although adjacent, were the products of quite different kinds of colonial relation.

The history of Lessing's family is typical of white Rhodesian settlement. Her parents were inexperienced colonists driven by dreams of fortune through growing maize (or tobacco, or various other cash crops). They remain dependent on long-term loans from the Land Bank, unable to thwart a slow decline into poverty, and connected to Britain through an overwhelming sense of exile and loss from the place where 'life' really happens. Lessing captures brilliantly the detritus of Englishness which fills the settler's 'first houses': Liberty prints, catalogues from the Army and Navy Stores, English jam, heavy silver and, in the case of the Tayler family, many books shipped regularly from England. These things are arranged on and around furniture made from paraffin tins and packing-cases; there are flour sack curtains, and bookcases made from petrol boxes. Lessing argues that there is a history of white poverty in Rhodesia which is obscured by histories of white supremacy. In autobiography it is obscured, as we have seen, by the 'out of Africa' mythography, which was grounded in the elitist 'public school' settler colonialism in Kenya. Rhodesia, on the other hand, was represented as the colony where poor settlers could make good, and the population itself took pride in its diverse and lowly origins.[22] Whereas indigents were culled from the white Kenyan population, the financial, ethnic and social composition of the Rhodesian settler society was more mixed. Various kinds of financial aid (such as assisted passages to the colony and renewable loans from the Land Bank) were vital to the maintenance of a white settler presence.

The comparison between these two autobiographies of childhood is also a reminder of the very different uses and contexts of *Thika* and *Under My Skin*. As I have argued, Huxley uses the child to envisage forms of indigenization for the settler in Kenya, imagining an ongoing presence and relevance at a crucial moment in negotiations for Kenyan independence in 1959. Lessing, on the other hand, writes of a place that no longer exists, Rhodesia, and with a sense of history which stresses conflict, change and the impossibility of translating white supremacy into an inter-racial post-independence state. Problems of history haunt the narrator of Lessing's autobiography:

> One reason for writing this autobiography is that more and more I realise
> I was part of an extraordinary time, the end of the British Empire in
> Africa, and the bit I was involved in was the occupation of a country that
> lasted exactly ninety years. People no longer know what that time was
> like, even those who live in Southern Africa.[23]

The problem is how to write of this time in the last decade of the twentieth century. How does one connect to that self in those pre-independence social landscapes of Africa irretrievably tainted by colonialism? How does one come to terms with that child, and what remains of the child within, given that this child was shaped in a state of racial apartheid, a 'slave state'? Lessing is very explicit about these issues. Although she remarks that this first volume is written 'without snags and blocks of conscience' (11), one of the problems which must be negotiated through the narrative is the relationship between the reader and the autobiographic narrator, and that narrator and the child.

In *Under My Skin* the relations between memory and autobiography are constantly under review. Lessing has written about her African years in a variety of autobiographic forms: *In Pursuit of the English*, *Going Home*, the first four volumes of the *Children of Violence* pentalogy, *The Golden Notebook*, a number of short stories, and *Memoirs of a Survivor*, a kind of 'dream autobiography'. She holds on to the different forms of truthfulness which are enabled by these various genres and styles of autobiographic writing, and refuses to privilege *Under My Skin* as more authentic or truthful. Lessing remarks at the outset that she writes her autobiography because her life is in the process of becoming the focus of a small industry of biographers. This is a useful reminder of the *kind* of information which is included here as opposed to, say, the first two volumes of *Children of Violence*, or the Black Notebook in *The Golden Notebook*. It does not tell more, or more truthfully, but it tells differently:

> when I wrote *Martha Quest* I was being a novelist and not a chronicler. But if the novel is not the literal truth, then it is true in atmosphere, feeling, more 'true' than this record, which is trying to be factual. *Martha Quest* and my African short stories are a reliable picture of the District in the old days. That is, from a white point of view. (162)

As a writer, Lessing is almost always aware of the various historical and discursive contexts of her writing, and readings of it. As an autobiographer, no less than as the author of *The Golden Notebook*, she will rehearse and 'stage' different styles of writing to induce different forms of memory. For example, there is an exercise in describing the bush in terms of what the child hears as a way of capturing that lost Africa, and there is the mode of 'fond lying memory' which is all sensuousness and pleasure. There are 'hallmarked memories', 'invited memories', 'concocted memories', and so on. Lessing is quite explicit about the influences of Olive Schreiner and Virginia Woolf, among others, on her writing about memory and childhood — as a writer she is always conscious of the small industry of critics which attach to her writing. In this autobiography, as before, she foregrounds and historicizes her readers and critics, and their relationship to her writing: 'I do not think it can be said too often that it is a mistake to exclaim over past wrong-thinking before at least wondering how our present thinking will seem to posterity' (50); 'But one of the difficulties of this record is to convey the contradictions of white attitudes' (72).

Rhodesia: the lost world

These strategies manage the relationship between reader, author and autobiographic narrator now, and the child produced in a lost world. Unlike Elspeth Huxley, or (more recently) Kuki Gallmann, Lessing has no investment in perpetuating the heroic pioneering narratives of Rhodesian settler writing from a white point of view. Lessing remarks in her review of Karen Blixen's *Out of Africa* that 'Blixen never saw the 6,000 acres were not hers', and that she too was a squatter in central Africa.[24] Yet when Lessing returns, it is to be reminded in complex ways of how that occupation and her childhood remains embedded within the adult so that she remains in some ways 'African'. She writes, as she points out herself, 'from the white point of view', and this produces ongoing contradictions in her autobiographic writing. How to connect to the experiences of the Africans who were there? When she speaks to one of her black contemporaries, who was a 'piccanin' working on the farms in Banket during her childhood, it is evident that they inhabited entirely different spheres: 'It seemed to him all the farm compounds were the same – poor, ugly, badly built places' (162). In this way the volumes of autobiography continue that desire to *write through* and *write out* her problematization of form which characterizes Lessing's writing, and which, as Rebecca O'Rourke suggests, 'is arguably grounded in the problem of how, as a white settler, to represent the relation of oppression: the internal and external dimensions of her situation as exile, both within and when distant from "her" country'.[25] From the beginning, Lessing's writings about Africa are caught in 'the contradictions of white attitudes'.

Like Alyse Simpson's Kenyan memoir, *The Land That Never Was*, the Rhodesian experience in *Under My Skin* draws on dystopian traditions. The tendency of the child to see the adult world in terms of the grotesque is established from the very start of the autobiography, and is related not just to place but also to Lessing's remark that her early childhood 'made me one of the walking wounded for years' (25). By this she means the psychological pressures which for her, like many others, produce an 'emotional wasteland' within. Thus in her earliest 'real' and 'authentic' memories of her parents, they are recalled as grotesque and obscene figures, 'enormous pale bodies, like milk puddings, sloshing about in out-of-control water that smelled cold' (19). Lessing's writing has always been a rich resource for critics interested in Freudian and Jungian approaches, and the autobiography provides further evidence for psychoanalytic criticism which focuses upon Lessing's sense of the different personalities within, and the problematic relations between mother and daughter in particular. My interest is in how colonial relations, that white occupancy of Rhodesia, feeds into this dystopian memoir of childhood, and how this autobiographic narrative compares to the series of childhood stories that recur across Lessing's writing. These African years reappear in her semi-autobiographic fiction, and these appearances must be gauged against ongoing political and social transformations in southern Africa. Lessing's sense of her African past is always keyed through the ongoing processes of decolonization and neocolonialism there, as well as her own changing perspectives as a writer.

The shifting subject of childhood across Lessing's autobiographic writing is cross-hatched by history and genre. For example, its first manifestation is in *Going Home*, a hybrid of journalism, fiction and autobiography first published in 1956. Lessing has revisited this volume a number of times, and written a series of Afterwords which review the context of her writing across time. The first, 'Eleven years later', begins, 'Always salutory to read over something written years ago. Particularly something written in emotion – that was 1956, a climactic year for everybody' (238). Changes in southern Africa and in the politics of East and West continue to change Lessing's sense of the relationship between her memoir of Africa and its readership. Thus 'Twenty-six years later': 'A new reprint, and I have just finished checking for errors that may have crept in. I have been forced to read, then, the record in my changes of mind about communism. Embarrassing' (253). Finally, in 1992, 'When I was writing this book and the postscripts that I added almost in desperation to try to keep up with events, I don't think anyone believed there would be a black government in Zimbabwe so soon – in 1980' (255). As Jenny Taylor has argued in her consummate reading of *Going Home*, this book does not simply reflect Lessing's social and historical situation, it is a stage on which the dilemmas of authorial identity, committed writing and historical stance are acted out: 'the text enacts a political and cultural crisis, not least in its ability to produce either a stable narrative voice or a fixed implied reader.'[26] In *Going Home* there is an unstable present and a collection of pasts. In this context the return to the scenes of early childhood foregrounds the problems of writing about Africa without reproducing the perceptions and legacies of colonialism. Like Lively, Lessing worries about the child within:

> many people had asked me how it was I had been brought up in a colour-bar country and yet had no feeling about colour. I had decided that a lucky series of psychological chances must have made me immune. But it was surely impossible that I should be entirely unlike other people brought up in the same way. Therefore I was watching my every attitude and response all the time I was in Africa. (12)

This is, in part, why she feels such a visceral affinity with Olive Schreiner, who struggled against the prejudice, taught 'from the moment you see anything, you see Africans as inferiors'.[27]

It is in *Going Home* that Lessing writes most engagingly of her 'Ur-house'. Here she lays claim to an intimacy with the African landscape, and an indigeneity which comes through belonging in the oneiric 'first house on the kopje'. The earth for the walls of the house is worked by the feet of the builders and two small children, 'my brother and myself'. It is originally taken from an anthill that contains the bones of three chiefs of a tribe, 'and so the walls of our house had in them the flesh and the blood of the people of the country'. This house is a living thing, 'built with affection'. The child knows the geography of the mud wall near her bed 'as I knew the lines on my palm'. Here she alone sees the patch where Tobias the painter put his hand flat on the whitewash: 'at a certain moment of the sunrise, when the sun was four inches over the mountains in the east, judging by the eye, that hand came glistening out of the whitewash like a Sign of some kind'(42). The child is one of a number of ghosts who come to the surface during this return to Rhodesia in *Going Home* – the 'perverted patriot' is another! These figures are dissonant and heterogeneous, and Lessing writes of Rhodesia in a series of guises: the witness, the historian, the journalist, the socialist, as well as through the memories of the child. Each of these has its illusions, and its unease. And yet here, in the most intimate moments of longing, memory and identification, Lessing insists on the 'Sign' of prior occupation, the mark of Tobias. She makes the reasons for this very clear: 'The basis of white domination in Southern Rhodesia was the Land Apportionment Act, which took away land from the Africans and gave it to the Europeans, and laid down where and under what conditions Africans were to live in "white" areas' (240).

It is a sign of the heterogeneity of *Going Home* that the text incorporates such subjective, eutopian expressions of intimacy and belonging in Africa alongside factual information about the legislation that made settler society a white enclave. If we follow Lessing's autobiographic child across to other episodes in her writing about Africa, we find other instances where Lessing describes how the kind of articulation of race and space produced by group area legislation is attached to identity. In one of Lessing's earliest published stories, 'The Old Chief Mshlanga', yet another autobiographic version of the white child appears. Reading and education make this child an alien, she

> could not see a msasa tree, or the thorn, for what they were. Her books
> held tales of alien fairies, her rivers ran slow and peaceful, and she knew
> the shape of the leaves of an ash or an oak ... the words 'the veld' meant
> strangeness, though she could remember nothing else.[28]

African and European societies in and around the farm are both rigidly stratified and in close proximity:

> The black people on the farm were as remote as the trees and the rocks. They were an amorphous black mass, mingling and thinning and massing like tadpoles, faceless, who existed merely to serve, to say 'Yes, Baas', take their money and go. They changed from season to season, moving from one farm to the next, according to their outlandish needs, which one did not have to understand ... The child was taught to take them for granted: the servants in the house would come running a hundred yards to pick up a book if she dropped it. She was called 'Nkosikaas' – Chieftainess, even by the black children her own age.
>
> Later, when the farm grew too small to hold her curiosity, she carried a gun in the crook of her arm and wandered miles a day, from vlei to vlei, from kopje to kopje, accompanied by two dogs: the dogs and the gun were an armour against fear. Because of them she never felt fear.
>
> If a native came into sight along the kaffir paths half a mile away, the dogs would flush him up a tree as if he were a bird. (12)

'Nkosikaas' both is, and is not, Martha Quest, or the child remembered in *Going Home*, or the young Anna Wulf, who spends all morning 'trying to remember myself back into sitting under the trees in the vlei near Mashopi',[29] or 'Tigger Tayler' who features in *Under My Skin*. Childhood and adolescence recur in an ongoing process of representing and reflecting upon what it means to be formed in and through this particular colonial relation. In 'The Old Chief Mshlanga' the adolescent girl out of curiosity reads books 'about the time when this part of Africa was opened up, not much more than fifty years before'. She learns for the first time that this was the Old Chief's country, and the settlers have imposed a new grid of names and distinctions which erase African possession of the land in the very recent past. In this story the child recognizes the various boundaries and categories of settlement which are no longer 'natural': homestead, farm, compound, vlei, village, reserve, district, town. Through the child, Lessing brings into view not only the racialized mentality and subjectivity which is learned in the states of apartheid, but also the articulation of this across the landscapes of southern Africa in apportionment legislation which began in the early twentieth century.

When Lessing refers to Rhodesia as a 'modern version of a slave state', and when I speak of her autobiographic writing in terms of crises of authority and dystopian forms of representation, there is a return to the specific discourses of slavery which were the subject of earlier chapters. What apartheid, as it emerged in southern Africa, and slavery, as it was practised in the Caribbean and the United States, share is a binary organization of racial difference, which produced a distinctive set of relationships, discourses and institutions. It also produced a complete articulation of race and space where black and white are in intimate proximity and yet remote. As the passage from 'The Old Chief Mshlanga' suggests, Europeans' daily routines were carried out in the constant presence of Africans, and yet legislative and symbolic boundaries organized every aspect of black/white relations. However, what sets apartheid apart from slavery is a recurrent theme of Lessing's African writings: the recognition of signs of prior occupation all around her. Africans were enslaved following invasion and occupation of their lands. In this way, what happened in Rhodesia connects to another set of colonial settler histories, as Lessing suggests:

> Australia, and New Zealand, Canada and the United States, Brazil, Africa – it is always the same story. The white men came, saw, coveted, conquered. The children and grandchildren of these invaders condemn their parents, wish they could repudiate their own history. But it is not so easy.[30]

Thus when Lessing finally comes to write her autobiography most explicitly, she re-presents a childhood that has already been displayed in a series of quite different generic facets and historical moments. She courts this inter-textuality quite explicitly in *Under My Skin*: 'I don't propose to elaborate on white settler attitudes, there's nothing new to say about them. My African stories describe the District – Southern Rhodesia – at that time. I would pick out ... ' (113). The child in *Under My Skin* is familiar, like and unlike Matty and 'Nkosikaas' and Anna. The reader can see refracted through and about the Tayler family a series of characters from elsewhere: Mr and Mrs Quest, Jonathan, the permutations of daughter, father and mother which recur in the African stories, the dream figures in *Memoirs of a Survivor*. To be tied to fact and to memory are represented by the autobiographic narrator of *Under My Skin* as a constraint. Yet it is not this generic shift to fact which changes the view of childhood here, but the shifting perspectives produced by time and change: 'for you see your life differently at different stages, like climbing a mountain while the landscape changes with every turn in the path' (12). The interest in this explicitly autobiographical childhood (rather than its semi-autobiographical fictional precursors) is not truth and evidence: 'Facts are easy. It is the atmospheres that made them possible that are elusive' (16).

Accessing the past

Lessing's writing, with the series of semi-autobiographic African childhoods and the ongoing postscripts to *Going Home*, makes it very clear that access to the past changes, and it is the subject of ongoing negotiation even within the domain of the individual life. The writer must constantly manoeuvre not only with 'lying memory' and the 'damn lying nostalgia' which dogs Anna Wulf's attempts to write of her past in the 'Black Notebook', but also the shifting ideoscapes and ethnoscapes of contemporary culture. In *Under My Skin* Lessing is scathing about 'political correctness', 'the new dogma that whites cannot write about blacks' (113). The point is that what can be said, and how and where it will be read, is subject to change. Those earlier representations of the rebellious semi-autobiographic girl and adolescent were written against Rhodesia, that Frankenstein of settler cultures, in the 1950s and 1960s. How does the return to the African childhood stand now, given the establishment of black rule in central and southern Africa?

Ironically, it may be that what falls to Lessing now is the work of fleshing out the atmosphere of white supremacy, exploring its 'atmosphere' and contradictions. *Under My Skin* incorporates several cameo presentations of stories of white poverty in Rhodesia, narratives which Lessing hopes can be incorporated into the history of Zimbabwe. When she remarks that 'people no longer know what that time was like, even those who live in Southern Africa' (160), her autobiography suggests, more clearly than its preceding semi-autobiographic fictions, that what they lack is the memory of the tenuousness and anxiety of white supremacy. Not 'tenuous' in the sense that it would be easily removed, but bizarre and irrational. Like Alyse Simpson, Lessing's dystopian account records the poverty and labour of British settlers as 'poor whites', a history almost always obscured by the more acceptable view of the wealthy élite in Kenya, and more recently by the urgent need to write the black history of colonization and resistance. As Dane Kennedy has suggested, the settler populations of Kenya and Rhodesia were in effect quarantined from their surroundings by political, linguistic, economic, social and physical boundaries that organized the arrangement of bodies and space, to the smallest detail, according to race.[31] Lessing has, from the very first African stories, written about this state from a subjective point of view, presenting the enclave from the perspective of the dissident within. In this she is unique.

The question remains as to what is the relation of contemporary white African autobiography to the circulation of ideas and the making of memories in and around Zimbabwe, and southern Africa more generally, during a phase when memories are being constructed in terms of the nationalist narratives of decolonization. Peter Godwin's memoir *Mukiwa: A White Boy in Africa* is also presented to us against a background where 'Rhodesia' has no meaning in contemporary Zimbabwe.[32] The question of what meaning it might have, and for whom, is an important one. At the end of his memoir, when Godwin's autobiographic narrator returns to Zimbabwe, there is little for him to do other than visit graves and monuments. Melsetter, the small town where he grew up, is almost purged of settlers, and renamed Chimanimani. The pioneer memorial is destroyed, although the grave of Thomas Moodie, the leader of the Gazaland pioneers, remains untouched.[33] Godwin remarks that there are now limited opportunities for the white man to bear witness. And, probably, the white woman.

The theme of the empty and uncreated land recurs in Lessing's African writings, and this, as Anthony Chennells points out, separates her from black African writers.[34] Traditionally, Rhodesian settler writing is organized around a series of myths and iconic figures, with a strong Arcadian element of moving into a land that is empty and full of promise.[35] These figures and myths continue to circulate in popular fiction, for example, in the masculinist adventure novels of Wilbur Smith. In Lessing's autobiography, more than any other account of her African childhood, the idea of the empty land reappears, although in a dystopian rather than an Arcadian mode. The autobiographic narrator tries to attach memory to history and logic, but the chronicle retains the child's estranged view. Her sense of loss, failure and futility is recurrent, in part because the war continues to cast a pall, and also because it was clear that within a few years the family would continue to slide into poverty despite dreams of abundant harvests. There is little sense of community in this dystopian view; rather, overwhelming isolation and loss, an 'exile from good'. In fact the absence of others, black and white, marks this more than any other recollection of the African years. This occupancy is doomed to fail, and is caught in sterility and exile.

We might contrast the effect of this with black autobiographic writing from Zimbabwe. For example, Sekai Nzenza-Shand writes of her community in terms of its lengthy occupancy of the land, and a long and continuous history. As we have seen, one of the important distinctions which Lessing's child learns in the short story 'The Old Chief Mshlanga' is the difference between the labourers from Nyasaland on the farm, who live in the compound and are constantly on the move, and the occupants of the village, who owned the land prior to white settlement. Nzenza-Shand recalls that the 1933 Land Apportionment Act severed her people from the land that was the traditional royal burial place. This is to say that there are important distinctions to be made among the black African population in terms of region, tenure and occupancy, and the dislocations produced by white colonization. Thus when Lessing writes in her autobiography that her parents 'were colonizing an

almost empty land', when she describes the African population as itinerant, and
when the only Note to her two volumes of autobiography is on population,[36]
describing the dramatic increase in the black population of Rhodesia following
white settlement, the question of meaning remains open and contentious. The
mark of Tobias, the reminder of an African presence which remains throughout
Going Home, is not there to the same effect in *Under My Skin*.

As the epigraph to this chapter suggests, writers must manoeuvre to engage
with a readership in the present. *Under My Skin* implies some of the difficulties
and contradictions of writing the years of white occupation into the collective
history of Zimbabwe, and into the confines of the individual life, at this time.
How can Rhodesia be a locus for the production of memory now? *Going Home*,
a juxtaposition of different styles of writing and with a series of postscripts
that grow with each reprint, is perhaps a more appropriate record of Lessing's
resistance to colonialism and racism during her years in Africa, and
subsequently in Britain. The empty vistas of the farm, with the occasional
glimpse of the African servant in attendance, which emerge again in *Under My
Skin*, remind us that white histories of Rhodesia come into the present
freighted with an unbearable weight from the past.

Reading across the Straits

The childhood in *Under My Skin* takes place in an extreme state, a site of
degeneration, paralysis and denial. Long before the advent of Zimbabwe,
Lessing wrote of white settlement in Rhodesia as doomed, an enclave which
must be abandoned. Penelope Lively too grew up in an 'island of white', a
place where beliefs, behaviours and appearances were policed and disciplined,
and where the spatial organization of British occupation was carefully
managed. These spaces, enclosures where each individual has a place and
each place an individual, are the essence of the colony, where multiplicity is
reduced to a unitary, vertical, hierarchical order.[37] One way and another,
these cells and enclaves, in the form of the garrison, the plantation, the estate,
the mission, the prison, the school, the farm, the household, for example,
were the building blocks of colonial settlement and rule in both its benign
and authoritarian forms. These enclaves and islands, and the internalization of
boundaries and behaviours they induced, are the spatial and psychological
enclosures of colonial childhood. The connections across memory, experience
and identity in these small places of colonialism preoccupy the autobiographer.

In *Taken*, the Canadian writer Daphne Marlatt uses a semi-autobiographic
approach to explore the connections across the island spaces of her life. The

ghosts from her childhood on the islands of Australia and Penang, the love-making and loss of her lover from the island home near Vancouver, and the Gulf War which is going on as she writes, need to be connected: 'A wet morning here and the war there in the late afternoon of the desert – they coexist.'[38] Marlatt too is a child of a colonial enclave; although unlike Lively she does not write of her return there, the traces of that childhood recur and remain embedded in the body: 'What i[sic] left behind is not left so much as embalmed in my childhood. Like a ghost it goes on living alongside this reality, occasionally felt, an inner twinge, the merest flicker of memory, unlocatable, indistinct'. (121) Like Lively, Lessing, Lorde and Kincaid, Marlatt too 'left this world behind to belong in the new one' in the metropolis, and for her too the ghost of childhood remains a haunting presence, an unfinished story. The exploration of coexistence in *Taken* anneals the colonialism of childhood and the neo-colonialism of the present, and explores her complicity with and accountability for each. For Marlatt, like Lively, memories of childhood in the English enclave, at Penang in her case, are written to openly court the inventions of romantic orientalism, although in *Taken* the spectre of difference is written *into* the child's narrative, rather than posed through juxtaposition in the retrospective lens of the camera:

> Making waffles, pouring melted butter into milk in this West Coast kitchen, why should i [sic] be visited suddenly by the smell of new cloth at the Chinese tailor's in Penang? Memory, a flash, flush of sensation through the body. Unbidden. The only time she took me with her to wait while she tried on a half-made evening gown ... I think her gorgeous, the tailor, squatting on the floor to pin up the hem as she stands on thin brown paper, properly deferential. Gazing at her, i [sic] breathe in the air of his shop, the richness of its smells a batik layering, all the bolts of colour laid out to touch, faded odours of cooking from the back, but most of all the hot scratchy stillness as if the cloth itself were soaking up the air ... Endless it seems my staring out between the blinds at the usual stream of shoppers, loiterers, hawkers, everything slowing down so that i[sic] see the teacups on the sidewalk, a bowl of rice, and not the syce-driven cars. See, just for a second, what it might be like to be that girl, younger than me, hanging round the kedai across the way, spoken to and speaking to the others but all the while staring with that territorial rudeness i [sic] know, staring between people and cars at me, outsider in her fathers? uncles? shop, while i [sic], guardian of this gorgeous mother, just as rudely stare back. (43)

Marlatt's writing explores intimacies by syncopating the public and the private, colonialism and neo-colonialism, in extraordinary ways. It is no accident that the love-making on the island in Victoria is between women; for Marlatt, this eroticism ruptures familiar connections and opens other stories and disclosures, a making strange which produces different ways of writing about the female body and its entry into language and subjectivity. This connects to that stare in the above passage, that linkage between the autobiographic narrator in the kitchen, the palpable and nostalgic eruption of the past into the present, and the presence of that other child who remains an object of curiosity and fantasy rather than the subject of acquaintance. This episode, like the image of 'PL' and the donkey, brings into view the boundaries of the enclave, and the incarceration of both children within the enclosures of colonial states.

Readers have more freedom to engage with both sides of this stare if they choose. In postwar Malaya, across the Straits from Penang in Malacca, Shirley Geok-Lin Lim's father managed a Bata shoe shop – briefly. She was a child of the streets. In their household the 'exotic other' was not the batiks and Amah's congee, as in Marlatt's childhood, but Jean Harlow, Hollywood and eau-de-cologne. Lim describes her family as saturated by the American imaginary. In her autobiography, *Among the White Moon Faces: An Asian-American Memoir of Homelands*, Lim fleshes out the location of that other girl in Marlatt's memory. This location is no less hybrid and conflicted than that of the white occupants, for Lim was born into 'a mélange of Chinese, Malay, Indian, Portuguese, British and American cultural practices' which is unique to the *peranakan* people of the Straits, who engage in elaborate cultural plays between Chinese and Malay, Asian and Western influences.[39] This mélange is the product of five centuries of migrations and occupations across east Asia, and is a reminder that hybridity is not the prerogative of postmodern postcolonial subjects alone.

It is also a reminder of the limitations of Anglocentric 'Raj revival' approaches to colonial memory. Both Marlatt and Lim recall their Malayan childhoods from their present location within the literary intelligentsia of North American West Coast feminism. Both are part of a recent inclination to look west from that coast, across to Asia and the Pacific, and to understand the connections there, out of Europe. This is to raise a different set of questions, and to be reminded that memories of British colonialism circulate in networks beyond Britain and Europe, and nor are they defined by Atlantic connections alone. The ideoscapes of feminism and of postcolonialism in particular produce new conduits for the circulation of postcolonial materials – as we saw with the return of *The History of Mary Prince*. The child spaces of Audre Lorde's Carriacou, and Jamaica Kincaid's Antigua, like the Malayan childhoods recalled by Marlatt and Lim, are framed within the discursive networks of North American neo- and postcolonialism. What does it mean to pull Malayan childhoods into this present? Here the dominance of discourses of nostalgia may be replaced by feminist discourses of empowerment and independence – these certainly marked the site of enunciation of Lim's child-self and her invocation of an implied readership for the autobiography. In a quite different way *Among the White Moon Faces*, subtitled *An Asian-American Memoir of Homelands*, is pulled into the gravity of the American narrative of immigrant inclusion – stories of the Asian immigrant's journey from a foreign strangeness to assimilation and citizenship – which attempts to construct symbols of cultural integration on the national terrain.[40] In the case of *Taken*, Marlatt's memoir responds to the issue of lesbian autobiographical difference. By exploring coexistence, Marlatt moves away from what Biddy Martin calls the 'bound singularity' of the lesbian autobiography, the insistence that sexuality defines a life.[41] The exploration of connections between sexuality and colonialism returns to the theme which Marlatt explored in her earlier fiction, *Ana Historic*. In *Taken* this becomes a more explicitly autobiographical pursuit of what it means to be seen as the object of the colonized gaze, and part of a history of colonialism which erupts into the present in unexpected and intimate ways.

Connected reading: the agency of the reader

By putting Marlatt in touch with Lim on the shores of the Straits and again on the coasts of North America, by reading *Under My Skin* as one of a series of autobiographic episodes of childhood in Lessing's *oeuvre*, and by connecting Lessing to Lively, and Lively to 'PL' and the fellaheen, I mean to suggest that now, in the ruins of colonialism, the grounds of autobiography present the reader with room to manoeuvre, and different ways of sifting through the debris. Agency is too often seen as the prerogative of the writer, and yet one of the legacies of recent postcolonial criticism is the renewed sense of the agency of the reader, and the urgency of reading. There is both agency and responsibility here, as I suggested in Chapter 5. That Moodie and Melsetter might enter into a discussion of nineteenth-century Canadian autobiography in Chapter 2, and resurface in a memoir of contemporary Zimbabwe in Chapter 6, is a kind of synchronicity which should not surprise. It is a reminder of the need to make connections across the intimate empire of autobiography, which is an imperium 'stuck together with words'.[42] The reader, no less than the writer, has the power and authority to pursue the other stories, histories, knowledge and experience that remain suppressed, unwitnessed and unauthorized between the lines.

To this end, the process of connected reading is important. This pursues those other stories, not by returning to any single text to retrieve a body or entire truth, but by making links between and across various narratives, tropes, sites, figures and moments. It is, if you like, a reading for supplementation rather than completion, for complexity rather than closure, for the making of truth rather than its revelation. Connected reading pulls at the loose threads of autobiography, and uses them to make sutures between, across and among autobiographical narratives, and so configure the intimate empire in a series of (sometimes improbable) links. This is a method of a critic in search of contiguities, who uses rogue connections as a way of navigating the terrain of postcolonial autobiography and negotiating with the past. It is to know autobiographies as they cannot know themselves, and to use criticism and reading as a means of suggesting new ways of thinking about ourselves.

Notes

1   Meena Alexander, *The Shock of Arrival: Reflections on Postcolonial Experience*. Boston: South End Press, 1996, p. 127.
2   Audre Lorde, *Zami: A New Spelling of My Name*. Freedom, CA: The Crossing Press, 1982, p. 14.
3   James A. Clifford, 'Diasporas', *Cultural Anthropology*, 9(3) (1994): 302. A lengthier discussion of this issue and a comparative reading of *Zami* and Dany Laferrière's *L'Odeur du café* is in A. James Arnold (ed.), *A History of Literature in the Caribbean. Volume 3. Cross-Cultural Studies*. Amsterdam/Philadelphia: John Benjamins Publishing Co, 1997, pp. 325–338.
4   Jamaica Kincaid, *My Brother*. London: Vintage, 1998.
5   Gary Saul Morson, *The Boundaries of Genre: Dostoevsky's 'Diary of a Writer' and the Traditions of Literary Utopia*. Austin: University of Texas Press, 1981, p. 92.
6   This is evident in, for example, Eric Michaels' AIDS diary, *Unbecoming*. See Ross Chambers, *Facing It: AIDS Diaries and the Death of the Author*. Ann Arbor: University of Michigan Press, 1998.
7   Vron Ware, *Beyond the Pale: White Women, Racism and History*. London: Verso, 1992, pp. 229–230.
8   Sarah Nuttall, 'Telling "free" stories? Memory and democracy in South African autobiography since 1994', in Sarah Nuttall and Carli Coetzee (eds), *Negotiating the Past: The Making of Memory in South Africa*. Cape Town: Oxford University Press, 1998, pp. 75–88.
9   Roger Bromley, *Lost Narratives: Popular Fictions, Politics and Recent History*. London: Routledge, 1988, p. 3.
10 See e.g. Joy Hooton, *Stories of Herself When Young: Autobiographies of Childhood by Australian Women*. Melbourne: Oxford University Press, 1990; Richard Coe, *When the Grass Was Taller: Autobiography and the Experience of Childhood*. New Haven: Yale University Press, 1984.
11 David McCooey, *Artful Histories: Modern Australian Autobiography*. Oakleigh, Victoria: Cambridge University Press, 1996, p. 26.

12 Arjun Appadurai, *Modernity at Large: Cultural Dimensions of Globalization*. Minneapolis: University of Minnesota Press, 1996, p. 30.

13 Penelope Lively, *Oleander, Jacaranda: A Childhood Perceived*. Harmondsworth: Penguin, 1995, p. 1. Further references to this edition in text. (First published by Viking in 1994.)

14 Ali Behdad, *Belated Travelers: Orientalism in the Age of Colonial Dissolution*. Durham, NC: Duke University Press, 1994, p. 16.

15 Lively, between pp. 54–5.

16 Helen Tiffin, 'Cold hearts and (foreign) tongues: recitation and reclamation of the female body in the works of Erna Brodber and Jamaica Kincaid', *Callaloo*, 16(4) (1993): 913.

17 Carolyn Steedman, *Past Tenses: Essays on Writing Autobiography and History*. London: Rivers Oram Press, 1992, p. 11.

18 *Ibid.*, p. 23.

19 Doris Lessing, *Walking in the Shade*. London: HarperCollins, 1997, p. 4. Further references in text.

20 Jana Sawicki, *Disciplining Foucault: Feminism, Power and the Body*. London: Routledge, 1991, p. 43.

21 Doris Lessing, *Going Home*. London: HarperPerennial, 1996, p. 239.

22 Dane Kennedy, *Islands of White: Settler Society and Culture in Kenya and Southern Rhodesia, 1890–1939*. Durham, NC: Duke University Press, 1987, p. 65.

23 Doris Lessing, *Under My Skin*. London: Flamingo, 1995, p. 160. Further references to this edition in text.

24 Doris Lessing, 'A deep darkness: a review of *Out of Africa* by Karen Blixen', in *A Small Personal Voice*. New York: Vintage Books, 1975, p. 151.

25 Rebecca O'Rourke, 'Doris Lessing: exile and exception', in Jenny Taylor (ed.), *Notebooks, Memoirs, Archives: Reading and Rereading Doris Lessing*. London: Routledge & Kegan Paul, 1982, p. 222.

26 Jenny Taylor, 'Memory and desire on going home: the deconstruction of a colonial radical', in Eve Bertelsen (ed.), *Doris Lessing*. Isando: McGraw Hill Book Company (South Africa), 1985, p. 55.

27 'Afterword to *The Story of an African Farm*', in *A Small Personal Voice*, p. 116.

28 Doris Lessing, 'The Old Chief Mshlanga', in *This Was the Old Chief's Country: Collected African Stories, Volume One*. London: Michael Joseph, 1973, p. 11. Further references in text.

29 Doris Lessing, *The Golden Notebook*. London: Flamingo, 1993, p. 72.

30 Preface, *This Was the Old Chief's Country*, p. 9.

31 Kennedy, p. 188.

32 Peter Godwin, *Mukiwa: A White Boy in Africa*. London: Macmillan, 1996, p. vii.

33 Thomas Moodie is a descendant of John Dunbar Moodie's brother, who remained at the Cape when J. D. Moodie returned to England, and then went to Canada to establish a 'Melsetter' there. See Chapter 2, 'Settler Subjects'.

34 Chennells, in Bertelsen, *Doris Lessing*, p. 35.

35 Lessing describes these in *Going Home*:

The myths of this society are not European. They are of the frontiersman and the lone-wolf; the brave white woman home-making in lonely and primitive conditions; the child who gets himself an education and so a status beyond his parents; the simple and brave savage defeated after gallant fighting on both sides; the childlike and lovable servant; the devoted welfare-worker spending his or her life uplifting backward peoples. (52)

For excellent presentations of the Rhodesian context of Lessing's writing, see Anthony Chennells, 'Doris Lessing and the Rhodesian settler novel', and Murray Steele, 'Doris Lessing's Rhodesia', in Bertelsen, *Doris Lessing*, pp. 31–54.

36 'A note on population' to Volume 1 reads:

It is believed that when the whites arrived in the area that later became Southern Rhodesia, there were a quarter of a million black people. By about 1924 there were half a million. When I left the country in 1949 there were one and a half million. In 1982 the estimate was nine or ten million. In 1993 they think there are twelve to thirteen million. Some demographers believe there will be thirty million by 2010. Now, in 1993, ninety per cent of the population are under the age of fifteen. It is currently thought by most experts that the continual increase of population since the whites arrived is because the Portuguese introduced maize which is easily grown, abundant, easily stored and nourishing.

37 Foucault writes of these cells of 'micro-power': 'its fundamental reference was not to the state of nature, but to the meticulously subordinated cogs of a machine, not to the primal social contract, but to permanent coercions, not to fundamental rights, but to infinitely progressive forms of training, not to the general will but to automatic docility' (*Discipline and Punish: The Birth of the Prison*. Harmondsworth: Penguin, 1979, p. 169).

38 Daphne Marlatt, *Taken*. Concord, ON: Anansi, 1996, p. 37. Further references included in text.

39 Shirley Geok-Lin Lim, *Among the White Moon Faces: An Asian-American Memoir of Homelands*. New York: The Feminist Press, 1996, p. 4. Further references included in text.

40 See Lisa Lowe, 'Immigration, citizenship, racialization: Asian American critique', in *Immigrant Acts: On Asian American Cultural Politics*. Durham, NC: Duke University Press, 1996, pp. 1–36.

41 Biddy Martin, 'Lesbian identity and autobiographical difference[s]', in Bella Brodzki and Celeste Schenck (eds), *Life/Lines: Theorizing Women's Autobiography*. Ithaca, NY: Cornell University Press, 1988, pp. 77–106.

42 Mary Louise Pratt, *Imperial Eyes: Travel Writing and Transculturation*. London: Routledge, 1992, p. 2.

Select bibliography

Adams, James Eli. *Dandies and Desert Saints: Styles of Victorian Masculinity*. Ithaca, NY: Cornell University Press, 1995.

Alexander, Meena. *The Shock of Arrival: Reflections on Postcolonial Experience*. Boston: South End Press, 1996.

Anderson, Benedict. *Imagined Communities*. London: Verso, 1991.

Andrews, William. *To Tell a Free Story: The First Century of Afro-American Autobiography, 1760–1865*. Urbana: University of Illinois Press, 1986.

Anzaldúa, Gloria. *Borderlands/La Frontera: The New Mestiza*. San Francisco: Spinsters, 1987.

Appadurai, Arjun. *Modernity at Large: Cultural Dimensions of Globalization*. Minneapolis: University of Minnesota Press, 1996.

Armstrong, Nancy. *Desire and Domestic Fiction: A Political History of the Novel*. Oxford: Oxford University Press, 1987.

Arnold, James A. (ed.). *A History of Literature in the Caribbean. Volume 3. Cross-Cultural Studies*. Amsterdam/Philadelphia: John Benjamins Publishing, 1997.

Ashcroft, Bill, Gareth Griffiths and Helen Tiffin, *The Empire Writes Back: Theory and Practice in Post-Colonial Literatures*. London: Routledge, 1989.

Ashcroft, Bill, Gareth Griffiths and Helen Tiffin (eds). *The Post-Colonial Studies Reader*. London: Routledge, 1995.

Ashley, Kathleen, Leigh Gilmore and Gerald Peters (eds). *Autobiography and Postmodernism*. Boston: University of Massachusetts Press, 1994.

Asmal, Kader, Louise Asmal and Ronald Suresh Roberts. *Reconciliation Through Truth: A Reckoning of Apartheid's Criminal Governance*. Cape Town: David Philip Publishers and Mayibuye Books, 1996.

Attwood, Bain. 'Portrait of the Aboriginal as an artist: Sally Morgan and the construction of Aboriginality', *Australian Historical Studies*, 25 (1992): 302–18.

Attwood, Bain and John Arnold (eds). *Power, Knowledge and Aborigines*. Melbourne: La Trobe University Press, 1992.

Ballstadt, Carl. '"The Embryo Blossom": Susanna Moodie's letters to her husband in relation to *Roughing It in the Bush'*, in Lorraine McMullen (ed.), *Re(Dis)covering Our Foremothers: Nineteenth Century Canadian Women Writers.* Ottawa: University of Ottawa Press, 1990, pp. 137–45.

Ballstadt, Carl, Elizabeth Hopkins and Michael Peterman (eds). *Susanna Moodie. Letters of a Lifetime.* Toronto: Toronto University Press, 1985.

Ballstadt, Carl, Elizabeth Hopkins and Michael Peterman (eds). *Letters of Love and Duty: The Correspondence of Susanna and John Moodie.* Toronto: University of Toronto Press, 1993.

Ballstadt, Carl, Elizabeth Hopkins and Michael Peterman (eds). *I Bless You in My Heart: Selected Correspondence of Catharine Parr Traill.* Toronto: University of Toronto Press, 1996.

Behdad, Ali. *Belated Travelers: Orientalism in the Age of Colonial Dissolution.* Durham, NC: Duke University Press, 1994.

Benstock, Shari (ed.). *Feminist Issues in Literary Scholarship.* Bloomington: Indiana University Press, 1987.

Benstock, Shari (ed.). *The Private Self: Theory and Practice of Women's Autobiographical Writings.* London: Routledge, 1988.

Beresford, Quentin and Paul Omaji. *Our State of Mind: Racial Planning and the Stolen Generations.* Fremantle: Fremantle Arts Centre Press, 1998.

Bertelsen, Eve (ed.). *Doris Lessing.* Isando: McGraw Hill Book Company (South Africa), 1985.

Bhabha, Homi K. *The Location of Culture.* London: Routledge, 1994.

Birbalsingh, Frank. *Passion and Exile: Essays in Caribbean Literature.* London: Hansib Publishing, 1988.

Bird, Carmel (ed.). *The Stolen Children: Their Stories.* Sydney: Random House Australia Pty, 1998.

Bird, Delys and Dennis Haskell (eds). *Whose Place? A Study of Sally Morgan's 'My Place'.* Sydney: Angus & Robertson, 1992.

Blixen, Karen (Isak Dinesen). *Letters from Africa 1914–1931.* London: Pan Books, 1983.

Blixen, Karen. *Out of Africa.* Harmondsworth: Penguin, 1982.

Blunt, Alison and Gillian Rose (eds). *Writing Women and Space: Colonial and Postcolonial Geographies.* New York: Guilford Press, 1994.

Boehmer, Elleke. *Colonial and Postcolonial Literature.* Oxford: Oxford University Press, 1995.

Boyce Davies, Carole. *Black Women, Writing and Identity: Migrations of the Subject.* London: Routledge, 1994.

Brennan, Timothy. *Salman Rushdie and the Third World: Myths of Nation.* London: Macmillan, 1989.

Brewster, Anne. *Literary Formations: Post-colonialism, Nationalism, Globalism.* Melbourne: Melbourne University Press, 1995.

Brewster, Anne. *Reading Aboriginal Women's Autobiography.* Sydney: Sydney University Press, 1996.

Bringing Them Home: The Report of the National Inquiry into the Separation of Aboriginal and Torres Strait Islander Children from Their Families. Canberra: Commonwealth of Australia, 1997.

Brodzki, Bella and Celeste Schenck (eds). *Life/Lines: Theorizing Women's Autobiography*. Ithaca, NY: Cornell University Press, 1988.

Bromley, Roger. *Lost Narratives: Popular Fictions, Politics and Recent History*. London: Routledge, 1988.

Brydon, Diana and Helen Tiffin. *Decolonising Fictions*. Sydney: Dangaroo Press, 1993.

Bruss, Elizabeth. *Autobiographical Acts: The Changing Situation of a Literary Genre*. Baltimore: Johns Hopkins University Press, 1976.

Buss, Helen. 'Canadian women's autobiography: some critical directions', in Shirley Neuman and Smaro Kamboureli (eds), *Amazing Space: Writing Canadian Women Writing*. Edmonton: Longspoon/NeWest, 1986, pp. 154–66.

Buss, Helen. 'Women and the garrison mentality: pioneer women autobiographers and their relation to the land', in Lorraine McMullen (ed.), *Re(Dis)covering Our Foremothers: Nineteenth Century Canadian Women Writers*. Ottawa: University of Ottawa Press, pp. 123–36.

Buss, Helen. *Canadian Women's Autobiography in English*. Ottawa: CRIAW/ICREF, 1991.

Buss, Helen. *Mapping Our Selves: Canadian Women's Autobiography in English*. Montreal: McGill-Queen's University Press, 1993.

Butler, Judith. *Gender Trouble: Feminism and the Subversion of Identity*. New York: Routledge, 1990.

Butterfield, Stephen. *Black Autobiography in America*. Amherst: University of Massachusetts Press, 1974.

Carrithers, Michael. *The Category of the Person: Anthropology, Philosophy, History*. Cambridge: Cambridge University Press, 1985.

Carroll, John (ed.). *Intruders in the Bush: The Australian Quest for Identity*. Melbourne: Oxford University Press, 1989.

Carter, David. 'Tasteless subjects: postcolonial literary criticism, realism, and the subject of taste', *Southern Review*, 25(3) (November 1992): 292–303.

Carusi, Annamaria. 'Post, post and post: or where is South African literature in all this?' *Ariel*. 20(4) (1990): 79–95.

Chambers, Ross. *Room for Maneuver: Reading Oppositional Narrative*. Chicago: University of Chicago Press, 1991.

Clare, Monica. *Karobran: The Story of an Aboriginal Girl*. Sydney: Alternative Publishing Cooperative, 1978.

Clifford, James. 'Diasporas', *Cultural Anthropology*, 9(3) (1994): 302–38.

Clifford, James and Dhareshwar, Vivek. *Traveling Theories, Traveling Theorists*. Santa Cruz, CA: Center for Cultural Studies, University of California, 1989.

Coe, Richard. *When the Grass Was Taller: Autobiography and the Experience of Childhood*. New Haven, CT: Yale University Press, 1984.

Cohen, Patsy and Margaret Somerville (eds). *Ingelba and the Five Black Matriarchs*. Sydney: Allen & Unwin, 1990.

Coleman, Daniel. *Masculine Migrations: Reading the Postcolonial Male in 'New Canadian' Narratives*. Toronto: University of Toronto Press, 1998.

Collis, Christy. 'Siting the second world in South African literary culture', *New Literatures Review*, 27 (summer 1995): 1–15.

Couille, Judith Lütge. ' "Not quite fiction": the challenges of poststructuralism to the reading of contemporary South African autobiography', *Current Writing: Text and Reception in South Africa*, 3 (1991): 1–23.

Couille, Judith Lütge. 'Self, life and writing in selected South African autobiographical texts'. Unpublished PhD thesis, University of Natal, 1994.

Couille, Judith Lütge. '(In)continent I-lands: blurring the boundaries between self and other in South African women's autobiographies', *Ariel*, 27(1) (January 1996): 133–48.

Darian-Smith, Kate, Liz Gunnar and Sarah Nuttall (eds). *Text, Theory, Space: Land, Literature and History in South Africa and Australia*. London: Routledge, 1996.

Davidoff, Leonore and Catherine Hall. *Family Fortunes: Men and Women of the English Middle Class, 1780–1850*. London: Hutchinson, 1987.

Davin, Anna. 'Imperialism and motherhood', *History Workshop Journal*, 5 (spring 1978): 9–65.

Daymond, Margaret. 'Class in the discourses of Sindiwe Magona's autobiography and fiction', *Journal of Southern African Studies*, 21(4) (December 1995): 561–72.

Daymond, Margaret. 'On retaining and recognising changes in the genre "autobiography" ', *Current Writing: Text and Reception in Southern Africa*, 3(1) (1991): 31–41.

Dean, Misao. *Practising Femininity: Domestic Realism and the Performance of Gender in Early Canadian Fiction*. Toronto: University of Toronto Press, 1998.

de la Campa, Roman, E. Ann Kaplan and Michael Sprinker (eds). *Late Imperial Culture*. London: Verso, 1995.

de Lauretis, Teresa. *Alice Doesn't: Feminism, Semiotics and Cinema*. Bloomington: Indiana University Press, 1984.

de Lauretis, Teresa. *Technologies of Gender: Essays on Theory, Film and Fiction*. Bloomington: Indiana University Press, 1987.

de Man, Paul. 'Autobiography as de-facement', *Modern Language Notes*, 94 (1979): 919–30.

Donaldson, Laura E. *Decolonizing Feminisms: Race, Gender and Empire-Building*. Chapel Hill: The University of North Carolina Press, 1992.

Donnell, Alison. 'Cultural paralysis in postcolonial criticism', *Ariel*, 26(1) (1995): 101–16.

Driver, Dorothy. ' "Woman" as sign in South African colonial enterprise', *Journal of Literary Studies*, 4(1) (March 1988): 3–20.

Driver, Dorothy. 'M'a-Ngoana O Tšoare Thipa ka Bohaleng – the child's mother grabs the sharp end of the knife: women as mothers, women as writers', in Martin Trump (ed.), *Rendering Things Visible: Essays on South African Literary Culture*. Johannesburg: Ravan Press, 1990, pp. 225–55.

Driver, Dorothy. 'Imagined selves, (un)imagined marginalities', *Journal of Southern African Studies*, 17(2) (June 1991): 337–54.

duCille, Ann. 'The occult of true black womanhood: critical demeanour and black feminist studies', *Signs*, 19(3) (spring 1994), 591–629.

Eakin, Paul John. *Fictions in Autobiography: Studies in the Art of Self-Invention.* Princeton, NJ: Princeton University Press, 1985.

Eakin, Paul John. *Touching the World: Reference in Autobiography.* Princeton, NJ: Princeton University Press, 1992.

Emberley, Julia V. *Thresholds of Difference: Feminist Critique, Native Women's Writings, Postcolonial Theory.* Toronto: University of Toronto Press, 1993.

Ferguson, Moira. *Jamaica Kincaid: Where the Land Meets the Body.* Charlottesville: University Press of Virginia, 1994.

Ferguson, Moira. *Colonialism and Gender Relations from Mary Wollstonecraft to Jamaica Kincaid: East Caribbean Connections.* New York: Columbia University Press, 1993.

Ferguson, Moira. *Subject to Others: British Women Writers and Colonial Slavery, 1670–1834.* New York: Routledge, 1992.

Ferguson, Moira (ed.). *The History of Mary Prince, A West Indian Slave, Related by Herself.* London: Pandora, 1987. Revised edn Ann Arbor: University of Michigan Press, 1997.

Ford Smith, Honor (ed.). *Lionheart Gal: Life Stories of Jamaican Women.* Toronto: Sister Vision, 1987.

Foucault, Michel. *Discipline and Punish: The Birth of the Prison.* Harmondsworth: Penguin, 1979.

Fox-Genovese, Elizabeth. 'To write myself: the autobiographies of Afro-American women', in Shari Benstock (ed.), *Feminist Issues in Literary Scholarship.* Bloomington: Indiana University Press, 1987.

Frankenberg, Ruth. *White Women, Race Matters: The Social Construction of Whiteness.* Minneapolis: University of Minnesota Press, 1993.

Frankenberg, Ruth and Lata Mani. 'Crosscurrents, crosstalk: race, "Postcoloniality" and the politics of location', *Cultural Studies,* 7(2) (1993): 292–310.

Friewald, Bina. ' "Femininely speaking": Anna Jameson's winter studies and summer rambles', in Shirley Neuman and Smaro Kamboureli (eds), *Amazing Space: Writing Canadian Women Writing.* Edmonton: Longspoon/NeWest, 1986, pp. 61–73.

Friewald, Bina. ' "The tongue of woman": the language of the self in Moodie's *Roughing It in the Bush*', in Lorraine McMullen (ed.), *Rediscovering Our Foremothers: Nineteenth Century Canadian Women Writers.* Ottawa: University of Ottawa Press.

Gaffney, Ellie. *Somebody Now.* Canberra: Aboriginal Studies Press, 1989.

Gagnier, Regenia. *Subjectivities: A History of Self-Representation in Britain, 1832–1920.* Oxford; Oxford University Press, 1991.

Gallmann, Kuki. *I Dreamed of Africa.* London: Penguin Books, 1992.

Gallmann, Kuki. *African Nights.* London: Penguin, 1995.

Garfield, Deborah M. and Rafia Zafar. *Harriet Jacobs and 'Incidents in the Life of a Slave Girl'.* New York: Cambridge University Press, 1996.

Gates, Henry Louis, Jr (ed.). *The Classic Slave Narratives.* New York: Mentor, 1987.

Gates, Henry Louis, Jr. *Colored People: A Memoir.* New York: Vintage Books, 1995.

Gaunt, Mary. *Alone in West Africa.* London: T. Werner Laurie, 1912.

Gaunt, Mary. *Where the Twain Meet.* London: John Murray, 1922.

Gaunt, Mary. *Reflection – in Jamaica.* London: Ernest Benn Ltd, 1932.

Gavron, Jeremy. *Darkness in Eden: The Murder of Julie Ward*. London: HarperCollins, 1991.

Gelder, Ken and Jane M. Jacobs. *Uncanny Australia: Sacredness and Identity in a Postcolonial Nation*. Melbourne: Melbourne University Press, 1998.

Gerson, Carole. 'Mrs. Moodie's beloved partner', *Canadian Literature*, 107 (winter 1985): 34–45.

Gerson, Carole. 'Nobler savages: representations of native women in the writings of Susanna Moodie and Catharine Parr Traill', *Journal of Canadian Studies*, 32(1) (spring 1997): 5–21.

Gikandi, Simon. *Maps of Englishness: Writing Identity in the Culture of Colonialism*. New York: Columbia University Press, 1996.

Gilmore, Leigh. *Autobiographics: A Feminist Theory of Women's Self-Representation*. Ithaca, NY: Cornell University Press, 1994.

Gilroy, Paul. *The Black Atlantic: Modernity and Double Consciousness*. London: Verso, 1993.

Godard, Barbara (ed.). *Collaboration in the Feminine: Writings of Women and Culture from 'Tessera'*. Toronto: Second Story Press, 1994.

Godwin, Peter. *Mukiwa: A White Boy in Africa*. London: Macmillan, 1996.

Goodman, David. *Gold Seeking: Victoria and California in the 1850s*. Sydney: Allen & Unwin, 1944.

Goodwin, June and Ben Schiff. *Heart of Whiteness: Afrikaaners Face Black Rule in the New South Africa*. New York: Scribner, 1995.

Grewal, Inderpal. *Home and Harem: Nation, Gender, Empire and the Cultures of Travel*. Durham, NC: Duke University Press, 1996.

Grewal, Inderpal and Caren Kaplan (eds). *Scattered Hegemonies: Postmodernity and Transnational Feminist Practices*. Minneapolis: University of Minnesota Press, 1994.

Grimshaw, Patricia, Marilyn Lake, Ann McGrath and Marian Quartly. *Creating a Nation*. Ringwood,Victoria: McPhee Gribble, 1994.

Gusdorf, Georges. 'Conditions and limits of autobiography', trans. James Olney, in James Olney (ed.), *Autobiography: Essays Theoretical and Critical*. Princeton, NJ: Princeton University Press, 1980, pp. 28–49.

Hall, Catherine. *White, Male and Middle-class: Explorations in Feminism and History*. New York: Routledge, 1992.

Hardy Aiken, Susan. *Isak Dinesen and the Engendering of Narrative*. Chicago: University of Chicago Press, 1990.

Harlow, Barbara. *Resistance Literature*. London: Methuen, 1987.

Healy, Chris. *From the Ruins of Colonialism: History as Social Memory*. Melbourne: Cambridge University Press, 1997.

Hearn, Jeff and David Morgan (eds). *Men, Masculinities and Social Theory*. London: Unwin Hyman, 1990.

Hewitt, Leah. *Autobiographical Tightropes*. Lincoln: University of Nebraska Press, 1990.

Hiltzik, Michael A. *A Death in Africa: The Murder of Julie Ward*. London: Bantam, 1991.

Holst Petersen, Kirsten and Anna Rutherford. *A Double Colonization: Colonial and Post-Colonial Women's Writing*. Mundelstrup: Dangaroo Press, 1986.

hooks, bell. *Bone Black: Memories of Girlhood*. New York: Henry Holt & Co., 1996.

hooks, bell. *Feminist Theory: From Margin to Center*. Boston: South End Press, 1984.

Hooton, Joy. *Stories of Herself When Young: Autobiographies of Childhood by Australian Women*. Melbourne: Oxford University Press, 1990.

Huggins, Jackie. *Sister Girl*. St Lucia: University of Queensland Press, 1998.

Huggins, Rita and Jackie Huggins. *Auntie Rita*. Canberra: Aboriginal Studies Press, 1994.

Hulme, Peter. *Colonial Encounters: Europe and the Native Caribbean 1492–1797*. London: Routledge, 1992.

Hurley, Michael. *The Borders of Nightmare: The Fiction of John Richardson*. Toronto: University of Toronto Press, 1992.

Huxley, Elspeth. *The Flame Trees of Thika: Memories of an African Childhood*. London: Penguin, 1962.

Hyam, Ronald. *Empire and Sexuality: The British Experience*. Manchester: Manchester University Press, 1990.

Jay, Paul. *Being in the Text: Self-Representation from Wordsworth to Roland Barthes*. Ithaca, NY: Cornell University Press, 1984.

Jelinek, Estelle C. (ed.). *Women's Autobiography: Essays in Criticism*. Bloomington: Indiana University Press, 1980.

Jolly, Margaret. 'Colonizing women: The maternal body and empire', in Sneja Gunew and Anna Yeatman (eds), *Feminism and the Politics of Difference*. Sydney: Allen & Unwin, 1993, pp. 103–27.

Jolly, Rosemary. *Colonization, Violence, and Narration in White South African Writing: André Brink, Breyten Breytenbach, and J. M. Coetzee*. Athens: Ohio University Press, 1996.

Jolly, Rosemary. 'Rehearsals of liberation: contemporary postcolonial discourse and the new South Africa', *PMLA*, 110 (1995): 17–29.

Joubert, Elsa. *Poppie Nongena*. New York: W. W. Norton & Co, 1980.

Kadar, Marlene (ed.). *Essays on Life Writing: From Genre to Critical Practice*. Toronto: University of Toronto Press, 1991.

Kaplan, Caren. *Questions of Travel: Postmodern Discourses of Displacement*. Durham, NC: Duke University Press, 1996.

Kennedy, Dane. *Islands of White: Settler Society and Culture in Kenya and Southern Rhodesia, 1890–1939*. Durham, NC: Duke University Press, 1987.

Kidd, Rosalind. *The Way We Civilise: Aboriginal Affairs – The Untold Story*. St Lucia: University of Queensland Press, 1997.

Kincaid, Jamaica. *My Brother*. London: Vintage, 1998.

Kincaid, Jamaica. *A Small Place*. New York: Plume, 1988.

Krog, Antjie. *Country of My Skull*. Johannesburg: Random House South Africa Pty, 1998.

Kuzwayo, Ellen. *Call Me Woman*. Randburg: Ravan Press, 1996.

Lane, Christopher. *The Ruling Passion: British Colonial Allegory and the Paradox of Homosexual Desire*. Durham, NC: Duke University Press, 1995.

Langford, Ruby (Ginibi). *Real Deadly*. Sydney: Angus & Robertson, 1992.

Langford, Ruby (Ginibi). *My Bundjalung People.* St Lucia: University of Queensland Press, 1994.

Langford Ginibi, Ruby. *Don't Take Your Love to Town.* Ringwood, Victoria: Penguin Books, 1998.

Langton, Anne. *A Gentlewoman in Upper Canada: The Journals of Anne Langton,* ed. H. H. Langton. Toronto/Vancouver: Clarke Irwin & Co., 1950, 1964.

Langton, Marcia. 'Aboriginal art and film: the politics of representation', *Race and Class,* 35(2) (April–June 1994): 89–106.

Laqueur, Thomas. *Making Sex: Body and Gender from the Greeks to Freud.* Cambridge, MA: Harvard University Press, 1990.

Lawson, Alan. 'A cultural paradigm for the second world', *Australian-Canadian Studies,* 9(1–2) (1991), pp 67–78.

Lawson, Alan. 'Un/settling colonies: the ambivalent place of discursive resistance', in C. Worth *et al.* (eds), *Literature and Opposition.* Clayton, Victoria: Centre for Comparative Literature and Cultural Studies, Monash University, 1994, pp. 67–82.

Lecker, Robert (ed.). *Canadian Canons: Essays in Literary Value.* Toronto: University of Toronto Press, 1991.

Lecker, Robert. *Making It Real: The Canonization of English-Canadian Literature.* Concord, Ontario: Anansi, 1995.

Lejeune, Philippe. *On Autobiography,* ed. Paul John Eakin, trans. Katherine Leary. Minneapolis: University of Minnesota Press, 1989.

Leps, Marie-Christine. *Apprehending the Criminal: The Production of Deviance in Nineteenth-Century Discourse.* Durham, NC: Duke University Press, 1992.

Lessing, Doris. *A Small Personal Voice.* New York: Vintage Books, 1975.

Lessing, Doris. *The Golden Notebook.* London: Flamingo, 1993.

Lessing, Doris. *Under My Skin.* London: Flamingo, 1995.

Lessing, Doris. *Going Home.* London: HarperPerennial, 1996.

Lessing, Doris. *Walking in the Shade.* London: HarperCollins, 1997.

Levine, George (ed.). *Constructions of the Self.* New Brunswick, NJ: Rutgers University Press, 1992.

Levy, Anita. *Other Women: The Writing of Class, Race and Gender, 1832–1898.* Princeton, NJ: Princeton University Press, 1991.

Lewis, Desiree. 'Myths of motherhood and power: the construction of "black woman" in literature', *English in Africa,* 19(1) (May 1992): 35–51.

Lewis, Reina. *Gendering Orientalism: Race, Femininity and Representation.* London: Routledge, 1996.

Lim, Shirley Geok-Lin. *Among the White Moon Faces: An Asian-American Memoir of Homelands.* New York: The Feminist Press, 1996.

Lionnet, Françoise. *Autobiographical Voices: Race, Gender, Self-Portraiture.* Ithaca, NY: Cornell University Press, 1989.

Lionnet, Françoise. *Postcolonial Representations: Women, Literature, Identity.* Ithaca, NY: Cornell University Press, 1995.

Lively, Penelope. *Oleander, Jacaranda: A Childhood Perceived.* Harmondsworth: Penguin, 1995.

Llewellyn, Kate. *Gorillas, Tea and Coffee: An African Sketchbook*. Hawthorn, Victoria: Hudson Publishing, 1996.

Lorde, Audre. *Zami: A New Spelling of My Name*. Freedom, CA: The Crossing Press, 1982.

Lowe, Lisa. *Immigrant Acts: On Asian American Cultural Politics*. Durham, NC: Duke University Press, 1996.

McClintock, Anne. *Imperial Leather: Race, Gender and Sexuality in the Colonial Contest*. London: Routledge, 1995.

MacKenzie, John M. *The Empire of Nature: Hunting, Conservation and British Imperialism*. Manchester: Manchester University Press, 1988.

McMullen, Lorraine (ed.). *Re(Dis)covering Our Foremothers: Nineteenth Century Canadian Women Writers*. Ottawa: University of Ottawa Press, 1990.

McWatt, Mark (ed.). *West Indian Literature and Its Social Context*. Cave Hill, Barbados: Department of English UWI, 1985.

Magona, Sindiwe. *Forced to Grow*. London: The Women's Press, 1992.

Magona, Sindiwe. *To My Children's Children: An Autobiography*. London: The Women's Press, 1991.

Mamdani, Mahmood. *Citizen and Subject: Contemporary Africa and the Legacy of Late Colonialism*. Princeton, NJ: Princeton University Press, 1996.

Mandela, Nelson. *Long Walk to Freedom*. London: Abacus, 1995.

Mangan, J. A. and James Walvin. *Manliness and Morality: Middle-class Masculinity in Britain and America 1800–1940*. Manchester: Manchester University Press, 1987.

Mani, Lata. 'Multiple mediations: feminist scholarship in the age of multinational reception', in James Clifford and Virek Dhareshwar (eds), 'Travelling theories: travelling theorists', *Inscriptions*, 5. Santa Cruz: Center for Cultural Studies, 1989.

Markham, Beryl. *West with the Night*. London: Virago, 1992.

Marks, Shula (ed.). *Not Either an Experimental Doll: The Separate Worlds of Three South African Women*. Bloomington: Indiana University Press, 1987.

Marlatt, Daphne. *Taken*. Concord, ON: Anansi, 1996.

Martin, Biddy. 'Lesbian identity and autobiographical difference[s]', in Bella Brodzki and Celeste Schenck (eds), *Life/Lines: Theorizing Women's Autobiography*. Ithaca, NY: Cornell University Press, 1988, pp. 77–103.

Martin Shaw, Carolyn. *Colonial Inscriptions: Race, Sex and Class in Kenya*. Minneapolis: University of Minnesota Press, 1995.

Mashinini, Emma. *Strikes Have Followed Me All of My Life: A South African Autobiography*. London: The Women's Press, 1989.

Midgely, Clare, *Gender and Imperialism*. Manchester: Manchester University Press, 1998.

Miller, Nancy. *Subject to Change: Reading Feminist Writing*. New York: Columbia University Press, 1988.

Mills, Sarah. *Discourses of Difference: An Analysis of Women's Travel Writing and Colonialism*. London: Routledge, 1991.

Minh-ha, Trinh T. *Woman, Native, Other: Writing Postcoloniality and Feminism*. Bloomington: Indiana University Press, 1989.

Moodie, J. W. D. *Ten Years in South Africa, Including a Particular Description of the Wild Sports of That Country* (2 vols). London: Richard Bentley, 1835.

Moodie, Susanna. *Roughing It in the Bush or Life in Canada*, ed. Carl Ballstadt. Ottawa: Carleton University Press, 1988.

Moore-Gilbert, Bart. *Postcolonial Theory: Contexts, Practices, Politics*. London: Verso, 1997.

Moreton-Robinson, Aileen. *Talkin' up to the White Woman: Indigenous Women and Feminism in Australia*. St Lucia: University of Queensland Press, in press.

Morgan, Sally. *My Place*. Fremantle: Fremantle Arts Centre Press, 1987.

Morgan, Sally. *Wanamurraganya: The Story of Jack McPhee*. Fremantle: Fremantle Arts Centre Press, 1989.

Morgan, Susan. *Place Matters: Gendered Geography in Victorian Women's Travel Books about Southeast Asia*. New Brunswick, NJ: Rutgers University Press, 1996.

Morley, David and Kuan-Hsing Chen. *Stuart Hall: Critical Dialogues in Cultural Studies*. London: Routledge, 1996.

Morris, James. *Farewell the Trumpets: An Imperial Retreat*. Harmondsworth: Penguin, 1987.

Morris, James. *Heaven's Command: An Imperial Progress*. Harmondsworth; Penguin, 1986.

Morris, James. *Pax Britannica: The Climax of an Empire*. Harmondsworth: Penguin, 1979.

Morrison, Toni. *Playing in the Dark: Whiteness and the Literary Imagination*. Cambridge, MA: Harvard University Press, 1992.

Mudrooroo (Narogin) [Colin Johnson]. *Writing from the Fringe: A Study of Modern Aboriginal Literature*. Melbourne: Hyland House, 1990.

Mudrooroo (Narogin) [Colin Johnson]. 'A literature of Aboriginality', *Ulitarra*, 1 (1992): 28–33.

Mudrooroo (Narogin) [Colin Johnson]. 'Couldn't ya cry, if ya couldn't laugh: the literature of Aboriginality and its reviewers', *Span*, 34–37 (1992–1993): 376–83.

Mudrooroo (Narogin) [Colin Johnson]. *Indigenous Literature of Australia: Milli Milli Wangka*. South Yarra: Hyland House 1997.

Muecke, Stephen. *Textual Spaces: Aboriginality and Cultural Studies*. Sydney: New South Wales University Press, 1992.

Murphy, Dervla. *The Ukimwi Road: From Kenya to Zimbabwe*. London: Flamingo, 1994.

Murphy, Dervla. *South from the Limpopo: Travels Through South Africa*. London: John Murray, 1997.

Murray, Pamela. 'Staking a claim: Mary Gaunt and *Kirkham's Find*'. Honours dissertatiion, Griffith University, 1991.

Neuman, Shirley. 'Importing difference', in Shirley Neuman and Smaro Kamboureli (eds), *Amazing Space: Writing Canadian Women Writing*. Edmonton: Longspoon/ NeWest, 1986, pp. 392–405.

Neuman, Shirley '"An appearance walking in a forest the sexes burn": autobiography and the construction of the feminine body', in Kathleen Ashley *et al.* (eds), *Postmodernism and Autobiography*. Amherst: The University of Massachusetts Press, 1994.

Neuman, Shirley (ed.). *Autobiography and Questions of Gender*. London: Frank Cass, 1991.

Neuman, Shirley. 'Autobiography: from different poetics to a poetics of difference', in Marlene Kadar (ed.), *Essays on Life Writing: From Genre to Critical Practice*. Toronto: University of Toronto Press, 1992, pp. 213–30.

Neuman, Shirley and Smaro Kamboureli (eds). *Amazing Space: Writing Canadian Women Writing*. Edmonton: Longspoon/NeWest, 1986.

Nicholas, Stephen and Peter R. Shergold (eds). *Convict Workers: Reinterpreting Australia's Past*. Sydney: Cambridge University Press, 1988.

Nnaemeka, Obioma (ed.). *The Politics of (M)Othering: Womanhood, Identity and Resistance in African Literature*. London: Routledge, 1997.

Norval, Aletta J. *Deconstructing Apartheid Discourse*. London: Verso, 1996.

Nussbaum, Felicity. *The Autobiographical Subject: Gender and Ideology in Eighteenth-Century England*. Baltimore: Johns Hopkins University Press, 1989.

Nussbaum, Felicity. *Torrid Zones: Maternity, Sexuality and Empire in Eighteenth-Century English Narratives*. Baltimore: Johns Hopkins University Press, 1995.

Nuttall, Sarah. 'Reading in the lives and writing of black women', *Journal of Southern African Studies*, 20(1) (March 1994): 85–98.

Nuttall, Sarah and Carli Coetzee (eds). *Negotiating the Past: The Making of Memory in South Africa*. Cape Town: Oxford University Press, 1998.

Obama, Barack. *Dreams from My Father: A Story of Race and Inheritance*. New York: Kodansha International, 1996.

O'Brien, Mary. *The Journals of Mary O'Brien 1828–1838*, ed. Audrey Saunders Miller. Toronto: Macmillan, 1968.

Olney, James. *Metaphors of the Self: The Meaning of Autobiography*. Princeton: Princeton University Press, 1972.

Olney, James (ed.). *Autobiography: Essays Theoretical and Critical*. Princeton, NJ: Princeton University Press, 1980.

Olney, James. *Studies in Autobiography*. New York: Oxford University Press, 1988.

Parker, Kenneth. 'Very like a whale: post-colonialism between canonicities and ethnicities', *Social Identities: Journal for the Study of Race, Nation and Culture*, 1(1) (1995): 155–74.

Pascal, Roy. *Design and Truth in Autobiography*. Cambridge, MA: Harvard University Press, 1960.

Perrault, Jeanne. *Writing Selves: Contemporary Feminist Autography*. Minnea-polis: University of Minnesota Press, 1995.

The Personal Narratives Group (ed.). *Interpreting Women's Lives: Feminist Theory and Personal Narratives*. Bloomington: Indiana University Press, 1989.

Pesman, Ros. *Duty Free: Australian Women Abroad*. Melbourne: Oxford University Press, 1996.

Pesman, Ros, David Walker and Richard White (eds). *The Oxford Book of Australian Travel Writing*. Melbourne: Oxford University Press, 1996.

Pile, Steve and Nigel Thrift (eds). *Mapping the Subject: Geographies of Cultural Transformation*. London: Routledge, 1995.

Poovey, Mary. *Uneven Developments: The Ideological Work of Gender in Mid-Victorian England.* Chicago: University of Chicago Press, 1988.

Pratt, Mary Louise. *Imperial Eyes: Travel Writing and Transculturation.* London: Routledge, 1992.

Probyn, Elspeth. *Sexing the Self: Gendered Positions in Cultural Studies.* London: Routledge, 1993.

Ramphele, Mamphela. *Mamphela Ramphele: A Life.* Cape Town: David Philips, 1995.

Riley, Denise. *'Am I That Name?' Feminism and the Category of 'Women' in History.* Minneapolis: University of Minnesota Press, 1988.

Roughsey, Elsie (Labumore). *An Aboriginal Mother Tells of the Old and the New.* Melbourne: McPhee Gribble/Penguin, 1984.

Rowse, Tim. 'The Aboriginal subject in autobiography: Ruby Langford's *Don't Take Your Love to Town*', *Australian Literary Studies*, 16(1) (1993): 14–29.

Rowse, Tim. *After Mabo: Interpreting Indigenous Traditions.* Melbourne: Melbourne University Press, 1994.

Rutherford, Anna (ed.). *From Commonwealth to Post-Colonial.* Sydney: Dangaroo Press, 1992.

Saba Saakana, Amon. *The Colonial Legacy in Caribbean Literature.* Trenton, NJ: Africa World Press, Inc, 1987.

Sander, Reinhard W. 'The Trinidad awakening: West Indian literature of the nineteen-thirties'. Unpublished PhD dissertation, The University of Texas at Austin, 1979.

Sawicki, Jana. *Disciplining Foucault: Feminism, Power and the Body.* London: Routledge, 1991.

Schalkwyk, David. 'The flight from politics: an analysis of the reception of *Poppie Nongena*', *Journal of Southern African Studies*, 12(2) (1986): 183–95.

Seacole, Mary. *Wonderful Adventures of Mrs. Seacole in Many Lands.* New York: Oxford University Press, 1988.

Sharpe, Jenny. *Allegories of Empire: The Figure of Woman in the Colonial Text.* Minneapolis: University of Minnesota Press, 1993.

Simon, Ella. *Through My Eyes.* Adelaide: Rigby, 1978.

Simpson, Alyse. *The Land That Never Was.* London: Selwyn & Blount, 1937.

Slemon, Stephen. 'Unsettling the empire: resistance theory for the second world', *WLWE*, 30(2) (1991): 30–41.

Slemon, Stephen. 'Introductory notes: postcolonialism and its discontents', *Ariel*, 26(1) (1995): 7–11.

Slemon, Stephen and Helen Tiffin (eds). *After Europe.* Sydney: Dangaroo Press, 1989.

Slovo, Gillian. *Every Secret Thing.* London: Little, Brown & Co, 1997.

Smith, Shirley with Bobbi Sykes. *Mum Shirl.* Melbourne: Heinemann, 1981.

Smith, Sidonie. *A Poetics of Women's Autobiography: Marginality and the Fictions of Self-Representation.* Bloomington: Indiana University Press, 1987.

Smith, Sidonie. *Subjectivity, Identity and the Body.* Bloomington: Indiana University Press, 1993.

Smith, Sidonie. *Getting a Life: Everyday Uses of Autobiography.* Minneapolis: University of Minnesota Press, 1996.

Smith, Sidonie and Julia Watson (eds). *De/Colonizing the Subject: The Politics of Gender in Women's Autobiography*. Minneapolis: University of Minnesota Press, 1992.

Somerville, Margaret. 'Life (hi)story writing: the relationship between talk and text', *Hecate*, 17(1) (1991): 95.

Soyinka, Wole. *Aké. —Isarà: Memoirs of a Nigerian Childhood*. London: Minerva, 1994.

Spivak, Gayatri Chakravorty. *In Other Worlds: Essays in Cultural Politics*. New York: Methuen, 1987.

Stanton, Domna C. *The Female Autograph*. Chicago: The University of Chicago Press, 1987.

Stasiulis, Daiva and Nira Yuval-Davis (eds). *Unsettling Settler Societies: Articulations of Gender, Race, Ethnicity and Class*. London: Sage, 1995.

Steedman, Carolyn. *Landscape for a Good Woman: A Story of Two Lives*. New Brunswick, NJ: Rutgers University Press, 1987.

Steedman, Carolyn. *Past Tenses: Essays on Writing Autobiography and History*. London: Rivers Oram Press, 1992.

Stewart, Frances. *Our Forest Home: Being Extracts from the Correspondence of the Late Frances Stewart*, ed. E.S. Dunlap. Montreal: Gazette Printing & Publishing Co, 1902.

Stoler, Laura Ann. *Race and the Education of Desire: Foucault's 'History of Sexuality' and the Colonial Order of Things*. Durham, NC: Duke University Press, 1995.

Stratton, Florence. *African Literature and the Politics of Gender*. London: Routledge, 1994.

Strobel, Margaret. *European Women and the Second British Empire*. Bloomington: Indiana University Press, 1991.

Suleri, Sara. *Meatless Days*. Chicago: The University of Chicago Press, 1989.

Suleri, Sara. *The Rhetoric of English India*. Chicago: The University of Chicago Press, 1992.

Suzman, Helen. *In No Uncertain Terms*. London: Mandarin Paperbacks, 1994.

Taylor, Jenny (ed.). *Notebooks, Memoirs, Archives: Reading and Rereading Doris Lessing*. London: Routledge & Kegan Paul, 1982.

Thomas, Nicholas. *Colonialism's Culture: Anthropology, Travel and Government*. London: Polity Press, 1994.

Thompson, Elizabeth. *The Pioneer Woman: A Canadian Character Type*. Montreal: McGill-Queens University Press, 1991.

Thurston, John. *The Work of Words: The Writing of Susanna Strickland Moodie*. Montreal/Kingston: McGill-Queens University Press, 1996.

Tidrick, Kathryn. *Empire and the English Character*. London: I. B. Tauris, 1992.

Tiffin, Helen. 'Cold hearts and (foreign) tongues. Recitation and reclamation of the female body in the works of Erna Brodber and Jamaica Kincaid', *Callaloo*, 16(4) (1993): 909–21.

Traill, Catharine Parr. *The Backwoods of Canada: Being Letters from the Wife of an Emigrant Officer, Illustrative of the Domestic Economy of British America*, ed. Michael A. Peterman. Ottawa: Carleton University Press, 1997.

Trollope, Joanna. *Britannia's Daughters: Women of the British Empire*. London: Pimlico, 1994.

Walvin, James. *Black Ivory: A History of British Slavery*. London: Fontana Press, 1992.

Ward, Glenyse. *Unna You Fullas*. Broome: Magabala Books, 1991.

Ward, Glenyse. *Wandering Girl*. Broome: Magabala Books, 1998.

Ward, John. *The Animals Are Innocent: The Search for Julie's Killers*. London: BCA, 1991.

Ware, Vron. *Beyond the Pale: White Women, Racism and History*. London: Verso, 1992.

Ware, Vron. 'Moments of danger: "race", gender and memories of Empire', *History and Theory*, 31(4) (1992): 116–38.

Whitlock, Gillian (ed.). *Autographs: Contemporary Australian Autobiography*. St Lucia: University of Queensland Press, 1996.

Whitlock, Gillian and David Carter (eds). *Images of Australia*. St Lucia: University of Queensland Press, 1992.

Whitlock, Gillian and Helen Tiffin (eds). *Re-Siting Queen's English: Text and Tradition in Post-Colonial Literatures*. Amsterdam: Rodopi, 1992.

Wicomb, Zoë. *You Can't Get Lost in Cape Town*. London: Virago, 1987.

Wilson, Robert R. 'Seeing with a fly's eye: comparative perspectives in Commonwealth literature', *Open Letter* 8th Series, 2 (winter 1992): 5–27.

Wolff, Janet. *Feminine Sentences: Essays on Women and Culture*. Berkeley: University of California Press, 1990.

Wolpe, AnnMarie. *The Long Way Home*. London: Virago, 1994.

Worth, Chris, Pauline Nestor and Marko Parlyshyn (eds). *Literature and Opposition*. Clayton, Victoria: Centre for Comparative Literature and Cultural Studies, Monash University, 1994.

Young, Robert. *White Mythologies: Writing History and the West*. London: Routledge, 1990.

Young, Robert. *Colonial Desire: Hybridity in Theory, Culture and Race*. London: Routledge, 1995.

Index

Lawson, Alan 71 n11
Leakey, Richard 113, 115
see also ivory fire
Lecker, Robert 69, 71 n1
Lessing, Doris 6, 183, 186, 189, 190–200,
 201, 203
 dystopias 183, 193, 199
 genre of autobiographical writings 192,
 194
 see also Going Home; Under My Skin
 memory 192, 193, 195, 198–9
 political consciousness 186, 193, 191, 198
 see also childhood; childhood, colonial;
 *Children of Violence; Going Home; The
 Golden Notebook; In Pursuit of the
 English; Martha Quest; Memoirs of a
 Survivor; Under My Skin; Walking in the
 Shade*
Levy, Anita 36 n17, 37 n31, 73 nn26 & 27
life history writing, *see* autobiographic
 writing; slave narrative
Life of Olaudah Equiano, The 30, 80
life story, origins in social anthropology 163
life writing, *see* autobiographic writing, slave
 narrative
Lim, Shirley Geok-Lin 202–3
Lively, Penelope 183–9, 194, 200, 203
 'ghost' of childhood 184, 186, 201
 making of Englishness 186–9
 see also Oleander, Jacaranda
Llewellyn, Kate; *Gorillas, Tea and Coffee* 112,
 117, 131, 132, 136, 138, 143
Long Way Home, The 154
Lorde, Audre 179, 180, 181, 182, 201, 202

McClintock, Anne 67
McCooey, David 181
MacKenzie, John M. 137
Magona, Sindiwe 147, 150, 166, 180
 links between public and private 146,
 153–4
 resistance to apartheid 148, 153, 172
 *see also Forced to Grow; To My Children's
 Children*
Makhoere, Caesarina Kona: *No Child's Play*
 147
Malaya, *see* Lim; Marlatt
Mamphela Ramphele: A Life 168, 172
 see also Ramphele
Mandela, Nelson 142, 143, 148, 169
Mansfield Park, and slavery 80
marginalia 12–14, 16, 25, 31, 32
 and authentication 13, 16, 31

Call Me Woman 149, 150–1, 169–70
challenge to narrator's authority 21, 22
reflection of ambivalence 22
Wonderful Adventures 86
see also collaboration, inter-racial; *History of
 Mary Prince*
Markham, Beryl 115, 116, 117, 124, 133,
 134–7
 identity as 'white' African 126, 128, 130–1
 safari 135–6, 137
Marks, Shula 163
Marlatt, Daphne 200–4
 see also Ana Historic; Taken
Martha Quest 192
 see also Lessing
Martin, Biddy 203
Martin Shaw, Carolyn 74 n50,
 140 nn11, 16 & 18
masculinity 6, 44–5, 47, 48, 51, 58, 65
 in African colonial discourse 60, 121, 138
 domesticity and 58–9
 identity 59
 and John Moodie 42, 59, 62, 70
 paternity 65–6
 redefinition in colonies 53, 54
 safari and 129
 see also white hunter
 and temperance 59, 62, 63–4
Mashinini, Emma 147, 148, 152, 161
master narrative 96–7, 102, 117
 see also Gaunt
maternalism 148, 151
 see also motherhood
Matshoba, Debra Nikiwe 149
Mau Mau revolt 125, 131, 139 n3
Meatless Days 5
 see also Suleri
Melsetter 199, 203
 see also Moodie, John
memoirs, *see* autobiographic writing; slave
 narrative
Memoirs of a Survivor 192, 197
 see also Lessing
memory 2, 82, 180–2, 192–3, 195–7, 200
 and colonialism 189, 198, 202
 and postcolonial autobiographic
 writing 180–1, 198
 social 181, 190
 see also nostalgia
Mendes, Alfred 107
middle class
 and abolitionism 51
 development 53, 57